Jeanne's Gift: Finding Home is not only an engaging story of one woman's journey in later life. In its pages, the author raises many soul-searching questions for readers about the meaning of home, family, friendship, identity and purpose, particularly in the third chapter of our lives.

Dori DeSantis
Healthcare Executive

Jeanne's Gift
Finding Home

Lynne C. Levesque

Cover design and interior layout: Caitlin Bechtel.
Original watercolor of Dieppe, France, on the front and back cover: Ilir Stili.
Author's photo: Jacques Normand.
All other photos: the author unless otherwise credited.
Developmental editing: Mary Carroll Moore.
Copyediting: Charlie McKee of Editor's Proof.

ISBN: 978-0-9979516-5-3

Lynne C. Levesque
Seattle, Washington
www.lynnelevesque.com

For Joël because I think you would have enjoyed the read.

For Jacques because, well… you know why.

For all my dear connections — family, friends and colleagues — who have contributed so much to my life and for whom I am most grateful.

TABLE OF CONTENTS

Map of Northwest France

Map of 17th Century Quebec

Adapted from Marcel Trudel, Introduction to New France, p. 119

MAP OF DIEPPE

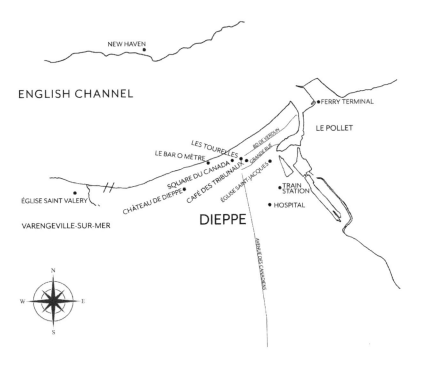

NEW HAVEN

ENGLISH CHANNEL

FERRY TERMINAL

LE POLLET

LES TOURELLES

BD DE VERDUN

LE BAR O MÈTRE

GRANDE RUE

SQUARE DU CANADA

CAFÉ DES TRIBUNAUX

ÉGLISE SAINT-JACQUES

CHÂTEAU DE DIEPPE

TRAIN STATION

ÉGLISE SAINT VALERY

HOSPITAL

DIEPPE

VARENGEVILLE-SUR-MER

AVENUE DES CANADIENS

N
W   E
S

JEANNE CHEVALIER TO LYNNE C. LEVESQUE

Jean-Alexandre (Jean or Jacques) Chevalier
m. Marguerite Scorban (Scorinan)
Circa 1642 Normandie, France

Robert Lévesque m. Jeanne Chevalier
22 April 1679, L'Ange-Gardien, Québec

François-Robert Lévesque m. M-Charlotte Aubert
7 November 1701, Rivière-Ouelle, Kamouraska, Québec

Jean-Baptiste Lévesque m. M-Josephte Bérubé
18 July 1736, Rivière-Ouelle, Kamouraska, Québec

Charles Lévesque m. Catherine Beaulieu-Hudon
17 January 1769, Rivière-Ouelle, Kamouraska, Québec

Germain Lévesque m. Geneviève Charrois
13 October 1794, St-Roch-des-Aulnaies, Québec

Joseph Lévesque m. Léocadie Lavoie
19 January 1841, Église de St-Louis-de-Kamouraska, Québec

Martial Lévesque m. Thècle Dufour
9 February 1864, St-Denis-De La Bouteillerie, Québec

Joseph M. Levesque m. Clara April
7 January 1890, Nashua, New Hampshire

Treffle George Levesque m. Marie Brodeur
3 September 1917, Nashua, New Hampshire

Gerard Joseph Levesque m. Judith Hallstrom
27 December 1943, Nashua, New Hampshire

Lynne C. Levesque

PROLOGUE

We almost didn't make it, the trip that I had been planning for so long.

This most recent adventure had begun roughly seven months previously during a two-month research trip to France in the spring of 2016, when I decided, shortly before turning seventy-two, that I should spend a "sabbatical" year in France. Although it's something I had dreamed about doing some fifty years earlier after graduating from college, it was a rather sudden decision to make on that day in May because I hadn't really thought of it since then, or didn't think I had. It was, however, a decision I believed I was destined to make, especially given that I had found the perfect place to rent for a year and had reached an agreement with the landlord for the rental, all in the space of one hour on my last day in Dieppe (a small town on the English Channel in Normandy) and three days before leaving France.

There were many reasons behind the decision. I had been writing a book about the life of my ancestor Jeanne Marguerite Chevalier. Although the first version was to be published on November 24, 2016, questions still remained concerning her life and that of her three husbands. The book needed to be translated into French. There was publicity to generate for both the English and French versions. I also planned to write a sequel to describe the many extraordinary and marvelous experiences I had had and the amazing number of outstandingly kind people I had met along the way. Perhaps most importantly, I wanted to finally become fluent in the language of my father. As it turned out, there would prove to be other reasons as well.

Expected and unexpected hurdles appeared on the way toward

realizing this dream. I had to complete an incredible number of forms for the French consulate in Boston in order to apply for the long-stay visa required for visits of more than six months in France. That process included finding alternative healthcare since Medicare wouldn't cover me for the year in France, and some sort of health insurance was required for the visa. I needed to arrange for routine doctor and dentist visits to last me the year since any affordable health and travel insurance did not include such visits. I had to figure out what to do about my fixed and mobile telephone lines, my plants, my mail, and my car, determine how to manage routine chores and other responsibilities around my third-floor condominium in the Charlestown neighborhood of Boston, and decide what to take and what to store and where. And, needless to say, I had to arrange for the transport of my nine-year-old cat Quincie all the way to France.

Everything seemed to be falling in place. I didn't really think there would be any impact on my family since I am the oldest child, I am single and without children, and our parents had died years ago. I did check, nevertheless, with my younger sister Carla to be sure I was not being too irresponsible. I spoke with the other two condominium owners in the building and with my financial advisor to let them know my plans and to see if they had any feedback; no one could foresee any problems.

While I at first believed I could manage the trip to France alone and wouldn't need any help, I reconsidered when I thought about all my suitcases and Quincie. I asked Carla if she would come with Quincie and me to help us get settled in Dieppe. It was a good idea since she's a lot of fun and a good traveling companion and would be a great support. We bought our plane tickets to leave Boston on January 1, 2017, and reserved a rental car to drive from the airport in Paris to Dieppe. I found house sitters to take care of my apartment, plants, mail, and routine chores and arranged with them to keep one room in my apartment closed off as my private storage space.

In October I received the approval of my application for a long-stay visa from the French government (although not without one last little, unexpected hiccup). I started making lists and began cleaning out corners and cabinets that had really not had a thorough cleansing in the eighteen years I had lived in my place. I found solutions for my telephone lines and my health insurance coverage and sold my car. I learned that France did not have any quarantine rules for animals, unlike Great Britain, and discussed with my vet what we needed to do to prepare Quincie for the trip to France. I began the time-consuming but incredibly "healing" task of throwing out long-unused items and packing up what I wanted to keep in order to make room for the sitters.

I was crossing off action items on my lists and began to schedule in tasks to complete during my first week in Dieppe. Christmas 2016 came, and I was beginning to believe the trip was actually going to happen. I started envisioning our life in the little cottage that I had rented down the secluded lane beside the blue garage door, with its brick fireplace and its garden full of hollyhocks, camellias, roses, strawberries, and rhubarb. I arranged with Nadine, a friend from my visit to France in 2015 and with whom I had exchanged homes the prior May, to meet us at the cottage with a litter box and litter for Quincie and to provide a temporary loan of the linen that we needed. With some difficulty, I was finally able to transfer funds for the deposit on the rental to my new landlord. And I raced to the French consulate in Boston to obtain a stamp and signature that I realized were missing from my long-stay visa application just five days before departure, almost too late.

Then, on December 28, four days before our scheduled departure, the first unexpected hurdle appeared. I took Quincie to the vet for what I thought were the last items on the list — her rabies shot, implantation of a special identification chip required by the European Union, and completion of the seven pages of paperwork by the vet to arrange for her entry into France, paperwork that had to be completed no more than ten days before our arrival in France.

Unfortunately, it turned out that the US Department of Agriculture (USDA) had recently changed their rules, unbeknownst to our vet. Their permission was required on the forms. I quickly put Quincie back into her carrier and gathered up all the papers. Since I had sold my car, we then took the subway from the vet's office to the nearest FedEx office to open an account and arrange for overnight delivery of the forms to USDA headquarters in Albany, New York.

The next morning, Thursday, three days before departure, the USDA, upon review of the forms, informed the vet that we had misunderstood one of the requirements regarding her rabies shot. Quincie was supposed to have been vaccinated against rabies thirty days before leaving the US, not within ten days as we had thought. The USDA could not sign off on the forms without a waiver from the French immigration offices.

The staff at the USDA were kind enough to provide a phone number for animal immigration at the Paris airport. I called the number. I was transferred around until I finally reached an official who, after listening to my plea for a waiver in my very halting French, answered, "That's impossible, Madame." We would have to delay our departure by twenty-six days, the required number of days remaining to ensure that Quincie did not have rabies. I hung up the phone, obviously extremely upset.

I spoke with our vet and decided to try again. I called the animal immigration office back and this time explained to the officials that she was not an outdoor cat, had never been outdoors or encountered other cats, and that she would not be allowed outdoors in France. I pleaded with them for creative solutions that could involve arranging for quarantine or any other possible options. This time the answer was: "Send us an email explaining the situation."

Slightly encouraged, I drafted and sent off the email, apologizing for the need to write quickly in English, but knowing that the six-hour time difference meant they were getting ready to close. A few minutes later, at 5:15 p.m. in Paris, I received a response requesting additional information about Quincie's vaccinations. Gathering the documents they requested from the vet's office took almost an hour, but I sent the information off shortly after 6:00 p.m. in France. No response. Obviously, the office was closed.

I called Carla. We tried to figure out alternatives since, given all the other arrangements both of us had made in our lives, we could not delay leaving Boston. Perhaps Quincie could stay with friends in Boston for the required twenty-six days. Then I could arrange to have one of my friends fly her over to Paris, or I could fly back to get her. Under no circumstances would I ever think of leaving her behind for a year, no matter what the expense of any alternatives.

Friday morning, two days before departure and the last day that the USDA office in Albany would be open before our scheduled flight on Sunday, I woke up at 4:00 a.m. EST (10:00 a.m. Paris time) and hurriedly checked my email. Nothing. I kept checking. Forty-one minutes later at 4:41 a.m., I received a response, allowing me to bring Quincie into France — under certain conditions. I had to sign a commitment letter, agreeing to have her checked by a vet in Dieppe no more than three days after our arrival to ensure she was indeed the cat identified in all the documentation. I would have to keep her quarantined in my home in Dieppe for thirty days, to keep them informed about any changes to her health during the month, and to arrange for a blood test for rabies within that month. Finally, and worst of all, I had to agree that, if she were found to have rabies, she could be euthanized.

Believing that this last eventuality would never happen, I signed and returned the form to the French vet. He in turn sent an email for the USDA, confirming the waiver. I forwarded that email to the office in Albany right before 6:00 a.m. and arranged with FedEx for an overnight return delivery on Saturday of the required forms. At 7:35 a.m. on Friday morning, the USDA confirmed receipt of the waiver. Less than forty-five minutes later, I received notice that the senior vet in charge had signed off on the forms. I still had to wait twenty-four hours, relying on FedEx to make the Saturday delivery. They came through, and the package was delivered as promised, one day before departure.

Carla arrived on Friday evening, and we were able to take a yoga class together on Saturday morning before spending the day finishing up last minute details. The next day, Sunday, we managed to give Quincie some of the sedative the vet had provided and that we thought she needed, especially for putting on her TSA-required harness and getting her into her carrier (Quincie is not a docile cat!). She slept underneath my seat on the plane most of the way to Paris.

Since I had had to provide our flight information to the French vet to ensure that the customs check could be completed when we arrived at the Paris airport, I was not surprised upon our arrival the next morning when a tall, very imposing customs officer sought us out in baggage claim. After I responded *"Oui"* to his question about my identity, he then escorted us to the appropriate agent. Quincie's chip confirmed that she was the cat identified in the forms. All the documents that I gave them appeared to be in order, and so we were allowed to leave and to find our way to the rental car agency.

Quincie slept during the three-hour drive to Dieppe. Although my attempts during the drive to reach my landlord and Nadine via my US mobile phone failed, we were finally able to connect with them and get into the cottage. Once we were inside, Quincie jumped out of her carrier and began to make herself at home, obviously unaware of what it had taken to get her there. On Thursday, we went to the vet in Dieppe, where her chip was checked one more time, and we made an appointment for the blood test at the end of January.

We were, however, not yet living happily ever after in the little cottage down the lane beside the blue garage door. Two more unexpected hurdles also presented themselves. The research I had done on the requirements for opening a French bank account had not revealed a particular issue for Americans, instituted apparently after the 9/11 attacks in New York City and beyond, over fifteen years ago. Not all banks had the proper arrangements and systems required to manage these accounts. Nadine, who was continuing to help me get settled, and I regrettably picked one of those banks on our first try. That made it difficult to arrange for Internet access since a French bank account was required for a contract with an Internet service provider. Without a French bank account, I also couldn't transfer funds from my US bank account to live on in France.

Finding the right bank and arranging an appointment with a bank officer who would be available to open the account took almost three more weeks. But it eventually happened. I was able to arrange with my US bank for the conversion of US dollars to euros and then for their transfer to France. And while another three weeks went by before an Internet connection could be installed, that also finally happened.

Did I ever question why I had made this decision — even on those dark, rainy January days after Carla left, when I was alone and suffering from a cold? Not really, because I was old enough and wise enough to know that I needed to give myself some time. Quincie would adapt, and I knew I could as well. Of course, I did not know at the time how it was all going to turn out or how my life would be changed forever.

Nonetheless, I did realize that I, in fact, had no choice. This adventure did not really begin in May 2016. In truth, it had begun almost twenty-five years earlier when I first heard the name of Jeanne Chevalier, my eighth-great-grandmother. It became more real, a few years later, when she began to haunt me.

Note to readers: If you are unfamiliar with the history of my ancestor Jeanne Chevalier and want to know more before reading on, you can find details about her life on my blog at www.lynnelevesque.com.

Part One

HEADING FOR THE CITY OF FOUR PORTS

Timeline of Lynne's Life

1944   Lynne is born in Missouri

1966   Graduation from college, first trip to the then Soviet Union

1977   Discovery of French nose in Strasbourg

1978   Meeting with René Lévesque

1980   Biographers of René Lévesque discover Robert Lévesque

1989   Diane's death in Hartford, Connecticut

1992   Levesque family reunion in Nashua, New Hampshire

1994   First trip to Hautot-Saint-Sulpice; parents die

1995   Trip to Quebec, discovery of book; trip to Rivière-Ouelle

2002   Blue travel journal notes

2009   Quincie is adopted

2011   First trip to Coutances

2013   First visit to Dieppe

2014   Research trips to Quebec

2015   Return to France, three weeks in Rouen; speech in Rimouski, Quebec

2016   Two months in France; fall in Caen; month at Nadine's

2016   Decision to spend a sabbatical year in France

2017   Quincie and Lynne arrive in France, with Carla's help

ONE

SETTLING IN

In the early evening on Thursday, January 12, 2017, just ten days after my sister Carla, my cat Quincie, and I had arrived in France, a violent windstorm, called "Tempête Egon," struck Dieppe. As the night went on, Dieppe recorded the highest winds in France and Germany, with gusts up to 146 kilometers per hour (ninety-one miles per hour), the strongest in thirty years. Egon's destructive winds were accompanied by heavy rain, enormous waves crashing on the beach, hail, and even snow in some places. They also caused widespread flooding, fallen trees, damaged roofs, power outages, and an automatic shutdown of one of the nearby nuclear power plants. We didn't lose power at the cottage, but we did rush around, struggling to close all the shutters, with the wind howling and the rain and hail pouring down outside. It was absolutely shocking and scary. I was definitely glad that Carla was still there. Since I hadn't been paying attention to the news or the weather, we had had no warning. It was certainly a rather ominous welcome to my year in France.

The next day was windy, chilly, and rainy, but fortunately not wild and stormy. On Saturday, with the weather a bit calmer, we rose early to make sure that Carla made her 1:00 p.m. flight back to Seattle and that I could return the rental car and catch the train back to Dieppe before it was too dark. We did manage to lose our way on the three-hour trip from Dieppe to the Charles de Gaulle Airport but arrived with plenty of time to spare.

Before Carla's flight left, we spent a few moments reminiscing about our two weeks together and even had time to share some thoughts about our years growing up in New Hampshire and then about our brief time as roommates in San Francisco many years ago. I felt torn. I was certainly going to miss her, and I didn't know when I would ever see her again. At the same time, I was eager to begin my year in France. After promising to stay in touch by phone, with both of us shedding a few tears, I left the airport.

It was dark when I unlocked the door to the cottage. And a bit lonely, despite Quincie's greeting at the door. With a bit of a sigh, I told her, "Okay, Quincie, are you ready? This unfamiliar place is going to be our home for the next year."

It had been a busy two weeks. Carla and I had celebrated her birthday with Nadine at a restaurant overlooking the English Channel. We had explored the Saturday market and bought what we thought would be an easy solution for the dinner I had planned for some friends I had met in 2013. With a fire in the fireplace, we had spent an enjoyable evening, despite our struggles to carry on a conversation with my French friends who spoke hardly any English and despite the somewhat limited success of my first attempt at cooking a meal in France. Carla and I had not been able to agree on when the salad should be served. She wanted it with the main dish, and I felt we should follow the French custom of a salad afterwards. I had won.

We had also made time for a short trip to Hautot-Saint-Sulpice, the village where our ancestor Robert Lévesque had been born. It had not changed much in the seventeen years since we had both been there with Laurie, our other sister, and my four nieces. It was still a very small village with a nineteenth-century church, a town hall, two community centers, and a school but no sidewalks, grocery, bakery, or other commerce. Over glasses of champagne in the home of the family whom we had met during that visit, we had shared memories and stories of our lives since then.

Back in Dieppe, we had taken three long hikes up and down the cliffs, only getting lost once because of my failure to understand the French directions on our map. We had shopped for bed and bathroom linen, office equipment, and other items I needed for the cottage. We had built several fires in the fireplace to enjoy with our dinners, and Carla had purchased candles to add coziness to the cottage. I had unpacked my suitcases and managed to find places in closets and cupboards for all the clothes, papers, vitamins, cosmetics, and other items I had thought necessary for the year. I had still not found the right litter for Quincie, and I still didn't have Internet access. However, most fortuitously, the wallet Carla had lost on her second day in Dieppe was found at the municipal police station with all her money and credit cards intact on the day before she was scheduled to leave.

And now I was alone, and Carla was back in Seattle. I ignored the sniffles, sneezes, and sore throat from the cold she had left behind and the next day took a guided tour, an introduction to Dieppe's history. Although the cold symptoms lingered on for several more weeks, I felt well enough to get around and to finally open a checking account at a French bank, obtain a bus pass and library card, and switch my mobile phone service to a French Internet provider. While the landline and, more importantly, access to the web would not be installed for another few weeks, I did have a temporary solution so I could stay in touch with family and friends despite the thousands of miles separating us.

I spent the rest of my first month in Dieppe continuing to settle in and becoming used to living in a small town in France. I was able to connect with old friends and meet new ones, find resources to help with the translation of my book on my eighth-great-grandmother Jeanne Chevalier's life, and begin writing the sequel to it. And happily, despite the rather bleak and cold weather, Quincie appeared to be adapting reasonably well. The little cottage was starting to feel like home, at least to her.

Finding the cottage was another example of the role that the combination of synchronicity and perseverance has played in my life. I am not sure where the concept of fate comes into the picture. When I had started toying with the idea of spending a year in Dieppe towards the end of May 2016, I had made several inquiries via the web with owners who had holiday homes for rent. I had been trying to find a furnished cottage for a year-long rental for an American and her cat without any luck and mostly without any responses. The two places I had been able to visit were either too small or too noisy or not at all suitable for a cat who, at the sight of a bird in the garden below, might be inclined to jump out of first floor windows without screens or other barriers.

With but a few days remaining for me in Dieppe, I had made one last call to an owner of a particularly attractive cottage. At first, she had responded that she had no interest in a long-term rental. Then, two days before I was scheduled to leave, she had sent an email indicating that she had reconsidered and asking if I would like to see it. I had jumped at the chance.

As I walked over to the place, I had reviewed my prepared list of requirements, of course headed by "cats accepted" and "quiet." I still have the list which also included: two bedrooms, one of which could double as a space for guests and a workspace for my writing; a bathroom with a bathtub; a separate toilet (to ease bathroom congestion with overnight visitors); WIFI; a microwave oven; and a garden. Even though I didn't have a garden back in Charlestown, I had become accustomed to the serenity of the flowers, trees, and green lawn behind Nadine's home in Dieppe and figured it should be on the list.

The absence of an Internet connection did not concern me at the time since the owner told me it could easily be made available when I moved in. (Little did I know then what I would later learn.) Because the cottage had met all the other requirements on my list and also had a fireplace — not on my list but something I had always wanted — I agreed to the rental on the spot.

The cottage had a nice, welcoming spirit, with wooden beams and a narrow wooden staircase that made it feel older than it really was. The sofa, dining room table and chairs, solid-wood built-in cupboard next to the fireplace, and other pieces of furniture all appeared to be in fine shape. A tall sideboard held all sorts of glassware and serving pieces. In the small kitchen, there was barely enough room for that very important microwave, a sink, a half-sized dishwasher, and small refrigerator. Next to the kitchen was a "water closet" with an adjacent bathroom that had enough space for a washing machine and the most wonderful, long, deep bathtub. I would eventually become used to the presence of hard, heavily calcified water that left spots on dishes, messed up the coffee maker, and drove me crazy with what it did to my hair.

The sloping ceilings in the two bedrooms upstairs lent character and charm. Separating those two rooms was a small lavatory, something very important, the owner reminded me, for persons of a certain age who would want to avoid having to climb down the narrow staircase to the other toilet in the middle of the night.

The cottage could be difficult to find, given its location on a lane off the main street. (I'd had trouble finding it on my first visit.) I always had to let new visitors know, "It's down the lane beside the garage with the blue door." But its hidden location ensured the quiet that I needed to sleep and write. With a garden promising camellias, roses, lilies of the valley, hollyhocks, and rhubarb and strawberries, it was truly lovely. Later I would learn to make compote with the rhubarb and strawberries, but I never did figure out how to make soup out of the nettles and sorrel as my landlady had suggested. The patio would allow me to sit and watch Quincie in the garden, which she would come to love. The sunroom would let her sleep in the warm sun all year long.

Since the cottage was located near the castle on the western cliff above Dieppe's town center, it did require walks, or perhaps "treks," up and down the cliffs to reach bakeries, shops, the library, the train station, bus stops, and the Saturday market. There was a bus with an infrequent schedule, but I tried to walk whenever I could, telling myself, while huffing and puffing my way back to the cottage, that the exercise was good for my heart.

Living in that cottage and living in Dieppe without a car and having to walk everywhere, I could imagine I was back in the 1950s when I was growing up. Having to hang clothes on the clothesline, for example. Except, of course, for the dishwasher, the forty-inch TV, the satellite dish, and the World Wide Web. In 1679, when my eighth-great-grandmother Jeanne Chevalier moved to the home of her second husband in Rivière-Ouelle, a frontier village in eastern Quebec, Canada, she lived there for years with young children in a one-room cabin without a toilet, running water, or electricity and with little connection to the outside world. I told myself that, if she could live through that challenging situation, I could manage in Dieppe. The cottage would be perfectly fine for my one-year-long sabbatical, I thought. I didn't need much more at that point.

Finding the cottage and turning it into a comfortable place to live turned out to be two different things. Before the end of the month of January, I took down some of the owner's decorations and put away her ceramic knickknacks. I went through the kitchen cabinets, the sideboard with all the glassware, and a storage closet to become familiar with what was available and what I might still need to purchase. I sorted out which shopping bags to take to the market, said hello to the man I had bought cheese from during my prior two visits to Dieppe, shopped for needed supplies, and started to learn my way around Dieppe — at least the center of town. Fortunately, there was not another repeat of Tempête Egon. The weather finally turned rather pleasant, certainly compared to New England.

On a Saturday evening, I sat down at the dining room table and started to look over the list of action items I had followed to make the trip. I could check most of them off. It was, therefore, time to start a new list to give me discipline for the next few months in order to meet the goals I had set to become fluent in French, translate the book, continue my research, and write.

At the end of the month, after making sure I had all the necessary documents, I took the train to Rouen to complete the final steps required for my long-stay visa for the year. I first needed to make my way to the clinic, located near the Musée des Beaux Arts, for my chest x-ray appointment. I then had to wait for over an hour to have the x-ray taken and afterward close to another hour for the film to be processed. As I sat there, I nervously remembered that I had once tested positive for tuberculosis and wondered if that had anything to do with the wait. Evidently not, because I was finally able to collect the film and walk with it across the Seine River for my next interview in the much less polished, less historic neighborhood of Rouen where the French Office of Immigration and Integration (OFII) was located.

Fortunately, I had extra time between the two appointments since finding the OFII had not been easy, or perhaps I had not completely understood the directions in French. I wandered through the Saint-Sever shopping center, filled with both French and American chain stores, looking for the office. I had to ask for help a couple of times since I could see no signs for it. At last, I was directed to a building attached to the center on the other side of the main entrance.

In a sterile set of offices that did not seem to me very welcoming, I met with a doctor who reviewed the x-ray, took my weight and height, and asked several routine questions about my health. I was pleased to hear that I had not shrunk from my 5'7" height (1.7 meters) and that the sixty-two kilos on the scale indicated I had not gained any weight so far in France. Not bad for my age, I thought. The doctor agreed. After handing over all the necessary paperwork and paying the obligatory taxes at another desk, I received my visa. It was all an eye-opening introduction to the France that exists beyond the magical city of Paris, especially since I had had to sit or stand in line with many others at both the clinic and the OFII, all of us waiting to receive visas, but most of whom were asylum seekers from Africa or the Middle East.

On the train returning to Dieppe from Rouen with my long-stay visa in hand, I was both relieved after getting that step out of the way and hopeful about the months ahead. I decided to give myself a little pat on the back — for a change. December and January had been incredibly busy and stressful, but I was now "legal" and making progress toward my goals.

Two days later, my friends Carol and Arthur arrived from Boston for the weekend. We visited some of the tourist attractions around Dieppe so I could introduce them and me to my new residence. I showed them St. Valery, the little twelfth-century church in Varengeville with its George Braque stained-glass windows. As we walked through the adjacent cemetery, we wondered how it and the church were going to be saved since they were both in danger of falling off the cliff, given the erosion of the landscape over the centuries. In the village of Veules-les-Roses, we made the circular walk along the shortest "river" in France[1] and observed the farmers growing watercress in the stream. Before Carol and Arthur left, we had a party to introduce them to my French friends who lived in and near Dieppe. I was amazed that the cottage had enough room for the twenty-five people who arrived!

After my Boston friends headed back home on Monday, I took Quincie to the vet for her blood test. The results eventually cleared her of rabies, so she and I could now officially begin our sabbatical year in France.

---

1. In one of the many idiosyncrasies of the French language, there are two words for the English word *river*: *Fleuve* refers specifically to a river that flows into the ocean or into the English Channel; the word *rivière* is used for all the rest. The Veules river is only one kilometer long but flows from its source into the English Channel, making it the shortest fleuve in France.

TWO

QUINCIE

Whenever I would tell the story of my arrival in France to new acquaintances, they marveled at my attachment to Quincie, my lovely tricolor cat with four differently colored paws. When I would invite them to the cottage and they met Quincie, I always had to warn them about her idiosyncrasies in order to avoid any surprises. Then, when they asked me, as most inevitably did, why I had adopted a cat who did not like to be petted and was known to bite and scratch without warning, I had a story to tell. First, I explained, "I grew up with pets — cats, dogs. I even had a salamander once, for a very short time. I couldn't imagine living without a pet."

It was true. My mother had a very soft spot for animals, so we always had cats and dogs in our home. Except for my first few years after college when I was pet-less, I generally followed her example. When I

My beloved Quincie

was married, we had a beautiful golden retriever, who died at too young an age. After another hiatus from pet ownership and a couple of moves across country, I "inherited" three of my parents' cats when they moved to Arizona. They all eventually passed on to cat heaven, and a day after my dad died, I brought Simba home.

Not long after Simba's demise several years later, I adopted Quincie, my current and rather ornery, but quite beautiful, frisky, and playful cat. It wasn't until a day or so after I brought her home from the animal shelter that I realized why the rescue folks had never taken her out of the cage and why she had been in the shelter for so long. The folks there had told me, "Oh, it's just that she is nervous from all the noise of dogs barking around her." In fact, that was not the case. The truth was that she did not like to be held, and she was definitely not a cuddly cat. She didn't even like to be petted for many years. I could sneak in a head rub every now and then, but normally it was "hands off!" with a snarl and perhaps a scratch.

By the time I realized all this, I couldn't take her back to the shelter where she would possibly have been labeled "unadoptable." After hearing this story, my friends surmised that she was terribly mistreated as a kitten and grew up without a mother cat to teach her how to play nice. It was also possible that I hadn't been the best parent by letting her continue her bad habits and not spending enough time trying to domesticate her. Whether it was DNA, her early years, or poor discipline on my part, I suffered the consequences.

In any event, somehow, over the last several years of living together, we had bonded closely enough that there was absolutely no way I could have left her behind when I decided on a sabbatical in France. People wondered why I was so attached to her and would take her with me wherever I went, despite her refusal to give me the caresses that other more normal cats give their owners or to allow me to cuddle or pet her.

The reasons for wanting her with me were many: she was my companion; the house was empty without another presence; and it was definitely not a home without her. Quincie had been known to come to the front door and greet me with a bit of a kiss on the nose whenever I arrived home (or she used to, anyway, in the condo in Boston). She would make me laugh with her sometimes crazy antics and unpredictable behavior. I'd find her hiding in some of the strangest places. She frequently disappeared into a closet and then would casually walk out after I had spent several minutes trying to find her. Her strong-willed and rather independent character was somewhat like her owner's, some would say. She didn't require much attention except when she wanted to eat.

Because she seemed to enjoy riding in the car and the plane, we travelled together whenever possible. Upon arriving in France, she received her very own European passport. Indeed, when I brought her home from the shelter back in 2009, she had purred all the way in the car to my place, leading me to believe — as it turned out, foolishly and erroneously — that we might have a normal loving relationship. We had been to Quebec twice on trips that involved several stops at motels. She adapted quite easily to new surroundings, sometimes with a brief snarl saying, "Okay, here we go again!"

Despite her independent spirit, Quincie had evidently set limits on her desire for freedom and exploration. After one of our Quebec trips together, we stopped for a three-day visit with Carol and Arthur at their grand, three-storied summer home in Maine. On the second day there, she managed to slip through a slightly open screen door. After searching the entire place and finally realizing she had escaped, I opened the door to see her scampering back from the neighbor's home across the way. So she seemed to quickly realize what "home" meant, the place where she could count on being fed.

Her regular cat food was supplemented by certain quirks. She liked peanut butter, whipped cream, crème fraiche, butter, avocado, and most cheeses — but absolutely not Swiss cheese. Somehow, no matter how quietly I would try to open the refrigerator, or twist open a jar of peanut butter, or start to butter a piece of toast, she would run to the kitchen and sit politely while staring at me intently until I gave her a taste. Her very well-developed senses of smell, hearing, and sight were obvious. With her intense gazes and attentive crouches, she would make me notice spiders creeping up a wall or a ladybug or some other creature crawling on the floor.

Although the first vet I took Quincie to in Boston claimed she was feral, I didn't believe it then. I changed vets and found one who agreed that she wasn't. In fact, she could be somewhat social with me alone or when I had company. She liked to have me stand over her when she ate. She preferred to be in the same room with me. Despite her standoffish behavior, she would often come to find me if I disappeared into another room. As a very well-mannered cat, she would sit before she was given treats and was a neat and dainty eater. She would let me know when she had vomited up some fur or food by staying near the mess until I found it. And she would rub against me to let me know that she wanted something — either to eat or perhaps to drink; water out of the faucet was her preference. She managed to find a suitable faucet wherever we lived. It was always very interesting to watch her size up the height she needed to scale to reach the faucet in the bathroom. She would make strange little noises (was she telling herself, "Yes, you can do this, yes, you can"?) before jumping up.

At the cottage in Dieppe, Quincie quickly adopted the sunroom as her favorite space and loudly let me know when she wanted to go out there. She was never allowed outside when we were living in Boston, so this closed-in space with lots of sun was obviously close to heaven for her.

Whenever I was out in the garden, if I let her join me there as I sometimes did, she would lie among the flowers, all the time keeping a close eye on me. If I seemed to be too engrossed in a document or story or some gardening activity, she would quietly make a move to escape beyond the garden. She did manage to escape a few times, but she always returned home in short order.

The exposure to the outdoors must have ignited her inherently wild nature or refreshed memories of her time "on the streets" before I adopted her. Over the months during our time living in the cottage, she managed to find and trap at least three mice. I once found one left by her, at the entrance to my bedroom, and, later, a couple more on the floor of the sunroom.

As Quincie's little escapade in Maine and a couple of others indicated, her exploration outside the boundaries of our home was always relatively limited, clearly by her own preference. One afternoon, several months after our arrival in Dieppe, I apparently had not shut the sunroom door carefully enough before heading to a gym class. She let herself out, but when I returned two hours later, there she was, sitting patiently in the garden. As soon as I passed through the gate, she stood up and trotted over to greet me. I could have sworn her cat sounds meant something like: "So, Lynne, where have you been?"

In Boston, we had a veterinarian who specialized in cats and who knew how to handle Quincie for exams, rabies shots, and nail trims without tranquilization. The vets in Dieppe didn't have that same background and at first were almost afraid of her. They generally required her to be tranquilized to treat her. So I hesitated to bring her to them as often as I should have for a nail trim. Eventually, I figured out a way to cut her nails in order to avoid the scars caused by her scratches when she wasn't happy with me.

She seemed to be mellowing a bit with age since she did begin to let me pet her head and ears for a bit longer than before. In Charlestown, she never slept in my bedroom. That changed in France, and, while she usually spent at least part of the night sleeping in her bed on the floor in my room, she did start to spend more time with me on my bed — at least until I turned out the lights. And she appeared to have mastered some French because, when I would tell her in French that it was time to go inside, or sit, or eat, she responded — most of the time. Okay, it might have had something to do with the treat she received as a reward, but still.

As the months went by, Quincie would keep her peculiar habits. Although she didn't provide me with many cuddles, I would continue to love her anyway. She showed her love in very different ways, I guess. Besides, she was the only real family I had in France — at least at that moment.

THREE

MEMORIES OF MOM AND DAD

During the two weeks of Carla's visit in Dieppe, we shared some memories of our childhoods in Nashua, New Hampshire. Her memories were somewhat different from mine — understandably, given our ten-year age difference — but there were some that were similar. One such memory, shared by my other siblings as well, was that our mother had a schedule of supper menus for each day of the week. Although we couldn't all recall the same meal for the same day, I remembered that Thursday was usually spaghetti. On Friday, it was some sort of fish; on Saturday, we had hot dogs and beans; and Sunday was most often roast beef. I still am not sure why this memory has stuck with us for so many years.

Dad and Lynne in Southern California

After Carla returned to Seattle, I started having even more memories. They were helped by the scrapbooks that my mother had made for me, as she had done for each of her five children. I had found them when I was cleaning out a cabinet in my apartment getting ready for my year in France and decided to take a few pages with me for my sabbatical year. On one of the first pages, I had found this picture of my father and me. I must have been around one year old. It was taken probably somewhere in California when he was still in the service.

The same cabinet had held some of the letters Dad had written to Mom during World War II. Partially because other news could be censored, his letters were primarily full of his love for her and for me, calling us his sweethearts, his dream girls, sending us his hugs and kisses. I was his first child and thus special, his little angel. This was before there were other children and other priorities to compete with me for his attention.

Now that I think of it, since one of the major reasons for initially wanting to spend a year in France was to finally, at the age of seventy-two, become fluent in the language of my father, was I still trying to get his attention? Good question, but hard to answer. After all, I wasn't totally sure what I really knew or felt or remembered about my father, and I never had a chance to speak with him about his life. Could this writing be an attempt to connect with him decades after his death?

Gerard Joseph Levesque was born to a first-generation family of Quebecois origin on August 29, 1921, in Nashua, New Hampshire, a town where the name Levesque was the most common name in the phonebook at the time. Although his parents were born in the United States, they both spoke French at home. My father went to French parochial school through the eighth grade, finishing in 1934 before going on to public high school. Growing up, he was surrounded by a large French-Canadian family. His father had three brothers and five sisters, and they all married and had offspring.

As a child, Dad must have spent time with his grandparents, along with his cousins, siblings, and other relatives. His grandfather, Joseph Levesque, had emigrated from Quebec with his parents as a youth. Joseph became a prosperous and prominent member of the Nashua community. Dad's grandmother Clara April had also been born in Quebec and emigrated around the same age. Although she was not known to speak English publicly, she supposedly understood it. Once or twice a year, Clara would hold a family gathering where those in attendance spoke French. I remember Joseph, always attired in a three-piece suit, from visits to our home but not Clara, who had died when I was not quite six. And, as a child, I don't remember meeting many, if any, of the numerous relatives in Nashua. I positively don't have memories of being hugged and kissed all the time by them, the way my second cousin Peter later described to me in his memories of times with all these relatives.

Joseph and Clara lived not far from our home when I was growing up, but I don't recall ever visiting them there. When Joseph died in 1961, he left nine living children, twenty-five grandchildren, and thirty-two great-grandchildren. Several years later in 1992, approximately 150 of the couple's grandchildren, great-grandchildren, great-great-grandchildren, and other living relatives gathered in Nashua at a reunion in their honor.

A monument to Joseph and Clara and to Joseph's parents, Martial Lévesque and Thècle Dufour (my great-great-grandparents), stands prominently in the old Louis de Gonzague Cemetery in Nashua. At some point after my great-great-grandparents' arrival in the United States, the accent mark on the first *e* in Levesque was dropped. The reasons for that change remain unknown, perhaps merely as a result of the absence of that mark on the American typewriter. Other families at the time changed the name Lévesque to Bishop (an English translation of the French name) or to Laveck to avoid difficulties with pronunciation and spelling.

Marie Louise Brodeur at age 16

Dad's father, Treffle, died in 1977 at the age of eighty. His mother, Marie Louise Brodeur, who was also a first-generation Quebecois, had died when she was only fifty-seven in May 1950, five months after her mother-in-law Clara. We never heard how Dad reacted to his mother's death when he was not quite twenty-nine years old. I have a copy of a picture of her at around the age of sixteen, but I don't have any memories of her. (I had also not turned six when she died.)

On Marie Louise's side of the family, I know of one single sibling, a sister, who became my godmother when I was born. Although there is a picture of her father and me in a scrapbook, I don't know much about her side of the family except that this great-grandfather had also been born in Quebec and had emigrated to the United States at the age of twenty-four.

Dad was the second oldest of five in his family. Estelle, the third oldest and

Grandpa Brodeur and Lynne

the last to survive, was still alive when I left the States in 2017 but had lost most of her memory. She died on August 29 during my sabbatical year in France.

In Dad's high school graduation picture from the class of 1938 he was listed as Gerard Joseph or "Jerry." The caption to his picture reads: "He laughs and fools the whole day long. And life for him is but a song." It went on to summarize Dad at the age of seventeen: "'Jerry' enjoyed watching the world go around and himself with it…. The girls as well as the boys enjoyed his friendship and humorous nature." He was a member of the golf team and finished in the upper quarter of his class.

Until Alzheimer's disease struck him down and limited his ability to clearly communicate, Dad was indeed the life of the party and a great swing dancer. I have special memories of dancing with him at my wedding in 1970 and then at Carla's wedding in 1986. At the same time, he was also fairly private about his life. In piecing together his life from archives and scrapbooks, I learned he attended the University of New Hampshire, one of the first in his extended family to go to college. After two years there, he decided to become a dentist like one of his uncles.

Dad was drafted into the US Army in July 1943. A deferment allowed him to finish his dental education until February of the next year when he entered into active duty as a first lieutenant. He was sent to the Pacific Theater in early 1945. His job as a medical officer during the invasion of Okinawa didn't prevent him from being wounded in his right arm and shoulder from grenade shrapnel on April 24, 1945. My brother Marc still has his Bronze Star and Purple Heart, engraved with the date and the location of the battle.

The wound was severe enough, so the story goes, that the surgeon was considering amputation. Reportedly, Dad threatened to shoot the surgeon if he amputated since the loss of his right arm would end his prospects for a career as a dentist. It's not clear if this story was true or how severe the wound really was since he was able to begin writing Mom within a week, first with the aid of a typewriter and then by hand. What we do know is that the USS *Comfort* hospital ship that Dad was being evacuated on was hit by a kamikaze pilot during the night of April 28. The ship suffered considerable damage and a significant loss of life among those men and women onboard but somehow managed to make its way to Hawaii for repairs before finally arriving in Los Angeles. Dad stayed behind in Hawaii to recuperate and sometime later arrived in San Francisco where Mom met him. He was discharged from the Army on September 4, 1946, with the rank of captain and with both his arms intact.

For the most part, from my memory and from those of my siblings, Dad was rather reticent to talk about the war. We only picked up bits and pieces. His letters from fox holes before he was wounded didn't reveal a great deal. However, given the fact that Okinawa has been called the bloodiest land battle of the Pacific theater and the last major battle of World War II,[2] his reticence was not surprising. But the scars showing the entry of shrapnel into his arm and then into his chest were still visible, and he didn't hide the story of how they came to be.

On December 28, 1943, when my dad, dressed in his army uniform married my mother, he was one of the first in his generation to marry someone who was not of French-Canadian heritage. Like my ancestor Jeanne, Judith Ann Hallstrom had had to make a lot of choices in

---

2. SSgt Rudy R. Frame Jr. "Okinawa: The Final Great Battle of World War II," *Marine Corps Gazette*. www.mca-marines.org, accessed December 14, 2020.

her life, some of which affected my connection with my French roots. At the age of twenty, she had moved from her native Idaho to Washington, DC, to "seek her fortune."

There she met, fell in love with, and married my father. I was born eight months later on Dad's twenty-third birthday and was subsequently joined by two brothers and two sisters. There was an oblique reference to me in one of my parents' letters as their "love child," but that fact was never acknowledged and remained a private joke and source of winks among my siblings and me.

Mom and Dad's wedding photo

Unlike my dad, we did not grow up speaking French. We didn't live on French Hill or go to mass at the French Catholic churches in town or go to French schools. Both parents did not want us growing up with what was supposedly perceived as a bilingual "handicap" that my dad had had to overcome.

In Nashua, as in other northern New England cities and towns in the 1950s, '60s and early '70s, having French Canadian heritage for at least some of us came with a bit of a stigma. French Canadians were immigrants in early to mid-twentieth-century Nashua. Many of them didn't or wouldn't speak English and were ostracized by long-term New England residents and even by some of their own relatives who were struggling to assimilate. For example, although he was a prosperous businessman, my French-Canadian godfather was denied membership in the local golf club.

Because many of my father's relatives still spoke French at home and because my mother didn't speak French, we didn't socialize with Dad's side of the family in their homes. My great-grandfather, my grandfather, his wives (he was a widower three times), and a small number of other members of my dad's family were welcomed into our home. Mom did try her best to make sure they spoke English around us.

"They don't speak real French," I remember her saying. "It's not Parisian French." We didn't identify as French Canadian or as "Franco-Americans." "We're Americans," she would frequently say. This was partly because of the shame of being seen as a second-class citizen (a Canuck) and partly because they were trying to build new lives and a new business. They did not want to be associated exclusively with the French community; they wanted to expand their circle of patients and friends. We did, to be sure, every once in a while, enjoy *gorton*, also known as rillettes, an unhealthy mix of pork, fat, and spices. (I never was able to find an exact equivalent in Dieppe.) I sometimes wonder what Mom would say about my decision to spend so much time in France to connect with my French heritage.

In addition to limiting our exposure to any French connections in our early years, my mother left me with a memory (or was it a complex?) about my nose. She was beautiful, gorgeous in fact, and had a lovely nose with a bit of a ski jump at the end. In her mind, that was the perfect nose. A nose job for me, whose nose was different — coming straight out of my forehead — was frequently discussed. I lived for several years after high school sensitive to what I believed was a visual disfiguration. During a 1977 trip to Europe, I was to discover something different. On a guided tour in Strasbourg, I was apparently spending more time looking at the French tourists than I was trying to listen to the guide. I was shocked. Several of them had noses exactly like mine. My "French nose" wasn't something to be ashamed of, I decided. "I don't need a nose job," I told my then husband. "Mine simply isn't a cute pug nose like my mother's!"

It was also not until later that I found out I was related, distantly to be sure, to René Lévesque, the twenty-third premier of Quebec and one of the founders of the Quebec separatist movement. Before September 1977, I hadn't even heard much about him. Something about him must have registered, since I was in the audience when he spoke in the auditorium of the bank where I was working in San Francisco. He was there as part of an attempt to dispel concerns in the US business and financial community about the possible consequences of Quebec's separation from the rest of Canada. I have a vague recollection of going up to him after his talk, introducing myself, and admitting that despite being a Levesque, I did not speak French. He gave me a strong reprimand about needing to learn. I wish I had saved his words to me. I did, fortunately, save the newspaper clipping of his visit.

The discrimination against French Americans from Quebec that René Lévesque did so much to defuse was definitely there when we were growing up in Nashua. Dad struggled to rise above it all. He rarely spoke French at home with us — except to swear.

Since my mother's family remained in Idaho and travel with a growing family was difficult, particularly at that time, we grew up without deep family relationships on either side. Her side of the family had several individuals with mental illness, and we didn't talk about them a lot. Nor we were allowed to use the word "nervous" to describe any perturbing feelings we might have before a test in school, a part in a play, or a speech we had to give. For some reason, on the other hand, feeling "anxious" was okay.

We were able to see some of the Idaho family, but not very frequently. I recall at least one extended summer trip to Idaho, then a later visit of my grandmother Hallstrom to Nashua, and finally a rather lengthy visit by her husband, my grandfather.

Dad loved Mom deeply. I still have their letters from the war and then from later years, full of phrases about how much he loved and missed her. During his service in the Far East in April and May 1945, he had written, "If it were in my power of vocabulary to express my true feelings for you, I could easily write a book every day." Later he wrote, "I love you from the bottom of my heart and will never cease." And his love for her never did end.

She was a high-school beauty queen, very personable and very social. The highest compliment I ever received from others was, "You look exactly like your mother." I knew that wasn't true. In the mirror I could only see a definite resemblance to my father — with our French noses.

Mom adored traveling and often did so, by herself or with a friend and once with me on a two-week trip to the then Soviet Union. Unfortunately, as she grew older and as her face and body began to show signs of aging, she struggled with alcohol addiction. Dad tried to help, but always gave in when she wanted to come home from a rehabilitation clinic. Despite his profound love for her and his devotion to her, I am not sure how happy she really was, especially in the second half of her life.

I don't remember Dad ever talking much about Mom's drinking problems or reflecting on his origins or questioning any of his decisions — at least with us. Perhaps he was too busy, or perhaps that wasn't what his generation did. Or perhaps we never asked.

Both parents were certainly very busy: Dad with expanding his own dental practice and promoting the practice of dentistry and Mom with raising five children. They were both also very active in the community and in, what we would call today, rather moderate Republican politics. With her outstanding social skills, my mother helped my dad establish his practice and move into a middle-class life, one that was different from his French-Canadian upbringing in his hometown and from her youth in Idaho.

They also worked hard to give us a good home, make sure we did well in school, and grew up Catholic: mass every Sunday, Sunday school, and then Catholic Youth Organization activities. Over the years, we moved from military housing to a rented home and then finally to a much larger place on Taft Street. Mom's organizational skills helped her manage all her outside activities and her role as mother. She kept detailed notes and letters that we would later find and wonder about. She had those set menus that we all remember for each day of the week, to make cooking and shopping much easier. She was a den mother during our years as Brownies and Girl and Boy Scouts and made sure we had piano and dancing lessons.

All five of us did our best to gain our parents' love, approval, and attention — each in our own way. Somewhere along the way, I learned that love was directly tied to achievement. Since I could not come close to matching my mother's beauty or social skills, my way was to excel in school, to achieve, to be strong and independent, and to be a good girl. Although as a one-year-old I was described as a bit of a hellion, as a teenager I took responsibility for my brothers and sisters. I often, I was told, cooked dinners for them since Mom was frequently off with her political activities. (Thank goodness for those set menus, since I wasn't and still am not much of a cook!)

The scrapbooks with all my report cards and other school papers and so many photos that my mother kept for me through high school are proof that Mom and Dad were proud of my accomplishments. So why is it that I grew up believing that I was never quite good enough? "Stand up straight so you can be a model," was my mother's wish for me. She insisted we participate in fashion shows with her to develop our posture and presence. No matter, I knew I was never going to become a model or a stewardess, the other career she urged me to consider.

Carla feels that, in their efforts to rise above their pasts, our parents held themselves, and thus us, to extraordinarily high standards. "They were trying to overcome their own upbringing. Mom escaped from Idaho, and Dad was trying to rise above his origins. They pushed themselves to achieve a new standard of living, and they projected those goals onto us."

They pushed, and we strove, while growing up in a warm, safe and comfortable environment, with Mom's home-cooked, well-balanced meals, regular routines, and special touches. She made rather elaborate Christmas stockings by hand for each of us with our names in bold letters. I still have mine, lovingly repaired by Carla when some parts became worn with age. We grew up with sufficient resources and were able to all go to college and graduate without the loan burden that now encumbers my nieces and a nephew.

Except for my younger brother Dana, who excelled at golf — my dad's favorite recreation — I was probably the closest to my father. I was tall like him. I identified more with him than with Mom. He taught me to drive with a manual transmission in our red Plymouth station wagon. We went on college visits together and had some memorable

Dad at my wedding in 1970

times later in college during "Fathers and Daughters" weekends. I can still see him beaming at me as we put the final touches on my veil, then walking me down the aisle at my wedding in 1970, and later shedding a few tears before we left the reception. (Was that because of the man I was marrying or because Dad's oldest daughter was getting married?)

Despite my mother's increasingly erratic drinking problems, from which I was somewhat isolated since I was living in California by that time, my parents and I stayed in touch although not regularly. They did come out to California to visit, sometimes together, sometimes Mom alone. I don't believe they commented much about my divorce. Nor had they given me any words of advice about love and marriage before my wedding.

Dad developed Alzheimer's disease early, around the age of sixty-three. He soon had to give up his dental practice. My parents moved to Arizona around 1987, taking with them all those letters and notes that my mother had so carefully kept over all the years. We siblings had a huge house cleaning before they left, dividing up most of the things they did not want to take with them.

In Arizona, Dad tried to keep his mind active with some hobbies and interests because he knew something was not working right. A year or two after their move, he was scheduled to come back East with Mom for what was supposed to be a short visit, but he made the trip alone. My siblings and I decided he needed to stay closer to us. We found him a place in an assisted living home in Nashua. Mom stayed in Arizona. I tried to get up to Nashua to see him once a month, but it was usually not for an extended time. I was never completely sure how to handle the situation. We once went out to a golf driving range, but that didn't work out well at all. Regrettably, I didn't have the patience to handle his disease. And we never were able to have extended conversations or talk about his life since his memory was slowly drifting away.

It was painful to see his decline and to see him alone without my mother, who insisted on staying in Arizona, particularly after the intervention we held to try to get her to confront her drinking problem and her angry, hurtful outbursts. She did come back to the East Coast to visit Dad but would then return after a week or so to Arizona. She died unexpectedly, tragically, and alone, there in August 1994, shortly before she would have turned seventy-three. I remember telling Dad about Mom's death not long thereafter. He died a short time later, less than six weeks after his seventy-third birthday.

Both my parents left a legacy of hard work, a focus on results, constant striving (also known as "over-achieving"), never being afraid to take a stand, the importance of education, a bit of a biting sense of humor, and a commitment to giving back to the community — not necessarily of money but of their time. From them, my siblings and I understood that life was serious business. They also left us with constant reminders to take good care of our teeth and to floss every day, as well as with an ever-present fear of Alzheimer's disease and alcoholism and perhaps with a sense of never being good enough. And, for me at least, a fear of dying alone.

My memories of our lives growing up are for the most part pleasant but a bit vague. I am attached enough to that past to keep mementos: dishes, pictures, and other things that no one else wanted — like Dad's army trunk. I still have the pearls and matching earrings I received for my twenty-first birthday and the purple cups that my mother gave me as I went off to my first teaching job in Oklahoma.

I am sure that Mom and Dad loved all five of us. They did not show it perhaps as much as they could have or as much as we might have liked. Or perhaps they didn't know how. I surely don't remember being cuddled or coddled.

Somehow, in our family, there didn't seem to be enough love to go around. Or maybe it wasn't voiced as affection and appreciation but instead was reserved for our accomplishments, for what we did — not for who we were, and still are, all very different individuals. Or, as Carla observed, "They did not have the right role models to give us the praise or to show us the love we needed. They really weren't that much different from other parents of that generation." Dad did tell me once that he didn't have a lot of love growing up.

Was I now writing this memoir to produce yet another achievement to earn their love and approval? Or was I learning French to establish a deeper connection with Dad? Or to please René Lévesque? Or was it my story that I was trying to preserve for my nieces and nephews? Or even more mundane, was it an attempt to stay busy and make sure I kept my own memory free of Alzheimer's or dementia?

How could I possibly answer all those questions and continue my search for the rest of Jeanne's story at the same time, alone with Quincie in the cottage in Dieppe?

FOUR

THE SEARCH FOR JEANNE CHEVALIER

When I was cleaning out one of my desk drawers back in Charlestown in preparation for my sabbatical year in France, I found a small blue travel journal with large green rings. On the first page, I had written "My Journal/Notes" from the years 2000 to 2003. I leafed through it and came upon a note that I must have written sometime between a visit to the Dordogne region in France in 2002 and one the next year to Scotland. It read:

> In 1660, when the letter from King Louis XIV arrived, few of us could read. So we put it on the table by the door, waiting for the priest to stop by and read it to us....

I might have jotted down that passage, supposedly the words of my ancestor Jeanne Chevalier, as an idea for the start of a novel about her except for two problems: a faulty understanding of history and my lack of expertise in writing fiction. In reality, as I later learned, the king would never have written a letter to a poor orphan like Jeanne, who could not read or sign her name. In any event, the date was all wrong. And, after so many years in the business world and after the publication of one business book and several articles and cases during my time working at Harvard Business School, writing fiction was not my style nor was it something I was eager to tackle.

But where did those words come from? That was a mystery. In fact, the first time I had heard Jeanne's name was in April 1992, at that family reunion in Nashua in honor of my great-grandparents, Joseph and Clara Levesque. My parents weren't there, but my siblings and their children were along with relatives from all over New England and as far away as Virginia and South Carolina.

There we discovered that, twelve years earlier, researchers working on the biography of Quebec's Prime Minister René Lévesque had found a French ancestor: Robert Lévesque. The reunion booklet we received included our family tree, beginning with that same Robert Lévesque and his wife, Jeanne Chevalier, my eighth-great-grandparents.

Nieces Raina, Zoe and Maron at the family reunion.
(Photo used with permission Nashua Telegraph April 24, 1992)

Over the next decade, I was too busy to think much about Jeanne. I was consumed with a banking career, doctoral program, and some rather major changes in my life. The year I turned fifty, my parents both died within two months of each other. I left the bank and began a new career as an independent consultant. Not long thereafter, I finished the work for my doctorate, moved out of the place where I was living in Hartford, Connecticut, took a trip to Australia, and found a new home in the Boston neighborhood of Charlestown.

I had, to be sure, found time in 1994 for a three-week trip to Normandy that included a very short visit to Hautot-Saint-Sulpice, Robert Lévesque's birthplace, but there was no mention of his wife Jeanne in any of the documents I was shown by a woman who had welcomed me into her home. A year later, I found a book in an old bookstore in Quebec City that contained three paragraphs about Jeanne in a chapter on her husband. I didn't give much thought at the time, however, to what was written there about her. Seeing her name on the Lévesque monument in the cemetery in Rivière-Ouelle, the village 150 kilometers northeast of Quebec City along the St. Lawrence River where Robert and Jeanne had lived, also hadn't triggered any interest when my sister, her daughters, and I stopped there during that same Quebec visit. Nor was any curiosity awakened even five years later when my sisters and I took my four nieces to Hautot-Saint-Sulpice.

Looking back, I wonder if Jeanne was beginning to gently haunt or taunt me in the midst of all those visits and other preoccupations. If so, she was being rather subtle! I wish I had kept a careful record of all her little hints. But I really didn't — prior to 2011. Instead, every now and then, I would find brief notes of ideas and bits of dreams in various notebooks and calendars, like that passage about the book in 2002 or, nine years later, in a note about a dream.

Something must have finally caught my attention, nevertheless, and inspired me enough to write that first line down in that blue travel journal. Sometime prior, I must have started to be curious about Jeanne or at least the *Filles du Roi* (King's Daughters)[3] program, initiated by the French king Louis XIV in 1663 to send young women to Quebec to marry, have children, and thus help populate and colonize New France (the territory in North America claimed by Jacques Cartier in the name of the king of France in 1532).

Whatever information I had found must have been interesting enough to store away in the back of my mind, but at that point, I didn't know there was any connection between the program and my ancestor. I am not even sure why I would have been pursuing this research. If it wasn't a push from Jeanne, it might have been those two visits to France or a fleeting memory of something about the program in those pages about Robert Lévesque that I had found years earlier. Or perhaps

---

3. Appendix I provides background information for readers who are unfamiliar with the *Filles du Roi* program.

it was because of the tragic death of a beloved cousin who, at the time, had been my last real link to any French family in Nashua.

Strangely, when I checked back in that travel journal from 2002, I also found a list: "Things I must do before I die." The fourth entry was: "Write a book about my great-grandmother." Maybe it was then that Jeanne had begun to haunt me.

In any event, I was still too busy during the next several years to spend any more time exploring her story, to reengage in my study of the French language, or to relax long enough to listen to her gentle and perhaps not so gentle taunts. But every once in a while I would chew over that sentence from 2002. My nieces remember me reciting the line over and over again to them as young adults. If Jeanne was slowly getting through to me, it would take some more time. I did wonder why I was the single member of my immediate family who was infected with this "bug." (My Australian friend Theodora once remarked that I could be channeling Jeanne.)

For whatever reason, I was slowly growing more curious. After all, my father was one of Jeanne's descendants. My interest in his lineage, though, had been rather recent, and I never had a chance to talk with him about it because, just as we were beginning to hear about his family history, he was slipping away from us.

Finally in late 2010, I was able to start paying attention to Jeanne's taunts since I was slowly disengaging from my consulting practice and not sure of what I would do next. I knew I didn't want to retire since retirement to me meant long, lazy days of golf, bridge, cocktails, and TV. I needed something in my life that would give me purpose and keep me engaged so I could avoid the boredom that I detested.

I started seriously researching Jeanne's life on the web. I reread those paragraphs in the book from Quebec City and then found more information about Jeanne in another book on Robert Lévesque, written by Ulric Lévesque, one of his descendants. From those readings, I determined that Jeanne had indeed been a Fille du Roi. In 1671, at the age of twenty-eight, she had left France forever and made her way to Quebec, along with one hundred other women who were also making the journey that year, all charged by the king with that mission to help colonize Quebec for France. There, she had married and then outlived three husbands, survived the births of nine children, and mourned the deaths of six of them. When she died on November 24, 1716, she left behind a will, an uncommon document for women and men at the time. She was survived by three sons and thirty-two grandchildren with generations of Levesques to come, including not only René Lévesque, but also the American author Jack Kerouac and my father, of course.

After learning this story, I grew even more curious. I began sketching out a novel around Jeanne's life. Using that introductory line to the book about the letter from King Louis XIV, I came up with an incredibly romantic tale about an encounter on the ship between Jeanne, the orphaned peasant girl, and the nobleman who was underwriting the ship's voyage to Quebec. Glances would be exchanged, and then love strings would be strummed amidst the pain of knowing the impossibility of fulfillment of their romance because of their insurmountable difference in social status. Years of separation would pass until fate and the democratic spirit spreading throughout New France would allow a marriage in their later years between the widow Jeanne and the nobleman, now a widower, and they would live happily ever after.

I knew this idea would not work, at least not for me. I explored other possible ideas for a novel, but they all felt equally "thin" to me and didn't fit with my personal style.

While I was wrestling with *how* to write Jeanne's story, I was still searching for *what* to write — that is, the details of her life. I started exploring the web more vigorously in December 2010. I reread Ulric's book about Robert and discovered that there was a problem pinpointing where Jeanne had been baptized as well as the exact names of her parents.

The next year in February I visited one of my nieces who was living in Paris at the time. We made a side trip from Paris to Coutances in an attempt to resolve the conflicting information about where Jeanne had been baptized since her first two marriage contracts had listed two different possibilities. In doing some additional research, I had not found any evidence to place her baptism in Dieppe, the first possible site.

The other possibility was Coutances, a cathedral town located at the base of the Cotentin Peninsula in lower Normandy, not far from Mont-Saint-Michel. The archivist in Coutances, with whom I had been in contact via email, had found a baptismal record for "Jeanne Chevalier" and had been able to decipher the almost illegible, hand-written one-line entry.

The document was waiting for me when I arrived at the Coutances Visitors' Center. The record indicated that Jeanne had been baptized in Saint Nicolas Church on June 8, 1643, although there was no reference to her parents, something I learned was rather common for that church at the time. When I asked if I could visit the church, the receptionist handed me a rather strange key and took my driver's license as collateral.

Key to Saint Nicolas Church

I walked across the plaza opposite the magnificent gothic Coutances Cathedral that dominates the town and turned left for the short walk down the street to Saint Nicolas Church. After several tries, I managed to unlock the heavy wooden door of the fifteenth-century Romanesque church. There was nothing inside. No chairs, no pews, no altar. It was totally empty, or so I thought at the time. It was no longer a functioning church, but instead was used as an occasional venue for musical and theatrical events. Despite the desolate interior, I wanted to wait around for a message from Jeanne or a signal from the universe that I was on the right path. Unfortunately, I didn't have any more time on that cold, damp day in February.

However, from that day on, my mild interest in Jeanne and her story started to grow into an obsession that would take over my life. Little did I know then that this obsession would grow even stronger and turn into my life's passion. It would ultimately lead to several more years of research, extensive trips to Normandy and Quebec, and to a "sabbatical" in France. I would be pushed to resurrect my high-school French in order to travel, to manage my way through archives and archival materials, to meet historians, distant relatives, and colleagues, to make new friends, to explore birthplaces, and to have truly unforgettable conversations and meetings. This obsession would also force me to reach back to my short graduate-school pursuit of a history degree and relearn the fundamentals of historical research. I would eventually give up my consulting practice to concentrate on her. I would even try to reach her through some shamanic channeling sessions.

I truly had no idea where the search for Jeanne's story would take me or how many unexpected, weird, and wonderful experiences I would have. I also never imagined how much work was involved in the quest to tell her story, to keep it alive for generations of her descendants, and to give Jeanne a voice and the recognition she deserved. Nor did I realize how many remarkable people I would meet who would be willing and able to help and would be so incredibly generous with their time. I am not sure which would have a greater impact on my life: the research and the writing or all those encounters along the way.

But I didn't know any of that then, and I am not sure whether that knowledge would have stopped me from getting more serious about my research after that cold February day in Coutances. My curiosity and the obsession with finding Jeanne's story wouldn't stop. I talked about her to anyone who would listen: nieces, friends, and people I had recently met in person or on the phone, including a Cuisinart customer service agent who had a French accent and who, it turned out, was also interested in genealogy.

In September 2013, two years after that visit to Coutances, I arrived in Dieppe to begin a three-week research trip with the hope of learning more. After my short stay in Dieppe, I continued my search for more information about Jeanne and drove to Coutances. I had decided to try to speak with the archivist there. Her office, I was told, was "in the archives." I wasn't exactly sure what archives in France were supposed to look like, especially in a medieval French city like Coutances. So when I was directed, or so I thought, to the third floor of the building opposite the Visitors' Center, I was not too taken aback by the old wooden staircase that I climbed with some trepidation. At the top were two old doors. I opened the most promising one and gazed into a dark hole with pigeon droppings and feathers everywhere. There was no light or any living person in sight.

I quickly retraced my steps and then found the elevator stuck on the other side of the nineteenth-century building and made my way to the third floor. Finally the archives looked more like what I imagined archives should look like: dark wood bookshelves stacked with old manuscripts, which promised to reveal all sorts of secrets. Unfortunately, I was not able to have a good conversation with the archivist, who could not make out much from my stammering attempts at questions. I did understand that she had not found any more information about Jeanne, other than that register entry of her baptism.

At her suggestion, I next visited the main departmental archives in Saint-Lô. The archives there were in direct contrast to those in Coutances. Their sterile white walls, standard bookshelves, and plain tables and chairs reflected choices made during the rebuilding of that town after World War II. There, as in other archives I would subsequently visit, an ID was required for entry, and pens were not allowed. Instead, pencils were provided, and smartphones were encouraged for making copies, as long as I noted down the specific pages copied. At the same time, I could have gone through original land records without the gloves or additional precautions that other archives required. While I was able to locate the birth, marriage and death records for the church in Coutances, my search for specific information about Jeanne and her parents proved to be futile in Saint-Lô and elsewhere that fall.

In the summer of 2014, I spent five weeks in Quebec doing more research. In Montreal, after passing through the grand, bright, and airy entrance to the archives lined with giant statues, I found the staff dressed in white coats, many of whom could speak enough English and tolerate my attempts at French to help me in my search for records and other information. While they were not dressed in white coats, I somehow also managed to communicate with the very helpful staff and volunteers at the Montreal University library, at the *Société généalogique canadienne-française* (the French-Canadian Genealogical Society), and at the Maison Saint-Gabriel, a museum and former residence of some of the Filles du Roi.

I then spent two weeks at the archives located at Laval University in Quebec City, where many of their white-coated staff were also fluent enough to understand my questions. Such was not the case at the archives in the village of Château-Richer on the north shore of the St. Lawrence River. I had a very frustrating conversation with the man in charge because of my inability to converse in French. It was becoming even clearer to me that I needed to accelerate my studying of that language if I was ever going to finish Jeanne's story!

During my time in Quebec City, other events more than made up for any frustrations. One day, Patricia, the owner of the studio I rented there, alerted me to the *Fête de la Nouvelle France* (New France Festival) that was starting the next day. I had not known anything about the four-day-long festival, and I was just coincidentally in Quebec City. Together, we attended the celebration of the 350th anniversary of the arrival of the second contingent of Filles du Roi where I connected with the President and other officers of the Society of the History of the Filles du Roi.

My luck continued. One time at the archives at Laval, I was trying to figure out how to pay for parking in the kiosk, when a woman in the same situation came to my rescue. We started sharing stories about family research. Soon afterwards, she introduced me to volunteers at the Charlesbourg Historical Society. One of those volunteers graciously drove me around Charlesbourg. Despite the fact that the landscape was now covered with twentieth-century homes and surrounded by a great deal of commercial development, he helped me visualize the village as it might have appeared in 1671 when Jeanne lived there with her first husband.

After that rather productive time in Quebec City, I drove over to Rivière-Ouelle, Jeanne's residence for the last thirty-seven years of her life. In between visits to the archives in nearby La Pocatière, I tried to continue to write, hoping that Jeanne's spirit would help me. Indeed, one night in the cottage I rented along the banks of the St. Lawrence River, I did have a very vivid dream of her, dressed in a green peasant dress and wearing a matching bonnet, standing at the doorway and welcoming me into her home.

I also had lunch with Ulric Lévesque, whom I had contacted after reading his book about our common ancestor, Robert. During our meal, Ulric told me about the Lévesque Association, a group that had been formed to share information and activities for descendants of the ten known founders of Lévesque families in Quebec and that would soon become very important in my life. The next day, at Ulric's suggestion, I stopped by the town hall. It was closed for lunch, but a man happened to walk out right as I was getting into my car to leave. The man, who turned out to be the mayor, stopped me and asked if I needed help. After hearing my story, he arranged for me to meet his assistant, who eventually connected me to Nelly, the secretary of the *Cousins du Nouveau Monde* (the Cousins of the New World) in Hautot-Saint-Sulpice.

The next year, 2015, I spent almost two months in France. For the first three weeks, I studied at a French language school in Rouen, lived with a French family, and divided my time between school in the morning and the archives in the afternoon. I then spent a month in a studio apartment in the Pollet neighborhood of Dieppe. Dieppe became my base for research trips to the villages of Cliponville and Beaumont-en-Auge and return visits to Saint-Lô and Coutances, looking, without much luck, for more information about Jeanne and her three husbands. Then again, I did have the good fortune to meet Nadine at the suggestion of my Rouen homestay family. Over the course of the following year Nadine and I stayed in touch via email and video calls and eventually arranged to exchange homes.

Three months later that year, I made a trip back to Quebec, this time with my feline traveling companion, Quincie. We spent a few days near Rivière-Ouelle with me doing more research at the archives in La Pocatière and Quincie hanging out in our motel. I then drove us further east to Rimouski for the annual meeting of the Lévesque Association. After lunch, I gave a presentation on my research to date on Jeanne, beginning with a question: "How many of you have ever heard the name Jeanne Chevalier?" Since few people in the audience raised their hands, I realized clearly that I now had found a purpose in life!

In 2016, thanks to a wonderful friend who adores Quincie and who offered to take care of her during my research trips, I was able to go back to France, this time for eight weeks. First, I spent a week in Caen, intending to devote all my time researching in Caen's archives. However, on my second day there, I happened to fall face forward on a sidewalk, breaking my glasses and requiring a visit to the hospital, an x-ray, seven stiches, and at least one day of rest — my first real encounter with the French medical system. Two days later, the staff at the archives were kind enough not to mention my black eye and very bruised and bandaged face when I showed up to continue my research. They did laugh when I tried to explain that I had had a battle with a sidewalk, even though I wasn't sure they understood my attempt at humor.

The stitches were removed and my glasses replaced during my next stop, ten days in Coutances at the archives and library. My face was pretty much back to normal during the following week when I spent several days at the archives located in an old fort overlooking the center of Le Havre, continuing to search, futilely as it turned out, for information about Jeanne's first husband.

With my face recovered from my close encounter with the sidewalk, I then took the train to Dieppe, where I had arranged my month-long home-exchange with Nadine, my acquaintance from the prior year. During my time there, I gave two presentations on my research on Jeanne's life. The first was for the Cousins of the New World in Hautot-Saint-Sulpice, arranged by Nelly, and another, organized by *Les Amys du Vieux Dieppe* (Friends of Old Dieppe), at the Château-Musée in Dieppe. A few days after the presentation at the Château, while sitting at Nadine's dining room table looking out across the deck at her beautiful flower garden, I made the decision to spend a year in France, beginning the next January.

In between all these visits to archives in Quebec and France, I had also been doing more library research. After my first visit to Coutances, I had joined the New England Historical Genealogical Society in Boston. There, Jeanne's story started to become more defined as I read baptismal, marriage and death registers, and notarial records of land transactions that were now available online from microfilms in their filing cabinets or could be located in documents on their bookshelves. With the help of the Boston Public Library staff, I obtained a three-month permission to use the libraries at Harvard University, where I spent hours researching Jeanne's story. There, as in other archives and libraries — although not all — I was free to wander in the stacks, where I would come across more resources not uncovered via library catalog searches.

Fortunately, living in New England where genealogical research and, most significantly, interest in Quebecois heritage continued to grow, I was able to take advantage of other resources at libraries in Woonsocket, Rhode Island, and Manchester, New Hampshire. Those libraries were also headquarters for genealogical and historical societies whose volunteers and staff were most helpful in my search for Jeanne's story.

Internet searches also proved to be invaluable, even though they frequently required dogged persistence as well as careful discipline to avoid getting lost among too many possible, but potentially fruitless, leads. My experience with a volunteer researcher at the historical society in the town of Longueil, Quebec, was one example of determined perseverance on both our parts and his incredible willingness to help. Even though I never did meet him in person, he persisted in tracking down an obscure reference that I had found regarding Guillaume Lecanteur, Jeanne's first husband. While I was able to give him few details, he eventually provided an answer along with copies of articles with more facts on Lecanteur and his land purchases.

Through the power of the Internet, I managed to locate email addresses so I could send queries to authors and historians, most of whom responded and provided answers or further information where they could. Many of those contacts incredibly led me to others. Thanks to a colleague from work, I met the author of a book about immigrants from France, who happened to live near Boston and who invited me to tea and conversation in her lovely backyard. She in turn connected me with Yves Landry, the living French expert on the Filles du Roi, who then led me to another historian and his extensive research on the early Quebec pioneers.

Of course, I also tried to take advantage of the web to access archives to track down documents and information in France. I soon realized that online access to French databases of archives was not uniform, at least at that point in time. The archives for the Manche and Seine-Maritime departments in Normandy could be accessed online, but those for Calvados could not.

Whether online or not, in France or elsewhere, records were not easy to read. They were handwritten in the French of the time with inconsistent spelling on paper, which was often double-sided and covered with ink splotches. I sometimes was able to find databases of transcriptions created by volunteers from local genealogical societies, but the information could be confusing. When I couldn't locate the registry of an event in one of those databases, I didn't know what to think. It was possible that the original record of it didn't exist since not all events were documented, given the possible absence of a priest. It was also possible that the record had been destroyed or that the volunteers hadn't started the work on that period or that particular village.

Most archivists and volunteers were welcoming and tolerant of Anglophone researchers with faltering French. Sometimes, though, when my requests for information were met with blank stares, I couldn't be certain whether they hadn't understood me or simply didn't know how to answer me. I was never totally sure how to react, but gentle and courteous insistence usually paid off.

In the middle of all this sometimes frustrating but generally rewarding research, I was also trying to find a good structure for the book about Jeanne and the right theme. I had given up the romance novel idea, so was the book going to be about "courage," "choices," or even my own "identity quest"? I attended several writing workshops to sort these issues out and to try to improve my writing skills. I needed help since my background in business writing wouldn't really fit this project. Case writing did help a bit in forming a story, but it was not all that useful when it came to character development, dialogue creation, or structuring a book that others would want to read.

Sometimes my education and training got in the way. I would become obsessed and then overwhelmed in trying to understand context. My history-student persona from my two years of graduate study decades ago would suddenly take over. I was struggling between knowing and not knowing, constantly wanting to learn more: What was Jeanne's life like before she left France at the age of twenty-eight? Why did she choose, if indeed it was a choice, to leave France? Why did she agree to marry those three very different men? I wanted to be able to picture her but decided instead to rely on the Le Nain brothers' paintings of seventeenth-century peasants to help with the image.

I tried to imagine what life must have been like in those days without clocks, those instruments that organize my life. Instead, Jeanne would have been forced to rely on knowledge of the passing seasons and the sun, moon, and stars for directions and for telling time.

Possible likeness of Jeanne
(Cutout from a copy of the painting
"Peasant Family in an Interior" by the
Le Nain brothers, at the Louvre.)

How did Lord Deschamps, her third husband, assemble his "crew" of eight workers in France and persuade them to go with him to New France and help establish his estate that would become Rivière-Ouelle? Why did he wait twenty years after the death of his first wife before marrying Jeanne? Why did any of those men and women choose to leave France and set sail for Quebec?

I kept asking myself how I was going to be able to answer these questions and solve the mysteries during that period in the life of New France when I had so little to go on to form hypotheses. My research was part history and part detective story. To ease the stress and deal with the frustration, I kept telling myself, *Concentrate on the research and you can put the pieces together later.*

I frequently felt as if I had fallen down a rabbit hole like Alice, but instead of Wonderland and a smiling cat, I was faced with Info-Factland, and the facts didn't all agree. I tried to temper my quest by asking myself, *How much do I really need to know about women, children, and life in seventeenth-century Quebec in order to write Jeanne's story?*

I wanted to go to the original sources but soon realized the improbability of finding the documents and the impossibility of reaching that goal. Or, if it was not impossible, I wondered how long it would take me to find the documents, transcribe them from handwritten Old French, and then translate those that needed translation. I finally realized I was going to have to rely on other authors and knowledgeable researchers who could read old French better than I ever could.

A conversation with my German friend and colleague Peter when we met up in Amsterdam in October 2013 also helped. After a visit to see Rembrandt's *Night Watch* in the Rijksmuseum on that rather chilly day, we stopped at a cafe. While we sipped cups of delicious hot white chocolate, I shared my anguish over my research. Peter gave me some perspective based on our common interest in and knowledge of creativity: "Jeanne didn't know what her new life would be like, and she leapt. You have also taken great leaps in your career. You can fill in the gaps between knowing and not knowing as you've done in the past with your creative talents." He then added, "Just keep thinking about possibilities, as Jeanne must have done when she left France."

On the train back to Paris, I reflected on Peter's words. It did take an enormous amount of courage and perseverance for Jeanne to keep going on in spite of the challenges she faced in her life. In her case, she presumably had no choice. Unlike Jeanne, I did have a choice. I could stop this obsession. I could give up my search for her story and this drive to speak French. Should I? Could I really? Would she let me?

Recalling a dream I had had in Paris during my 2011 visit also helped me recognize that I didn't need to be perfect, that I could still tell her story without all the i's dotted and t's crossed. It had been a strange dream, on a night after I had seen the movie *The King's Speech* in English with French subtitles. In it, episodes from my financial analysis days in a bank were mixed with my knowledge of creativity. I interpreted the dream's message to be: *It will be a different sort of book, but it will be mine. I don't need to have exact numbers that all agree. I can round them. I can use my knowledge about creativity to make it work.*

The message of that dream was reinforced during a December 2013 talk that author Julie Orringer gave at a Radcliffe Institute event in Cambridge, Massachusetts: "Lies That Tell the Truth: Story and History in the Novel." The advice I took from her talk was that I could use my research, my creative imagination, and the right vocabulary to "lengthen the shadow" that Jeanne had cast on my life. I could deepen it, sharpen it, give it substance, "de-blur it," in Orringer's words, by "giving flesh to dry records" that had been lost, eaten, or destroyed long ago.[4]

I must have also been inspired and encouraged by the persistence and commitment of Jeanne, Robert, and all the other early settlers in Quebec as they cleared the land, seeded it, and harvested it to produce food and create a livelihood for themselves. With all of this help, I managed to do what I believed I had promised Jeanne I would do at some point over the years and what I wasn't sure I would actually be able to do. After two more weeks at the archives in Quebec City to wrap up my research, once again with Quincie, I published the book on November 24, 2016, on the three-hundredth anniversary of Jeanne's death with some measured feelings of accomplishment. I then started to pack up and get Quincie ready for our trip to France. Finally, on Sunday, January 1, 2017, we headed out to the airport with Carla for our flight, and Quincie and I began our next adventure in the little cottage in Dieppe.

---

4. https://www.radcliffe.harvard.edu/event/2013-julie-orringer-lecture.

FIVE

DISCOVERING DIEPPE

Often when I would tell people back in the States that I was spending a year in France, they assumed that meant Paris or perhaps Provence. So I would have to explain, "No, I've rented a cottage in Dieppe, a small town in Normandy on the English Channel, forty-five minutes north of Rouen and not much over a two-hour train ride, with good connections, from Paris."

For those who asked why I chose Dieppe, I would initially respond that I found it to be a very pleasant place, despite its ever-changing weather that was still far more comfortable than the frigid, icy, snowy winters and hot, humid summers of Boston where I lived for so many years. It could be easy to get around without a car, as long as walking up and down the cliffs didn't present a problem. For those of us over a certain age, riding the bus was free. The cost of living in Dieppe compared very favorably to Boston's. Its outstanding Saturday farmers' market was a major attraction as were the quays, the beach, the esplanade, and the boardwalk. And my mother would be happy: most everyone in Dieppe spoke "real French"! My dad could certainly get along fine with his French as well.

For those interested in hearing more about my choice, I would tell them that, in fact, the first time I saw Dieppe was in late September 2013. Since I had not done much research about the town before arriving, I actually didn't know what to expect. I was surprisingly charmed.

Dieppe is set between two chalk cliffs at the mouth of the river Arques, which empties into the English Channel, providing a harbor for all sorts of boats. Indeed, it's called the "city of four ports" because of its lively commercial, fishing, cross-channel transportation, and leisure activities. Two bridges — one a drawbridge and the other a historically important "bridge that turns" — connect the main part of Dieppe with the Pollet neighborhood, where fishermen and their families have lived for centuries in small stucco homes, some still adorned with hooks for hanging fishing nets. Along the quays on that September day, the many restaurants were filled with patrons — tourists and locals, sitting inside or outside as they often do year-round, weather permitting.

Yet, though I found Dieppe to be a lovely town, it turned out to be more than merely a pleasant stop for me in Normandy. It was Dieppe's history and its spirit that I found especially attractive. As I learned from several guided tours and conferences, the town was first mentioned as a small fishing village in 1030, although Roman ruins had been found around Dieppe from even more remote times. In its early years, the town was tossed back and forth between belonging to England and France. It was part of England during the time of William the Conqueror and his successors and then was annexed to France in 1204 after the victory over Richard the Lionheart by the French king Philippe-Auguste, one of my very distant ancestors. Dieppe was subsequently occupied by the English from 1420 to 1435 during the Hundred Years' War and may have been one of the stops made by Jeanne d'Arc on her way to her trial and execution in Rouen in 1431.

By the time my eighth-great-grandmother Jeanne Chevalier arrived in Dieppe in the late seventeenth century, the town was already well developed as a center for fishing, trading, cartography, and ivory and lace crafts. Dieppe fisheries, using relays of carriages, horses, and drivers, arranged for daily deliveries of their products over the roads to Paris making the 172 kilometer trip in twenty-four hours, arriving at Les Halles in the capital city via the Rue des Poissonniers.

Dieppe managed to survive a significant loss of population during the religious wars of the sixteenth century as inhabitants who embraced the reformed religion of Jean Calvin left for more welcoming lands. Its citizens were also able to recover from several epidemics that swept through the town in the seventeenth century.

Dieppe's merchants played an important role in exploring and mapping North America through their support of early maritime expeditions to other parts of the world, as well as to locations in what are now the United States and Canada. As a port city, the town served as a major point of debarkation for many emigrants to Canada throughout the seventeenth century. Since medieval times, it has also been one of the stops for pilgrims arriving from northern Europe making their way to the shrine of St. James in Santiago de Compostela in Spain.

While I might never know how long she lived in Dieppe, I did believe that it was from Dieppe that Jeanne Chevalier, along with the majority of other Filles du Roi, as well as her second and third husbands, left France to sail to Quebec. I could feel her spirit whenever I walked the cobblestone streets of old Dieppe. When I watched the ferry leave Dieppe headed for England, I would try to imagine what it was like to climb aboard a ship almost 350 years ago and embark on a journey of at least six weeks toward an unknown future in New France.

Jeanne's Dieppe was a very different place, but since so few vestiges of that time remain, trying to picture what Dieppe was like when she was there could be a challenge. The two oldest churches (Saint-Jacques and Saint-Remy) were still standing, although in varying states of needed repair. A fifteenth-century castle set above Dieppe on its western cliff continued to dominate the town from its setting overlooking the beach.

Erected to defend the population against the English in 1435, it survived numerous wars since then. During World War II, the castle served as headquarters for German forces who left behind underground tunnels and several bunkers. Converted to a museum in 1923, it houses a collection of ivory, local memorabilia, and a variety of paintings by local and not-so-local artists. In one of its rooms could be

Château-Musée, Dieppe France

found a large wooden sign from a seventeenth-century pharmacy that was located on Dieppe's main street and that Jeanne might easily have walked by or even visited.

Twenty-three years after Jeanne left Dieppe, English and Dutch warships bombarded the town, and the fire that ensued destroyed many of the homes built of wood in typical Norman style. When King Louis XIV had the city rebuilt, he prohibited the use of wood. The homes, apartments, shops, and other structures that make up Dieppe's town center are now a mix of styles from the late seventeenth century through more recent times. Many of the streets have disappeared, been remade, or at least had a name change. Jeanne could recognize the churches, the castle, remnants of the fortifications, some of the streets, and one or two other buildings, including one that remains from the Augustinian convent and that I considered buying in order to restore and save it from further deterioration. That was before my brother Dana (who was visiting me at the time) and I determined the cost and effort involved. Little else, however, has survived from Jeanne's time.

The main part of Dieppe used to be surrounded by walls that were first erected in 1360. As part of the "modernization" that began at the end of the eighteenth century, the walls were eventually demolished, reportedly to "beautify the town." Only one tower and a few remnants of the walls remain from Jeanne's time, although traces of the walls have been found in the basements of older buildings or in excavations for new ones.

Even the beach was very different when Jeanne was there. Then, she would have seen sheep grazing on what is currently a broad stretch of lawn and women along the beach, drying linen or gathering stones to be used for construction or munitions or to be sent to England for use in the manufacturing of ceramics. Now, the two-kilometer-long esplanade is treasured by both residents and visitors for its tranquil expanse of green and as a location for sports, entertainment, and leisure activities. And, despite the fact that layers of small and not-so-small pebbles and stones cover the sand and can make walking difficult, the beach has for years welcomed throngs of tourists from surrounding areas and even Paris who somehow manage to make themselves comfortable enough to enjoy the sun, the waves, and the sky.

In the early nineteenth century, the Duchess of Berry, an Italian princess who married into the French royal family and who was an influential patron of the arts, helped develop the town's reputation as a fashionable beach resort. A number of grand hotels were built along the waterfront and in the town. Several impressionist painters found the light on the cliffs, the clouds, and the water a major attraction, as did English visitors who built majestic homes along the shore beneath the castle.

During World War II, Dieppe suffered significant damage. The town was occupied by the Germans beginning in June 1940 and endured Allied bombing for the next four years. The population dwindled as children and other family members left for safer quarters or as men were sent off as forced labor to work in Germany or other parts of France. The beach was cordoned off with barbed wire and cement blocks in preparation for a suspected invasion. The worst disaster occurred on August 19, 1942, during the ill-fated Allied raid on Dieppe and its surrounding beaches, when six thousand soldiers landed and over half of them were killed, wounded, or taken prisoner. Most of the buildings along the beach and the quays were severely damaged. All those majestic houses below the castle were destroyed. Reconstruction of the town would take decades.

Until 2013, direct trains that had been established in 1848 brought Parisians to Dieppe as the closest beach to Paris and the nearest access to England. While there was talk about re-instituting direct trains on weekends, for the moment they just went back and forth to Rouen, where connections had to be made to reach Paris. Two or three times a day, depending on the season, a ferry left Dieppe to make the trip to and from New Haven on the southern coast of England, four hours and 103 kilometers away.

When I arrived on my initial visit to Dieppe on that late September day in 2013, my principal destination was the church of Saint-Jacques at the southern end of the town's main plaza. According to Jeanne's first marriage contract, this was her parents' parish church, although I had not been able to locate any other record that tied Jeanne or her parents to Saint-Jacques or gave any information as to how long the Chevalier family lived in Dieppe.

For centuries since Saint-Jacques was built in the twelfth century, it had been undergoing constant expansion, reconstruction, and restoration. It's a large church, the size of a cathedral, with a bell tower that holds three bells named Catherine, Geneviève, and Hélène. The church is a mix of different architectural styles. It offers gargoyles, flying buttresses, and an incredible assortment of symbols of nature, religion, and mythology, as well as of Dieppe's history of exploration and fishing — most notably the famous coquilles (scallops). The exterior of the church still suffers from corrosion caused by the sea air mixed with the limestone that was used in its construction, and from damage that took place during the sixteenth-century religious wars.

Inside the church, several chapels that were built after the flying buttresses were added in the seventeenth century line the walls. To the right of what was once the main altar with its two giant carved angels is the chapel of Jean Ango, one of the church's benefactors who also financed the voyages of Giovanni da Verrazzano and Jacques Cartier to North America. To the left of that altar is the Treasury Wall with its sixteenth-century frieze of carved figures, representing the peoples of America, Africa, and the Indian Ocean whom explorers and traders from Dieppe encountered on their many journeys. To the west of the Treasury Wall is the Canadian chapel. Its stained-glass windows depict the martyrdom of two Jesuit missionaries in seventeenth-century Quebec. Along the chapel's walls are hung several plaques in homage to brave family members who left France to settle in Canada.

Sometimes, in later visits to the church, I could imagine my ancestor Jeanne sitting in one of the straight-back chairs with her family. It would have been there, during one of the services in 1671, where she could have heard the news from the archbishop in Rouen about the plans of King Louis XIV to send young women to New France. I often wondered what she was thinking when she heard those words. Was she eager to answer the call? Did her parents encourage her to make the journey? Sadly, the reasons why Jeanne decided to leave Dieppe and sail off to Quebec that June with one of the last contingents of Filles du Roi will likely forever remain a mystery.

That September 2013 visit to Saint-Jacques and to Dieppe was too short. I didn't have time to wander around the town and find the Canadian Square and the stone pillar near the castle wall. I wasn't able to read all the dates engraved on the pillar that marked the events linking Dieppe with Canada from those days of early exploration five hundred years ago through that tragic raid of August 19, 1942, and even later. And it wasn't until sometime afterward that I discovered a family tie: among the close to one thousand Canadian soldiers who died that August day was Lieutenant Jean-Jacques Lévesque, a very distant cousin. He was buried along with the others in the Les Vertus cemetery, located not far from the center of town.

On that lovely fall day, I also failed to see all the other monuments that line Dieppe's boardwalk in remembrance of the Allied lives lost during that battle. If my dad had been with me and we had made that walk together, how would he have reacted? Would the monuments have brought back too many tortured memories of the horrors of war?

I returned to Dieppe in 2015 for a month and then again in 2016 for five weeks. That's when I decided to find a way to stay, initially for a year, fulfilling that college dream of mine to live in France. The more I visited, the more this town fascinated me. It's true that Jeanne's spirit pulled me to Dieppe, but I kept coming back for other reasons.

Despite its problems as one of the poorest cities in France, Dieppe offered many attractions besides its long history, the castle, the old churches, the clean air, the frequently swept streets and sidewalks in the center of town, and the essentially moderate climate. Farmers' markets are held on Tuesday and Thursday mornings in the main square. The much larger Saturday market, recently voted the most beautiful in France, occupies several blocks in the center and provides visitors and locals with an abundance of options for buying cheese, sausages, fish, meat, poultry, fruits and vegetables, flowers, all sorts of international delicacies, and incredible choices of clothing, hats, scarves, and household items.

From Tuesday morning until Saturday evening, small and mostly local clothing stores and boutiques offer an amazing selection of items that run the gamut from cheap to chic (and expensive). In addition, lining the pedestrian-only main street and several side streets is a wide variety of bakeries, cafes, restaurants, chocolate stores, bookstores, banks, travel and real estate agencies, and no Starbucks. A Domino's Pizza, a Subway, a McDonald's, and a Burger King are mostly hidden away on the outskirts, much to my delight.

Shortly after arriving for my sabbatical year in France, I started regularly packing up my shopping bags and list early on Saturday mornings to make my way down the cliff to the farmers' market. Sometimes, if I knew I had a lot to buy, I would take the straw shopping cart that I found in the cottage's sunroom, but I usually avoided doing so since pulling the cart back up the cliff required a good bit of extra effort.

Even in the winter, the market was usually crowded with locals — and sometimes a few tourists — sauntering through the stalls, checking on what was available, and stopping along the way to greet friends, thus clogging up the passageways, much to the annoyance of this impatient American shopper. I would stock up on cheese, vegetables, occasionally mushrooms — depending on the season — dried apricots, hummus, chicken, and other items on my list. Not infrequently, I would unexpectedly meet a friend in the market, and we would stop for coffee.

Unlike most of my French friends, I tended to shop once a week — to save both time and energy, despite the weight of the bags. My priority tended to be convenience versus the absolute freshness preferred by others. A friend once explained her rationale for shopping almost every day: "If I buy a steak today to eat tomorrow, what would I do with it if I were to be invited to dine out that day?"

If I did need something during the week, I would walk down to the grocery store in the town center or to a nearby bakery for a baguette. Sometimes I would take the bus up to the Belvedere shopping center where an Auchan, a large supermarket, was located. In nice weather, I would walk the thirty minutes to Auchan, partly for the exercise and partly for the joy of climbing up and down some of the many stairways that connect streets and alleys up and down the cliffs. Once Sylvie, a delightful French woman whom I met shortly after arriving in Dieppe, led me on a walk where we tried to find, climb, or descend all of them. I am not sure that we were able to accomplish that goal that day, but we did end our trek with a coffee at the very popular Bar-o-Mètre at the far end of the beach.

Beyond those stairways, Dieppe's location provided other advantages for me since it was ever so easy to walk out of the city limits and start hikes along the cliffs or elsewhere. A car was sometimes necessary, but I found I could walk most of the time. For a semi-monthly church meeting in Pourville, some three kilometers west of the cottage, I would walk past the grounds of the nearby high school along the cliff and the golf course, one of the oldest in France. I would often stop at a lookout point with a glorious view of the western cliffs and beyond before zigzagging down the road into Pourville's center. I would then make my way up another cliff to reach a church member's home, set high above the town with a magnificent view of the channel. Fortunately, a friend would offer to drive me back to Dieppe after the meeting.

Unquestionably, it was those friends — with or without cars — who also made Dieppe so very delightful. I was pleasantly surprised by the number of interesting people from all different walks of life who lived there, either because Dieppe was where they had lived all their lives or because they were born there and had decided to return to their roots. Increasingly, there were also many newcomers from the Paris region who decided to seek out Dieppe's attractions with its location on the channel, its beach, the boardwalk, the esplanade, and its relatively lighter demands on their finances.

In addition to the many wonderful new friendships I made in my various visits to Dieppe, I discovered something almost as incredible: the astonishing light. So clear and soft and changing with the seasons and the time of day, it would bathe the stucco, brick, and stone homes, the churches, and the buildings of the town with delicate pastels.

Watching the ribbons of color on the English Channel, I could easily understand why impressionist painters were so attracted to Dieppe and the region. Was Jeanne ever able to experience that light? Did she ever have an urge to paint, or would she have simply stood, like me, in amazement on the cliff above the castle and view the clouds and their shadows dancing across the water and the cliffs?

Even though there was not much left of the town from Jeanne's time, I could sometimes imagine her walking along the cobblestone streets amid the houses that were built right up to the sidewalk. I often felt her presence inside Saint-Jacques church. I once had a dream of her walking outside the walls along the Arques River. In another dream, she was sitting in a garden in the Augustinian convent that disappeared long ago. Remembrance of that dream led me down a street where I had not previously walked to find that old building, dating from the years of the convent, the one I had once considered buying.

Since that first visit to Dieppe back in 2013, I eventually learned a lot more about Jeanne and her history. But some questions remained, including how, when, and why she left Coutances where she was born and moved to Dieppe. Nevertheless, whether or not I would ever find the answers to these questions, I would forever thank her for enticing me to experience Dieppe's wondrous light, its history, the cliffs, the castle, the friendship of so many interesting, kind, and generous people, and the ever-changing palette of light and color — even the fading paint on the blue garage door.

Part Two

Charting the Course

SIX

THE SEARCH FOR COMMUNITY

Not long after arriving in Dieppe with Quincie in January 2017, I was sitting in one of the red upholstered chairs in a new church home and struggling with the French version of the Lord's Prayer. Certain parts of the service seemed familiar, and I recognized the music of some of the hymns, but the words were all foreign, of course. *How had I arrived here?* I wondered.

Back on November 24, 2016, when I had fulfilled my promise to Jeanne to publish the story of her life, I had awakened with the sudden realization that I had really not written much in the book about her religion. The omission was very odd for two reasons. First, religion must have played a major role in her life in the seventeenth century. Second, religion had become a very important part of my life as well, and my search for Jeanne's story was not the only journey I had been on in the latter part of my life.

From a twenty-first-century perspective, it's difficult to appreciate or understand how intricately integrated into everyday life religion was in France and New France at that time. There might not have been church bells ringing every quarter-hour in the frontier village of Rivière-Ouelle, as there surely would have been in Dieppe with its two Roman Catholic churches and five convents. However, on the ship carrying the Filles du Roi to their new home, there would have been frequent, if not daily, masses said by the priest who accompanied them on their journey.

Jeanne's life in Quebec must have been deeply tied to her Catholic faith. Her three marriages were conducted by priests. Her children were baptized in the Catholic Church. Her will, in which she left money for masses to be said for her soul at eight different churches, was further proof. So, why did I fail to more substantially and specifically describe the role of religion in Jeanne's life? Perhaps it was too speculative at the time, or I was in too much of a hurry to finish the book.

Hoping that she had forgiven me, I thought about my own spiritual path as I sat in my new church home. On that bucket list of items that I had composed in 2002, there was nothing about finding a church community despite the role that religion had been playing in my life for many years before then.

As I was growing up, my life, like Jeanne's, had also been tied to the Catholic faith, at least for the first few decades. Although my mother had been raised a Protestant, she converted to Catholicism in order to marry my father. Ours was a strict but superficial Catholicism, based on sins, confession, and penance. Being Catholic was a badge of honor and a significant part of our family life from First Communion at the age of six through Confirmation six years later. We had missals with the words for services for every imaginable saint or reason, including passages from the New Testament but hardly ever from the Old Testament. I don't remember seeing a Bible in the house.

Latin Mass was obligatory every Sunday, as was fish on Fridays. We went to confession at least once a month, usually weekly, often for "sins" made up in order to have something to confess. I would have promised to never again be "conceited," be "selfish," or fight with my brothers and sisters. I would then recite the Act of Contrition and receive my penance from the priest. There was also catechism every week and lots of indoctrination into the mysteries and rules of the Catholic tradition. In addition, much of my social life was centered around Catholic youth organizations and activities, including summer camp.

I remained a Catholic through college, seldom questioning its theology. After graduation, I explored the Episcopal Church during the two years I was teaching Russian and Russian History in a private Episcopal school in Tulsa, Oklahoma. I even dated the minister for a short time. Although I was married in the Catholic Church a few years later by a priest and a Protestant minister in deference to my husband's religion, we didn't practice either faith very often, only attending church on Easter and Christmas. After my divorce, I went back to being an active Catholic while living in California, to the point of obtaining a church sanctioned "dissolution of marriage."

My subsequent move to Connecticut to a much less liberal Catholic Church converted me to years of being "spiritual" rather than religious and to attending the "church of the Sunday morning walk around the reservoir." My religious beliefs, such as they were, floundered against the challenges of a new world of anti-war feminism, mixed in with the pressing needs of everyday life and a growing career. Faith, religion, and belief in God were wrapped up in Catholicism and got rejected in total with my increasing impatience over the direction of the Church.

Yet, I was always searching for some higher purpose in life, something more than having a good time. So I embarked on a several-years-long "new-age quest for the meaning of life," aspects of which I have maintained ever since. I explored crystals and therapy, devoured self-help books, and studied Carl Jung's work on dreams in depth. I learned that dreams were a gateway through which the unconscious communicates with our conscious minds. I followed Scott Peck's less-traveled road and read most of what Thomas Moore had written about finding soul, whether in a mate, in life, or in what he called "place."

I also had my astrological chart done. The reading explained my no-nonsense approach to life, my problems communicating my feelings, my belief that no one was ever going to take care of me, and that love was conditioned on achievement. The presence of certain planets in my "House of Relationships" supposedly adversely impacted my ability to have good partnerships and could help explain my divorce and somewhat spotty track record with members of the opposite sex.

Clearly, I was going to have problems finding a soulmate. Instead, I decided — consciously or unconsciously — that I could add depth and support in my independent life by finding a community. Still, all that new-age spirituality did not provide much of a community for me, and having one became significantly more important when a work colleague, who was much younger than me, had a stroke. Since I was living alone in Hartford with no family nearby, I wondered who would visit me in the hospital if something like that happened to me.

So I found a Congregational church that resembled a Catholic one, built of stone with stained glass windows, wooden pews, and a real organ. I eventually became a member after struggling with the emotional consequences of converting to being Protestant and my fear, a remnant of my years of Catholic Christian Doctrine, of going to hell since that's where all Protestants ended up. The minister could not offer me guarantees about my destination after death, but he did promise to visit me in the hospital!

Before I moved to Boston in 1996, I asked him for advice about another church that would suit me in terms of theology, the congregation, location (I didn't really want to have to drive to church), architecture (stained-glass windows continued to be a requirement), and music (a choir and organ were on that list). My requirements regarding the physical church and for community and convenience of location evolved over time. Twenty years later, I was comfortably a member of my third church home in Boston, complete with stained-glass windows and an organ and built of stone, bringing me back almost full circle to the Episcopal faith.

When I first arrived in Dieppe, I thought I might occasionally attend Catholic mass at Saint-Jacques, the church that had been, according to her first marriage contract, the parish home of Jeanne's parents. It was definitely built of stone and had the necessary organ and stained-glass windows. I also tried to find an Episcopal church but learned that the nearest one was in Rouen — a forty-five-minute drive from Dieppe and not very convenient for Sunday services or any other activities I might want to attend.

That left the United Protestant church in Dieppe, which at first didn't look all that inviting in its store-front location: plain interior, no pews, no stained-glass windows, and no organ that I could see. However, given the crowd of people in attendance at mass at Saint-Jacques and the lack of a "coffee hour" afterwards, I wasn't sure that

I would find a community there. And, besides, there were still all the problems that I had with the Catholic Church and its theology. So I decided to try the Protestant church.

That decision turned out to be a wise one and eventually would lead to an incredible number of new friends and totally unexpected new experiences. Through conversations, readings, and conferences, I learned that the church in Dieppe was started by Huguenots, or French Protestants, who at one time represented one-half of the town's population before being significantly reduced in numbers by the religious wars of the sixteenth century. As a "recovering Catholic" and "initiating Protestant," I had spent most of my years as a Protestant learning about the Bible, particularly the Old Testament. While I had heard the names of Martin Luther and Jean Calvin in history courses, my naïve perception until I arrived in Dieppe was that, at least in the United States, Protestantism started either with the early seventeenth-century arrival of the Puritans or Pilgrims in New England or as the legacy of King Henry VIII's decision in England to divorce and marry again. Needless to say, learning about these European roots and the Huguenots gave me quite an education.

I was also amazed by how much of a minority Protestants represent and how few Protestant churches there are in the Normandy region of France. In the United States, almost every town has a church and, for the most part, the primary church has a Protestant affiliation. In France, every village has a church as well, but it's a Catholic one.

Despite the prevalence of these Catholic churches, France is surprisingly much more secular in its political and everyday life than the United States, a result of a law passed in 1905 clearly separating church and state. In France, unlike in the United States, the separation is much more strictly observed. During my time in Dieppe, religion was rarely brought up as a topic of conversation around the dinner table and was not, to my knowledge, mentioned in any French political campaign as an issue or as a qualifying or disqualifying characteristic for a candidate. Because of the 1905 law, President Macron was not allowed to give a eulogy inside the church at the funeral of celebrated French singer

Johnny Hallyday. Only lately had religion entered public conversations as a result of concerns about terrorist activity and dress codes.

My arrival in France in early 2017 coincided with the celebration of the five-hundredth anniversary of the "posting" of the ninety-five theses by Martin Luther in Germany. Consequently, I was able to attend several lectures and group discussions about Luther and Calvin and the evolution of their theology into the twenty-first century. As a result, I was pushed to expand my thinking about my faith, helped along the way by our minister whose British origins were a great help whenever I needed a translation of something he or someone else had said.

I would continue to miss some of the pageantry and those stained-glass windows of my former Episcopal — and even the Catholic — church. I sometimes even missed the sight of candles, the smell of incense, and the reverence for the Virgin Mary and the saints in the church. Instead, I found a church family, offering new companions and interesting conversations, sometimes over coffee after the service. The Sunday services and sermons forced me to pause, reflect, and relax. I ultimately came to appreciate the simplicity of the room and the music of electronic piano, which could very nicely emulate the sound of an organ.

Sometime later, after an extended visit to the States, I was reminded of what all these experiences had added to my life. A long-time member of the church stopped me before the service and asked me where I had been: "You should have said goodbye and let us know your plans." He was concerned that I hadn't told anyone where I was going and for how long, and he wanted to be sure I was okay and still coming to services.

While finding a welcoming church home had strangely never been on any of my many written lists of goals over the years, it must have been on an unconscious one. In Dieppe, the city of four ports and a stop for pilgrims making their way to Santiago de Compostela in Spain, I apparently had found that community, whose members would most assuredly come visit me in the hospital.

SEVEN

QUEST OR OBSESSION?

The silk tree that had appeared dead for most of the months since my arrival in Dieppe had burst into full bloom in early July. Its strange red flowers and frond-like leaves were a pleasant distraction on that rainy day at the end of August 2017, five months after I had found my new church home. I was sitting at the dining room

Silk tree
(https://en.wikipedia.org/wiki/Albizia_julibrissin)

table in the cottage I had rented and reflecting on the fact that, two days prior, I had turned seventy-three. My mother had died a couple of months before she turned seventy-three, and my dad had followed two months later, shortly after his seventy-third birthday. And Jeanne died at the age of seventy-three over 300 years ago.

Instead of, or perhaps because of, these depressing thoughts, I was wondering again why I was doing this, following this obsession and letting it take over and disrupt my life, causing me to pick up roots and spend a year far away from family and friends in the United States. I've often tried to explain my reasons when asked this sort of questions by the people I would meet, whether in France or Quebec or even in the States. Once, on my research trip in 2014 to Quebec, I was enjoying a beer on a sunny afternoon at the Tête des Allumettes brasserie and brewery on its patio overlooking the St. Lawrence River, somewhere along the road a little north of Kamouraska in eastern Quebec. It was a glorious, lovely summer day, amazingly free of mosquitos and black flies. As I sipped my beer, the closest thing to a Stella Artois that the brasserie offered, I started to chat with the people sitting at the table next to me. When I told them about my research, they asked, "Why are you doing this?"

I tried to explain. "My ancestor Jeanne Chevalier was a Fille du Roi." Since many people in Quebec know the story of the Filles du Roi, those founding mothers of Quebec, I was not surprised when they nodded their heads and urged me to continue. "These women were just as important to Quebec's history as their husbands, yet little has been written about them. Jeanne's is a story that needs to be told because, without her, there would be no Levesques!"

To their question about whether she was someone special — besides being my eighth-great-grandmother — I answered, "Well, not unlike many other Filles du Roi, she faced many dangers, sorrows, and the deaths of husbands and children, as well as numerous other challenges, but she managed to live a long life. Yet, compared to young women in France at the time, she was indeed extraordinary, as were most of the other Filles du Roi." My high-school French didn't let me add: *They took a risk that very few women were willing to take in the seventeenth century since women seldom travelled around in France or even considered emigrating. Jeanne and the others risked everything, and at the same time, they risked very little to come to New France. An unknown future was better than one that offered little hope or promise, which was essentially what awaited them in France.*

After I said goodbye to my table companions, I headed back to Quebec City. On the two-hour drive, I started thinking about all the stories I could have told them about the mysterious forces that had driven my journey to date.

There was, for example, the story about Jeanne's will. My book about her life began with the writing of her will on January 30, 1713. On what must have been a very cold winter day with a fire in the fireplace to keep everyone warm, Jeanne, her notary, and two witnesses were gathered in her room in the home of her middle son. She was living there as a result of an agreement that had been made with her sons in July 1705. It was the search for that agreement that had led me to discover the copy of Jeanne's will in the spring of 2013, three hundred years after it was written.

I had been spending many days and hours in Boston's New England Historical Genealogical Society's library, exploring their vast resources, reading old records, and searching through microfilm in my attempts to learn more about Jeanne. I'd managed to figure out how to use their catalogues to track down notaries and their records, how to find the corresponding microfilm reels in the rows of steel gray cabinet drawers, and how to operate those tricky microfilm readers. I also had to get used to the handwriting and the French alphabet used by the seventeenth-century notaries. Not easy tasks!

On that particular day in 2013, I found a notation that the 1705 agreement with Jeanne's three sons had been ratified in 1717 and was filed under that later date. In order to find that agreement, I had had to carefully search through the film, winding the reel very slowly, since many of those handwritten documents had been misfiled when they were collected and microfilmed. I would never know why I happened to stop the reel where I did. Yet, if I hadn't been paying close attention and hadn't remembered that Jeanne by that time was also known as Madame de la Bouteillerie because of her third marriage to the French nobleman Jean-Baptiste-François Deschamps de la Bouteillerie, I might have missed the document. There it was — almost at the end of the reel: "Le Testament de Madame de la Bouteillerie." I hadn't really been looking for her will since there was no mention of it in Ulric Lévesque's carefully researched book on Robert Lévesque. I also knew that wills were quite rare in early eighteenth-century Quebec.

When I found Jeanne's will, I needed to have it transcribed since the notary's handwriting was very difficult to read. Even then, I still had to edit it to make sense of the run-on paragraphs and the old French spellings. When I was finally able to read her requests and bequests, chills went through my body.

Over the prior few years, I had been puzzling over how to structure the book to best tell Jeanne's story. After eliminating the "letter on the table" idea and the romance novel, I came up with a possible option of having Jeanne, on her death bed, tell the story of her life to a grandchild. In some preliminary research, I learned that she had only one grandchild who would have been old enough at that time to appreciate those memories. That was Marie Jeanne Lévesque, her first grandchild and goddaughter, born in 1702.

I played with that idea and others, all of them involving a book of fiction about Jeanne's life but finally had rejected that approach as too complicated — in my perfectionist, history-student mind — in terms of voice and style. In what language would I write? In what dialect? After some research and feedback in workshops, I found a better approach and decided that the book on Jeanne's life would be nonfiction. I put the idea about the deathbed narrative so far in the back of my mind that I actually forgot about it — that is, until I read her will. In it, she had left a small gift of money to one sole relative of the many she had at the time. And that one person was …. her goddaughter, Marie Jeanne Lévesque.

Many other strange, lucky, scary, mysterious, coincidental, and synchronous events have occurred in my search for Jeanne's story. One day, for example, while I was driving from Quebec City to the village of L'Ange Gardien in the summer of 2014, something inside me forced my car over the bridge to Ile d'Orléans, the large island in the St. Lawrence River slightly east of Quebec City. I stopped at the church in the village where I knew Jeanne's first husband had purchased some land. After hearing my story, the woman in the church shop told me that I really should visit the Maison de Nos Aïeux up the road. Having never heard of this "House of Our Ancestors," I decided to take her advice. There, twelve kilometers east in an old church building turned museum, I learned the exact address of the land Jeanne's husband had purchased. Even more remarkably, in that rather remote place, I found a DVD of a colloquium on the Filles du Roi that I had been searching for in France, in Quebec, and over the web during the previous nine months.

Later that day, back on the road to L'Ange Gardien, another mysterious force made me pull into the driveway of a winery located behind one of the houses abutting land where Jeanne and her first husband had lived. Inside, while tasting some lovely wines, I learned that the home in front of the winery was owned by a family who had lived there for centuries. Emboldened by my inner guide and perhaps by the wine, I walked down the driveway and found three women sitting on the porch. In my fractured French, I repeated the story of my search for Jeanne. I discovered that they were all members of the Letarte family, the same family who had been neighbors and close friends of Jeanne and her husband over three centuries ago. In fact, one of Jeanne's sons had married a Letarte woman in 1705, and that couple were ancestors of mine through another family line.

Looking out over the land to the north shore of the St. Lawrence, I felt Jeanne's presence. Although I knew that most of the homes and churches of that time had been destroyed, rebuilt, or replaced, I could imagine her looking out over this same view when she lived nearby 340 years ago. It was a peculiar feeling, similar to the one I had had earlier that year with Jeanne's will.

These weird experiences and chance discoveries, many of which remained unexplained, were not limited to Quebec. On a visit to Coutances two years later, I happened to walk by a bookstore with a poster in the window, advertising a talk about Jean Nicolet to be held the very next day. I recognized the name of this French explorer who had gone to Quebec to seek his fortune. There, he had married Marguerite Couillard, the mother of Catherine-Gertrude, the first wife of the nobleman Deschamps. Naturally, I attended the conference with great interest and unexpectedly picked up more information about that family's history.

Another unexpected experience came about as a result of my attempt to learn more about Deschamps. My interest in him arose shortly after I had begun my research on Jeanne in 2011. I wanted to learn more about him, not only because he was Jeanne's third husband, but also because he was the godfather of François-Robert, her son from whom

I am descended and the oldest of her sons with Robert Lévesque. So there was at least a spiritual connection.

In the spring of 2013, I had found a book online about the Deschamps family. It contained a reference to possible descendants living in the Dieppe area. After some additional investigation, I was able to find the name of a man in Dieppe that sounded promising. I sent off a letter to him, with only his name and the name of the street, without any house number. In the letter, I described my search for more information on his family and provided my contact information.

I was surprised to receive an email less than a month later. The letter had in fact been delivered and the recipient had given my letter to his father Jacques, who had spent a good deal of time studying his family history. Although he was familiar with the story of Jean-Baptiste Deschamps and his life in Quebec, he did not know that Deschamps had married a second time. By this time, I was able to provide documents confirming his marriage to Jeanne.

Our email exchange led to an invitation from the family to join them for tea during my planned visit to Dieppe later that year. Several weeks later, I walked up to the home where the Deschamps family lived on the eastern cliff of Dieppe. Their place was full of lovely things: velvet covered chairs, lace doilies on end tables, antique books, and knickknacks. On the walls were pictures of old French landscapes. It could have been the home of anyone's grandparents. However, it clearly belonged to a descendant of that noble family. Prominently displayed in the living room was a copy of a painting of Jean-Baptiste's grandson, Charles Deschamps de Boishébert, a hero of the Acadian war with the British that, unfortunately for the French, eventually ended with the surrender of Quebec in 1759.

While my host Jacques Deschamps and his family were descendants of Jean-Baptiste Deschamps's older brother Adrian and the Acadian hero Charles Deschamps was a very distant cousin, they were all quite interested in my research. Over tea in their dining room, we discussed some of the things I had learned, including a reference to their family's lineage back to the third crusade in the twelfth century. Jacques questioned whether this long lineage was more legend than fact. No matter, the family could trace its noble roots back at least several centuries. And they were understandably proud of their heritage.

Since then, I continued to stay in touch with both Jacques and his family. In subsequent visits, Jacques shared stories about listening to his grandfather describe reading the original document that conferred noble status on the family in 1437. It was among their family archives that had been housed in their

*Charles Deschamps de Boishébert
(Original in McCord Museum of Canadian
History, Montreal Quebec)*

chateau in Offranville, not far from Dieppe. The chateau had been occupied by the Germans during World War II. By the time the German soldiers left the area at the end of the war, they had burned the chateau, its contents, and all the archives. Consequently, that document and all the other ones that I would have loved to see no longer existed.

Disappointed but still eager to learn more about Jean-Baptiste's family in France, I moved on to a visit I had arranged in Cliponville, the village where he was born. On the web, I had discovered that the then mayor of the village was named Levêque. Thinking that he could possibly be a distant relative, I got in touch with him and invited myself to meet in his office during the hours that the town hall was open. We agreed on a time to meet.

The day after that first meeting with the Deschamps family in 2013, I drove to Cliponville, about an hour's drive southwest of Dieppe. I had no idea what sort of reception to expect since my correspondence with the mayor had led me to believe that it might be a short meeting. I suspected he might not be sure how well we would be able to communicate since he spoke little English and my letter in French had surely contained many errors. Instead, I was cordially greeted by him and his sister. They proceeded to give me a tour of the village, the church, and the home where he had been born, parts of which dated from the seventeenth century. I was then invited to join them at the home that the mayor had built right next door. First it was for cocktails and then for dinner, just like family, although we weren't able to find any familial tie at the time.

During this visit, I learned that Cliponville had been the property of the Deschamps family who had built a chateau there in the seventeenth century. As my new "cousins" explained over dinner, little remained of the chateau or from the seventeenth century in the rest of Cliponville. There were also no references to the noble family or their son who had left in 1671 to seek his fortune in New France. Most of the older buildings, including two small chapels, were destroyed during the French Revolution, although fortunately not the Levêque family home or the twelfth-century church where Jean-Baptiste Deschamps was most likely baptized.

Unfortunately, the mayor was clear: "No baptismal record for Jean-Baptiste has yet been found. It must have been lost as a result of wars and the revolution." Despite that warning, I would not give up my search for it.

These and other mostly unplanned events on my journey to date made me feel as if someone else was in charge, driving my research forward and directing me to continue. Were these synchronous and serendipitous experiences all a result of happenstance or my imagination, or were they caused by something more profound, some sort of connection with the collective unconscious, as Swiss psychologist Carl Jung might say?

Or was this journey perhaps simply my quest to take some pride in my French-Canadian heritage and get in touch with those French roots? As we were sitting in Carla's kitchen having tea in Seattle at Christmas 2013, three years before our trip to France, she observed that I might be trying to make up for the lack of family since our parents had both died almost twenty years earlier, I had no children, we did not grow up with a large extended family, and relations among my siblings and a few cousins were not particularly tight. "You feel closer to Jeanne than you do to most of the family," she remarked. "Look at you! You're ready to go back to France to do more research on Jeanne, but you won't take the time to visit [our brother] Marc in New Mexico!"

While there was probably some truth in her observation, for me, at that time anyway, this was more than an identity quest or a search for roots or for a substitute family. I sometimes felt chosen by Jeanne to take this journey. But why? Perhaps she wanted me to give up my consulting practice, take my high-school French lessons and my history degree off the back shelf, and make some major changes in my life. Perhaps she was unhappy with what had been written to date about the Filles du Roi, describing them with either too much romantic fiction or too many dry statistics. Perhaps she believed I'd have the perseverance to ferret out the facts, get them straight, and tell her story the right way. Perhaps she did indeed want to spur me on to connect with my French roots and find some lost pride in them. Perhaps she just wanted to take my imagination for a ride. Or perhaps she had other, even more important, plans for me.

For whatever reason, Jeanne would continue to prod me gently on — and sometimes not very gently. She wouldn't let me go, and I refused to abandon her as well. She visited me in my dreams. The search to tell her story became an obsession. Besides that Cuisinart customer service rep, I continued to talk about her to anyone who would listen. Members of my family — not only my nieces —would admit they were tired of hearing me talk about her and at times worried about my sanity. They would probably admit, nonetheless, that they were happy to see their elderly maiden aunt and sister so engaged in the project.

As I told Carla and anyone else who asked, there were several other reasons why I was willing to agree to Jeanne's demands. One was plain curiosity. Who was this woman? Where did she come from? Why did she embark on that dangerous journey without knowing what she would find in the new world? How did she manage to find the resolve to live the life she lived?

Perhaps I also wanted to learn what legacy Jeanne had passed on to me so that I could in turn pass that on to my nieces and nephews and their children. She was a brave, courageous woman who was able to strike out into unknown territory. Were her courage and strength part of my inheritance from her?

And there I was, several years later on that dreary day in August 2017, sitting in a cottage in France, thinking back on that conversation in the brasserie along the St. Lawrence River and continuing to ponder why I was doing this — this year in France without any definite plans for the years ahead. Okay, I had to admit that many years ago, in 2002, before the movie *Bucket List* was released, I had made my own list of things I wanted to do before dying in that little blue travel journal. One of those items, right after "Write a book about my eighth-great-grandmother," was "Live in France for at least six months." So now, I could check that item off.

What's next? I asked myself. I knew I needed to stay busy in this the third chapter of my life. This drive to tell Jeanne's story and to try to find answers to some remaining questions about her life — and maybe even about my own — could continue to keep me energized and engaged and ensure that my creative juices flowed on through my seventies and into my eighties and perhaps beyond. I hadn't felt the need, to date, to question what to do in the next phase of my life or how to keep my mind active in what my brother called my "encore career." I really hadn't had any choice.

Although I recognized that I was lucky, I also knew that I wasn't totally comfortable with the way things were turning out. I was used to being in charge — at least I believed I was in charge — of a fairly orderly, well-planned, logical life. I could have ignored Jeanne's entreaties — perhaps. But then what would I do to keep myself busy and stay challenged? I needed purpose. I needed structure. I didn't think I could live without to-do lists, goals, plans and objectives, and new oceans to explore. I refused to think about this new chapter of my life as retirement. I was not going to retreat. I never had.

I remember a former boyfriend telling me, "You're always searching,

Lynne. Always searching." I am not sure whether that comment was meant as a compliment, a criticism, or simply pointing out our differences. Whatever, that description would undoubtedly turn out to be true, although some might label it "overachieving."

Yes, search! Tell Jeanne's story! Spread the word about those courageous women. Find something constructive to do each day. Before it was too late.

EIGHT

TIME TO LEAVE

On the day before Thanksgiving 2017, not long after I had written those notes about my obsession to discover Jeanne's story, a mere few weeks remained of my sabbatical year before my scheduled return to Boston. As I was finishing up the preparation for the Thanksgiving dinner that I was hosting for friends the next day, I spent some time reflecting on the past eleven-plus months. *They had gone by so fast. What had happened to those goals I had set for my sabbatical year in France?*

Well, to be fair, I silently responded, *the initial tasks of getting settled, opening a bank account, obtaining my long-stay visa, arranging for phone and Internet service and other essentials for daily living had not all gone as quickly or as easily as I had hoped. They had all taken a lot more of my energy and time than I had first imagined.*

Once I managed to complete those tasks, despite the delay, the next item on my list had been to find a yoga class. During my 2016 visit, I had noticed a sign advertising yoga classes on a house near Nadine's. Upon my return in January, I decided to investigate. The first yoga class was certainly not what I was expecting after over twenty years of yoga in the United States. Apparently, at least in Dieppe, the French approach of Hatha yoga was more about breathing and relaxation and less about exercise and stretching. So I learned to practice breathing, holding my breath for thirty seconds, then sixty seconds, and only occasionally did a downward-facing dog.

The dressing room, or lack thereof, was also a bit of a revelation. Americans have been accused of being too puritanical in matters relating to the body, and that could account for my shock when I walked into the studio and found a very small reception area and no changing room. Unlike me who had walked over to the studio in my yoga clothes, most students arrived in what might be called street clothes and then changed into their yoga clothes — men and women alike taking off pants, skirts, panty hose, socks, and shoes and putting on yoga pants and tops, all in the same small room. And then after the class, changing back into their street clothes. All very discreetly to be sure, but it was a bit startling to this American.

Despite these sometimes awkward moments, I continued to attend the class for the rest of the year. It wasn't exactly what I thought I needed in terms of exercise, but it wasn't far from the cottage, and it would do until I could find an alternative. Plus it did lead me to Martine, my French tutor.

The next order of business for me had been to find some structure and discipline in my days in order to achieve my goal of becoming fluent in French. Unfortunately, a search of the Internet and of various possible schools and groups in Dieppe revealed that there was nothing suitable for foreigners at my level. I decided to look for a tutor. Shortly afterwards at my second yoga class, I rather fortuitously connected with Martine, a retired French teacher. For the rest of the year, we met once a week for an hour after yoga to cover lessons in the grammar book I had brought with me from the States or to correct any important email messages I wanted to send or articles I was writing for my blog.

A few weeks after starting to work with Martine, I was having coffee with my new church acquaintances after a service. I mentioned that I was looking for someone who wanted to have an exchange, sharing a couple of hours every week speaking half the time in English and half in French. Joël, a retired sales executive, happened to be passing by the coffee break room, overheard the conversation, poked his head in, and said he would be interested. We met up the next week at his home. Almost weekly thereafter, I walked up the hill to his home, which fortunately wasn't far away. We would spend time vigorously discussing politics, history, and whatever topic caught our attention. Joël turned out to be one of several "walking encyclopedias" whom I would meet in France, people with so many broad interests and so much knowledge.

One of the first discussions turned out to be about how I had arrived at his place. After trying several different walking routes, I had found a short cut from my cottage almost directly to his home. The path took me through the high-school property and sports field across from the blue garage door. Since I saw no signs indicating that such access was not allowed, I saw nothing wrong with walking through the high-school grounds. Joël was aghast at my lack of respect for property laws. According to him, what is not expressly allowed in France is considered illegal, quite the reverse of my experience in the United States. I later learned that the French do respect laws, perhaps more diligently than Americans, except when they didn't want to.

Despite the help from Martine and Joël, the goal I had set to be able to speak French fluently turned out to be close to impossible to attain. Had I really thought that one year was all I needed to reach that level and to lose my accent so that I would not be recognized as an American? That had absolutely not been the case for many reasons, one of which was that I had found it difficult to spend more than three or four hours a day reading, speaking, listening to, studying, and writing French. That work wore me out, and that was my excuse for reading the news in order to relax, if reading the news about the political situation in the States at that time could in any way be considered relaxing! In addition, the nuances of the French language, its structure, and the fact that it reflected a very different culture and mentality had likewise slowed my progress. Undoubtedly, age had played a role as well.

Those nuances and my probable underestimation of the effort involved meant that the work of translating my book about Jeanne's life also took significantly longer than I had originally thought. It had been an enormous, extremely complicated, and time-consuming project.

In February not long after my arrival in Dieppe, I had attended a book fair at a local hotel. The room was full of authors and their books. *Will I ever be able to attend an event like this someday once my book is published in French*, I wondered. I stopped to speak with a couple of authors about their work and mine. When I explained what I was doing, one woman suggested, "You should have at least three translators." Another author agreed. I finally ended up with nine. Those nine individuals sequentially read versions, corrected grammatical errors and misstatements of historical facts, put adverbs in the correct places in the French sentences, and made a lot more revisions to ensure that the text could be understood by French readers. Translating word for word from English to French was almost never possible.

We sometimes struggled between their recommendations and my style (too much repetition, I was told) and my voice, which I really didn't want to lose. Most of the translators had some sort of working knowledge of English, which sometimes helped and sometimes got in the way. We would have conversations about what I really meant to say because that meaning wasn't always evident, they had interpreted what I said differently, or my attempt at poetry didn't work in French. One woman had a problem with my perhaps too poetic description of life in Quebec during the winter that included a reference to the "sound of falling snow." That was untranslatable because it didn't make any sense to the translator who was not all that familiar with snowy winters. I was, nevertheless, able to convince her that it was reasonable, and we found a suitable translation.

Then there was the problem that evidently the French do not like to mix the concrete with the conceptual. In the English version of my book, my description of life in French cities in the seventeenth century was: "Life was noisy, dirty, and smelly." One translator told me, "No, no, no. *Life* cannot be noisy or dirty." After some back and forth, I learned it was correct to write something similar to: "In the city, the quality of everyday life was impacted by noise and dirt."

These sorts of conversations, and there were many others, resulted in a translation process that took a lot longer than planned. Looking back, I was not sure how much my personal involvement added to or subtracted from the effort, but I wanted to learn from the process as well. I was probably more involved than other authors might have been. I've been told that I have a rather controlling personality. I'd like to think it was because I wanted to learn.

In any event, after several revisions, re-readings, and more revisions by the nine translators and then two trips by me to Rouen to find a printer, the book was ready to be published on June 20, 2017, six months after my arrival and just in time to meet the date I had promised myself of "in the spring." The French version of the book turned out to be significantly better and more historically correct because of all that work, but it was a long, complex process.

Had I not been in France, I probably would have missed that June deadline, as well as many other opportunities to promote Jeanne's story, including several book signings. In late August, not long after the French version of my book was published, I sat at a small table in the corner on the ground floor of Le Plumier, a local bookstore, and signed copies of my book. Some were bought by friends who surprised me by stopping by and some by total strangers. At one point I had to commission my friend Sylvie to drive to the cottage and pick up more copies since we were running low!

The next month, I rented a car and drove to Cherbourg, not far from Coutances where Jeanne had been born, to take part in a conference and book signing with another author of a book on a Fille du Roi. The author, whom I had met through a mutual friend, had included in his novel anecdotes about the life of Jeanne's third husband, Jean-Baptiste Deschamps. While the historian perfectionist side of me bristled at what I believed were his misinterpretations of that nobleman's life, I did my best to remain neutral during our talk and gladly sold copies of my book.

These opportunities to promote Jeanne's story were not the only experiences I would have missed. Earlier in the year, one of my new acquaintances had suggested I come with her to a meeting of her monthly book group. After that first session, I decided to join the group and ended up reading some French classics, an American one, and other more recent arrivals on the French literary scene. I would buy the books in advance in order to have enough time to read them before the next month's meeting. As I read them, I diligently highlighted all the new words in order to look them up later in a dictionary and discuss any questions with Martine in our weekly meetings. During the monthly discussions of the book I remained uncharacteristically silent, something not that easy for me to do, since I found it difficult to follow the conversations, and I didn't want to make inappropriate comments.

Without being in France, I could not have attended the annual meeting of the Cousins of the New World in Hautot-Saint-Sulpice, the group that had been formed to welcome visitors from Canada and the United States who arrived in the area seeking information about their ancestor Robert Lévesque. Back in 2014, Nelly, the secretary of the group and an enthusiastic fan of all things related to Lévesque and Rivière-Ouelle, had contacted me shortly after my visit to that town at the suggestion of the Mayor's office. We had started exchanging emails. She had arranged for me to be welcomed by the group in 2015 and again in 2016 so I decided to become a member. Until I joined, interestingly, none of the other members had any familial connections to Robert Lévesque.

Then there were all those conferences that I would have missed if I hadn't been in France. Besides the ones on Luther and Calvin, there were lectures on the Franco-Prussian war of 1870, the origins of World War I, and the role of De Gaulle in fostering Quebec separatism. Other conferences introduced me to Roman architecture in Norman churches, to Dieppe's school of cartography, to William Turner and the English school of Romanticism, and to the lives of Walter Sickert and Jacques-Émile Blanche, two impressionist painters unknown to me prior to 2017, as in fact was all that other information!

I would also not have been able to dabble in French politics. Beginning in January, upon my arrival in France, and continuing through April and early May, I followed with great interest the progress of the French presidential election. I watched the rather astonishing rise of an unknown politician who would surprisingly top the field of eleven candidates in the first round of voting on Sunday, April 23. Two friends let me observe them as they voted in Dieppe that Sunday morning. Later that evening, I was glued to the television for the results that would determine the two candidates for the final round.

Thanks to a carpooling arrangement organized by his supporters, I attended the May 1st rally in Paris for that "upstart" Emmanuel Macron. In the stadium overflowing with boisterous, enthusiastic supporters of all ages, we waited for at least an hour. Finally, he arrived. I was a bit startled to watch his entrance directly onto the podium, without all the preceding short speeches given by a long list of politicians who appeared at similar events in the States. We did have posters and cards and waved them at appropriate moments during his ninety-minute speech. But there had not been and would not be any of the exorbitant spending, door-to-door campaigning, buttons, or bumper stickers that I was so familiar with after years of working in local, state, and presidential campaigns in the States.

The second round of voting occurred only six days after the rally, unlike the many months that follow the end of primaries before the final US election. That evening, after the voting was concluded, I watched the new president's dramatic entry onto the esplanade at the Louvre, accompanied by the European Union's anthem, also known as Beethoven's "Ode to Joy."

Without question, it had been a year full of revelations and unexpected activities that kept me from making significant progress on all of my original goals. While I had managed to publish the French version of my book on my ancestor Jeanne and to advance somewhat my ability to speak French, I had not become fluent and had not done much work on the sequel to that first book. Nor had I found time to do more research to fill in the missing pieces of her story.

There had been too many irresistible diversions. Indeed, even Jeanne played a role in disrupting my plans. While having a plaque made in her honor must certainly have been on a list of objectives somewhere, it was not on the list that I had explicitly made for 2017. Apparently, she wasn't going to let that task go unaddressed for very long.

In a visit to Saint-Jacques church one spring day, I was struck with the idea of having a plaque made in Jeanne's honor. At that point, I had no idea how complicated a project it would turn out to be but I soon learned. I first asked around for recommendations for a local company to make the plaque. Upon finding one, I somehow was able to communicate with the woman in charge exactly what I wanted to have made and then have hung in the Canadian Chapel in Saint-Jacques Church along with the other plaques to emigrating French families. To accomplish this plan, I needed the approval of the head priest, who thankfully was fluent in English, and the President of the Committee to Save Saint-Remy and Saint-Jacques, who was not. To come up with a design, I checked out other plaques in the chapel. To finalize the wording, the choice of marble, and the addition of the Lévesque coat of arms, I sought feedback and approval from the Lévesque Association in Canada, who also unexpectedly offered to help fund the project.

Finally, the plaque was ready to be installed, just two days before the ceremony I had arranged. I was not able to be there for the work but rushed down to see it as soon as I could, only to discover that it had been hung in the wrong place! I panicked, but happily there was time for the problem to be fixed. On September 15, we celebrated the installation in the Canadian Chapel in the presence of city officials, the press, a film crew, and visitors from Quebec, returning to their roots — some of them distant relatives. I believe Jeanne was also there, at least in spirit.

My second cousin Peter, a Roman Catholic priest, whom I did not know very well at all until I started my research on Jeanne and who had helped me enormously during the many months and years prior to the publication of her story, arrived in Dieppe on the ferry from England the night before the ceremony. After Peter blessed the plaque, I had to fight back tears — not totally successfully — during my short dedication speech. The talk on Jeanne's life that I gave the next week at the Lévesque family reunion in Hautot-Saint-Sulpice was, mercifully, not nearly as emotional.

Peter, who had been raised in a French-speaking home and went to French schools, stayed on with me for two weeks. In addition to visiting some of the tourist sites around Dieppe, we had several conversations about our very different childhoods, growing up in the same town and born a mere 366 days apart but in quite different circumstances. Proud of his Quebecois heritage, Peter had traced most of his ancestors back to France and had even visited many of the villages where they had been born. I was so jealous of his stories about being hugged by our great-aunts and about meals and visits with our great-grandparents and other relatives in their homes in Nashua that I finally had to beg him to stop.

We did laugh about some of the experiences I had had in my time to date in France. One evening sitting out on the patio after dinner, I described a couple of long Sunday or holiday meals with "relatives": "They began before noon with aperitifs and hors-d'oeuvres, followed by three or four courses, usually including a salad with homemade dressing, cheese, and some sort of dessert, followed by a long walk with conversation and then another two-to-three course meal."

Peter agreed that in the United States, we might spend that amount of time over a Thanksgiving or Christmas meal but probably not every Sunday. My French friends did tell me that this practice was dying out, at least in the cities, and my experience could have been the result of being in a small town and dining with friends who were retired. Then again, I had noticed that normal main meals, usually at noon, followed a similar order on a much simpler scale but almost always involved cheese and dessert. Even in schools and hospitals, meals concluded with an offering of cheese before a bit of dessert.

Another time, while sharing beers in a café overlooking the beach in Veules-les-Roses, Peter listened to my story about the ecumenical church walk I had taken in the summer. I had been told to bring something to eat for a lunch break. I had no idea what to expect, and I rather foolishly had not asked around for advice. In my American brain, "lunch" meant preparing a sandwich and bringing along a bottle of water and possibly a banana. However, when we stopped for our lunchbreak in the St. Valery church courtyard, the midpoint of our hike that day, I was in for another one of many new experiences. For this group of French people anyway, a picnic involved bringing enough food along to share, be it appetizers, main dishes, salads, cheese, or dessert. A hot water heater was plugged into a socket in the nearby church to make coffee. Someone had even brought along a bottle of wine. All this bounty made my peanut butter sandwich on whole-wheat bread look a bit meager, although it turned out to be sort of a hit since I tore off portions to share with group members who had never tasted such a typically American sandwich.

After these stories, more conversations, and a visit to the Museum of French Emigration to Canada in Tourouvre, Peter left to continue his planned trip in Europe. He was not the only relative to visit during the year. My nephew Cyrus, his wife Teresa, and their not-yet-two-year-old daughter Lexie had arrived in May to spend six days in Dieppe. We drove over to see the little church in Varengeville, took the walk in Veules-les-Roses — where this time the roses were in superb full bloom — visited the aquarium in Dieppe, and rode the funicular up the hill in the town of Le Tréport, not far from Dieppe.

In early November, Carla returned, this time with her husband David, bringing with them the Ocean Spray cranberry sauce and Pepperidge Farm cornbread stuffing mix that I needed for my Thanksgiving dinner later that month. I didn't realize until later that I should also have asked them to bring peppermint candy canes so I could make treats to share with friends at Christmas since that flavor of candy cane was not readily available in France.

Carla took a yoga class with me and found the different approach quite enjoyable. The three of us took the walk that she and I had tried to take in January, and this time we didn't get lost. We also walked along the shortest river in France, where neither roses nor watercress were to be seen. Even so, the walk was lovely, as was our short visit to Paris before they returned to Seattle.

The weather during the next few weeks was rather dismal. I caught a cold that lingered for several days. It did not keep me from attending a conference on Brexit, the upcoming separation of Great Britain from the European Union, a topic of great interest to the commercial interests in Dieppe and to the many British citizens with second homes in

Normandy. Nor did it interfere with a return to Hautot-Saint-Sulpice for the funeral of a long-time member of the Cousins of the New World, a man I had first met during the visit that I had made with my sisters and nieces back in 2000. Finally, the cold was a good excuse for me to spend the day on the sofa watching the funeral procession and services for Johnny Hallyday.

Towards the end of December, with my health returned to normal, I took the train to Paris, then the Metro, and the RER (the French commuter rail system) to the airport to pick up a rental car and meet my globe-trotting nephew Max. I had last seen Max in Paris in June 2016, after I had decided to spend a year in France and after he had spent a semester studying at a university in Morocco. We had stayed in Paris for a couple of days of sightseeing before I went back to Dieppe and he continued his visit in Europe. This time, when I picked him up at the De Gaulle airport, I almost didn't recognize him! He had grown both in height and in facial hair.

Together, we attended the Christmas service at the Protestant church in Luneray and afterwards took the Varengeville hike, where we almost got stuck twice in the unexpectedly deep mud. I would forever have memories of having to cling very carefully to a barbed-wire fence along the path in order to avoid one or two rather wide and very muddy puddles. We ate crêpes in Veules-les-Roses before doing the walk (obviously one of my favorite tourist offerings!). We climbed the clock tower in Rouen and joined friends at the Christmas market for a cup of mulled wine. Max came with me to visit that historic house that I was thinking of buying. He even offered to return and help me with all the work it needed. Ever the adventurer, Max also took a baptismal flight in a light plane over the cliffs and the channel. Even though he decided to cut his visit with me short by taking the ferry to England to meet up with friends in London, it was a truly wonderful way to end the year.

All the experiences during that sabbatical year had proven to be too enticing to abandon. Sometime in early summer, I had started thinking about the coming year and realized I was not ready to end the adventure. There was still too much to learn about the French language and French history, too many avenues still to pursue in my ongoing research, too much more work to do on my second book, and too many nascent relationships to continue to nurture.

Before really deciding what to do next, I wanted some input. I called my therapist in the States to talk about whether I should stay or go. Her suggestion was: "You can deepen your experience there with another year, so why not?"

Then I spoke with Carla and her husband. They gave essentially the same answer and added, "What are your other options?"

I checked with the consulate in Boston about how to arrange for a visa renewal. "You can do that in France," I was told. So, I didn't have to return to the States to renew my visa. That was excellent news! I began making arrangements to stay for another year.

Easily said but not easily done! Once I figured out what was involved, that task took up a significant amount of time. I needed to reach agreement with the renters of my condo in Boston to stay on for another year, renew my lease on the Dieppe cottage, and extend my health insurance in France. I had to obtain proof of residence from my landlord and of liability insurance from my French bank. And I also wanted to arrange lunch and dinner dates with friends and the necessary doctors' appointments during the short time I now planned to be in Boston.

With all the documents that I thought were required for visa renewal, I took the train to Rouen and found my way to the Prefecture, about a twenty-minute walk from the train station. After passing through security, I entered what was once a splendid hospital and these days served as the administrative headquarters for the department of Seine-Maritime in the region of Normandy where Dieppe is located. I was given a number at the reception desk and then joined perhaps fifty other applicants in a large hall. Our numbers were posted in turn on a large screen. Two hours later, my number came up.

I didn't know what to expect as I handed my documents over to the agent who checked them over carefully. She then told me I was missing the necessary bank statements to prove my financial independence in

France. Fortunately, this agent took pity on me and agreed to begin the process of preparing the visa, provided I sent in the statements as soon as I returned to Dieppe. She issued me a "receipt for a one-year visa request" that would be valid until it was replaced with the actual visa upon my return to the Prefecture in January. I made my way back to the train station for the trip back to Dieppe, breathing a huge sigh of relief.

Yes, it would have been easier to return to Boston and take up my life there again. I wouldn't have all the struggles to communicate in my daily life, to understand sermons, to ask questions at conferences, or to find time to stay in contact with family and my American friends. In the United States, I would at least have some illusion of control over my life.

Despite moments of exhaustion and feeling too frequently a bit out of balance, I had kept on going, inspired by thoughts of the perseverance with which I imagined Jeanne had lived her life. Indeed, something or someone (perhaps Jeanne?) was pulling me to stay in France. Or perhaps it was the lack of a pull to return to life in the United States. In truth, I really couldn't come up with many more desirable alternatives at the time to staying in France. I frankly didn't have an answer to Carla and David's question during our train ride to Paris when they were here: "What would it take to keep you in the States?"

Everything seemed to be falling nicely into place for me in France, although perhaps not as easily as I might have liked or in the way I had planned, and I was definitely having fun, at least in my definition of fun. How could I not continue the journey?

NINE

A WELL-PLANNED LIFE

"So, Lynne, what are your objectives for the year?" my Australian friend Theodora asked when we talked on the telephone in early February 2018, not long after my return to France. "What do you want to get done?" she gently prodded. Before I hung up, I told her I would have to think about an answer to her questions since I was still recovering from my visit to the United States after my first year in Dieppe.

I was back in Dieppe and sitting at the dining room table in the cottage that I had rented for another year. In late January, my younger brother Dana had flown from New Mexico to Boston to help me return to France and had carried in his suitcase some of my vitamin stock and other critical items that didn't fit in my luggage. After visiting for ten days, he had returned home.

Despite the somewhat sporadically dismal weather, we had been busy and a bit jet-lagged and hadn't had either time or interest in chatting about my plans for the coming year. We made a long daytrip to the D-Day beaches with Joël, my conversation-exchange buddy, as chauffeur. In Arromanches-les-Bains, a friend from my 2013 trip in France joined us for a visit to the World War II museum and for lunch afterwards. A couple of days later, Dana and I drove down to Hautot-Saint-Sulpice so he could visit the village where our eighth-great-grandfather, Robert Lévesque, had been born. After a brief tour given by Nelly from the Cousins of the New World and after a very pleasant meal with her in the nearby town of Yvetot, we returned to Dieppe via Veules-les-Roses. The sun finally came out as we arrived, so we were able to enjoy a walk along the "shortest river in France."

Dana came with me to Rouen to pick up my one-year visa, although he refused to spend the entire two hours in the Prefecture waiting for my number to be called. While he went off to find an internet boutique to try to improve the email connection with his wife, I waited somewhat patiently in the large hall at the Prefecture. As I looked around, I observed: *Not much had changed since my previous visit last November when I was here to apply for the renewal of my visa.*

When my number was finally called, it was close to noon. The agent reviewed my documents and took the fiscal stamps to pay the fees for the visa. She then said that I would have to return that afternoon to collect my visa since she was about to shut her window for lunch. When I asked if I would have to take another number, she replied, "Yes, you will have to wait in line again." I then insisted, somewhat politely I believe, that she take a minute to see if she could find my visa so that I would not have to return. She did, but not without a sigh and not without making it clear that she was doing so "exceptionally," solely for me.

With my visa in hand, I met up with Dana. Before catching the train to Dieppe, we grabbed a sandwich and then visited some of Rouen's historical sites. In Dieppe, we took a yoga class together and had dinner with Nadine. He also spent an evening with me and the group that some friends and I had formed to help them improve their English. That evening we chatted about an article written by one of my American colleagues. The topic — the importance of identifying personal strengths in order to reach higher levels of achievement — generated a rather lively discussion. As far as those French friends were concerned, the American focus on achieving and "being the best" was overrated. According to them, the majority of French people believed that "good enough" was absolutely fine. After barely fourteen months in France, I couldn't determine whether their observation truly did apply to the general French population, but Dana and I both found that lesson in cultural differences rather interesting.

The next day, the curator of Dieppe's museum came with us to inspect the old convent building that I was thinking of buying. Despite the curator's evaluation that the four-hundred-year-old building was in relatively good condition, Dana's reality check on the costs of its restoration ("a veritable money pit!") was sufficient to bring me back down to earth and give up my fantasy of turning the place into a museum honoring the role of women in colonizing New France.

Now, after spending two more surprisingly snowy days with him in Paris before his return to New Mexico and hopefully having assured him that my life in Dieppe was relatively safe and sane, I was back in the cottage, reunited with Quincie who had stayed with a friend during my time in the States. The place was quiet. With the chilly but relatively mild winter weather, Quincie had decided to forgo the sunroom and instead was sleeping on the living room couch. I decided to join her to try to absorb my recent experiences in Boston.

Those three weeks that I had spent in my Charlestown condo had truly been productive and busy. I cleaned out four filing-cabinet drawers of papers that I knew I would never need again since they were part of a chapter of my life that was now closed. I went through the storage containers and closets that held my clothes and got rid of a suitcase and its contents, mainly old ski clothes that the moths had attacked during my absence. I gave away six boxes of books that I thought at the time I would never want to read again. Appointments with my doctors and dentist resulted in a clean bill of health. I visited with friends and shopped for items I wanted to take with me to France. I shoveled the snow around the condo building and avoided falling on the ice that seemed to be on sidewalks everywhere. And then somehow I made it back to France — with Dana's help.

It felt good to be there. Instead of the cold and wind and snow and ice that continued into February and March in Charlestown, the camellia bush was in full bloom in Dieppe, and crocuses and hyacinths were starting to appear. Jonquils were even trying to open up. The flowers and the weather that had turned more pleasant all seemed to be welcoming me back.

While I felt more comfortable returning to France this time compared to a year earlier and I absolutely didn't regret the decision to spend another year in Dieppe, I was feeling a bit unsettled. Perhaps because it had been such a quick trip to Boston, and I never had time to breathe. Or because Quincie hadn't been with me. Or because I hadn't had enough time to relax with Dana. Or maybe it was because Charlestown, or even Boston, didn't feel like home anymore.

In trying to sort out these feelings, I thought back over the past year. I could check several important items off my list of objectives. Sales of the books on Jeanne's life in English and in French, while modest, continued on. Feedback from readers and from articles in the local press was good. My circle of connections with smart, thoughtful people who were patient with my learning of French kept expanding. I had updated my goals from the prior year with a missing item regarding maintaining my health and staying fit and flexible. Apparently, all the almost-daily walking up and down the cliffs of Dieppe and a weekly yoga class had managed to counteract my recently developed love of French cheeses and red wine. I had learned to make rhubarb compote and how to use white vinegar to fight calcium deposits in the tea kettle and coffee machine (but not my hair!). And at times I felt as if my French was improving. Not all the time, for sure, but there were moments when I could actually understand a good part of what was being said.

Of course, at the same time, as the shine of a new location had worn off a bit, I was feeling the stress of living in a foreign country. I found a note I had written on February 19, not long after that call with Theodora. I had just spent two days standing behind a folding table, trying to sell my book at the Salon des Livres in a large and cold room with few English-speaking participants and where no one seemed eager to talk to newcomers like me. "It is fair to say," the note said, "that it's not merely the psychological stress I am feeling, but the physical toll on my body as well."

Over dinner one night, a friend had asked me, "Do you miss the English language?" — a thought-provoking question. My answer then had been "not really." Several months later, it was still the same. "But," I had added, "what I do miss is the ease of communicating." That was and would continue to be true.

When I had taken the Eurostar train from Paris to London to attend a business school alumni event in March during my first year in France, I had been struck by how easy it was to ask directions from people on the street without having to think about the question in advance. Getting things done was certainly more difficult in a language I didn't grow up speaking. Everyday things, like getting a haircut and trying to explain "a little off the top and sides, but not the back." Or explaining Quincie's idiosyncrasies to a veterinarian. Or understanding gas company technicians who showed up to change the meters. All were conversations that demanded a good bit of effort from me.

After some additional reflection, however, I realized that some of the discomfort I was feeling could also be caused by the lack of a plan for my life ahead. Theodora's questions about my future plans had thrown me off balance since I couldn't answer her immediately. Usually, I had lots of objectives, or at least I had had in the past.

In 1986, I was living in California and was in a job and in a relationship, neither of which was going very well. I decided to take a break from both and visited my good friend Marion, with whom I had worked before she returned to her native state of Texas. The two of us were about forty-two years old at the time. Around her kitchen table drinking tea or one of her herbal-drink concoctions, we worked on our life plans with one-year, five-year, ten-year, and twenty-year time horizons. We even added a column for what we hoped people would say about us at our funeral. We also divided those goals into categories: financial, professional, health, and personal. It was quite a rigorous and detailed process, punctuated by meals in Mexican restaurants and long walks so she could introduce me to her home town. Interestingly, there was nothing about learning French on that list, although I had included a very long-term goal to "find a place where I belong, where I find peace, am never bored, and am making a valuable contribution."

Within six months of that visit, several of my one-year goals were well on their way to completion. I had ended the relationship with my partner in California, found a new job, and moved back to the East Coast.

Goal setting and checking on progress continued to be a pattern in my life. In January 1987, shortly after moving to Hartford, Connecticut, I connected with Diane, a work colleague. In between dinners, gym classes, and other activities, we talked about our goals for the future. I revisited the ones I had set with Marion. Not long afterwards, I also started working on a new longer-term goal of finishing a doctoral program.

At another critical period in my life, a few years later, I found two other women who were facing career decisions similar to mine at the time: what to do next. At first we met monthly at one another's homes for a Saturday morning. Soon, we added an annual weekend retreat devoted to working on our goals for the years ahead, usually on an island in Massachusetts or at one friend's winter home, where we could combine walks and shopping with serious discussion. On the ten-year anniversary of our first meeting, we even spent a week in Ireland, reflecting on our futures. In our two decades of working together, we managed to achieve many of our annual and longer-term goals thanks to regular meetings and mutual support of each other. Since our initial focus was on career challenges, once again learning French wasn't on that list of goals, although I did recently find some long-forgotten journal notes dated August 12, 1995, that mysteriously mentioned "learning French."

In 2003, around the time I started that bucket list in my blue travel journal, my college roommate Paula and I spent a couple of weeks in Scotland, sightseeing but also working on career and personal goals over coffee in the morning or a glass of whisky in the evening. We continued to work on them regularly in the States at her home in North Carolina. By now, learning French was prominently on the list, as was spending time in France and writing a book about my ancestor.

Despite all these experiences that confirmed my belief in the power of setting goals, I realized I hadn't done that sort of planning in a while. *Since I couldn't respond to Theodora's questions, that might help*, I thought.

Nonetheless, I now had to answer a tough question: At this point in my life, was it realistic to do a five- or ten- or twenty-year plan, something to which I was so addicted — without a plan for dying since I was now in my seventies? How do we set goals, or do we set goals and have a Plan B or a Plan C at the ready? Somehow that didn't seem to work or be so appealing.

In our half-French, half-English conversation session one Wednesday morning, Joël responded to my concern about the fragility, even the futility, of setting goals at the age of seventy-three. He made a very valid and helpful comment: "When we make goals at the age of forty or fifty, we don't know if we are going to live long enough to achieve them. Anything could happen to get in their way. You could have died any time during those years. Would that have made any difference in your planning process?"

Of course, in his somewhat predictable manner, he then reversed direction at our next meeting and asked, "Why do you need to have goals in the first place? Why not live in the here and now?"

Like most of his questions, it was also a good one. Later, I reflected and asked myself, *Why can't I let things germinate for a while and enjoy life?*

Because that's not me, I said to myself. Or was it to him? Sometimes I wish I were different. But if I were, I wonder if I would have accomplished as much as I have or made the many necessary and life-altering changes in my residence and career that I have without those plans in 1986? And what about that bucket list in 2002? What would have happened without it?

At the same time, I wondered if it was ever possible to balance planning for the future and living for the present. According to one friend from my past, "Life is about having a plan and then working that plan." But there's all that other advice: "Life is a journey. Enjoy it while you can." My life to date had revealed a definite preference for the former. That had been a very practical and purposeful choice that had led to many accomplishments. Was it time to change my thinking? Could I do so at this point in my life?

Did age make any difference in my attitude about long-term planning? Well, perhaps. There could be a shift in priorities from professional ones to more personal ones. Maybe I needed to put pen to paper and write down some goals and some possibilities for the next five years of my life. The goal-setting process could help deal with the decisions I needed to make for the years ahead and with some of the uncertainty about what's next. Or maybe not. Maybe I needed to let things flow. What a change that would be!

I had to admit, though, that the challenges of setting goals at my age definitely exacerbated my sense of not being in control of my life. How could I be when it was so difficult to communicate in a foreign language? Or was it my routines that were different, and I was having trouble adapting? I decided that probably was not the answer since I hadn't really changed my daily routines. I was still getting out of bed fairly early, having a large cup of tea that I sipped and constantly reheated all morning long, then eating a late breakfast with orange juice and all my vitamins, a snack in late afternoon, before a fairly substantial dinner and early bedtime. It was just that the location for the routines and the language with which I was living my life had changed. Or perhaps I was not in as much control of my life as I had always imagined. Perhaps I never had been.

Although I had been told multiple times in my life that I was too serious, as well as bossy and controlling, and that I needed to "lighten up" and add more fun to my life, I struggled to do that, at least the lighten up recommendation. In fact, I tended to bristle whenever anyone suggested I do that. I had certainly added that goal to my lists over the years but without a lot of success in achieving it. I found it quite difficult to focus on the pure adventure of life, without some reason or timeframe for the moment. I never seemed to be able to go with the flow or take things calmly and coolly. I wished sometimes that I could listen to the advice of a dear and very adventurous ninety-year-old friend who, when asked for his secret to such a long life, had replied, "You can't win if you don't play."

Reflecting sometime later on his words and chuckling at their double meaning, I wondered if the focus should be less on goals and more on having fun while still finding a purpose even in our later decades. Couldn't we have both? Last year, I had had tea with an octogenarian who explained why she was continuing to give piano lessons. "You always need a reason to get up in the morning. That's mine."

Afterwards, as I left her place and climbed down the stairway that led to town so I could climb back up the western cliff toward the cottage, I had asked myself, *Are you still living that purpose you set in 2015 at the Lévesque Association meeting? How much more time do you need to devote to sharing Jeanne's story?* Well, to be fair, I still needed to find some missing pieces to her story, including information on her third husband, before I could legitimately say that the research was done. And I still wanted to spread the story about the Filles du Roi in France, where it continued to be rather unknown. Oh, and there was also that sequel that I had promised to readers of my book about her. And perhaps there was something else I was supposed to be pursuing here in France?

Throughout the past fourteen months, what had kept me going when I was feeling a bit out of sorts or when the aches and pains of aging tried to get in the way? The forces were many to help me regain my balance. I would wander around Dieppe and suddenly discover the vestige of an arch dating from the late seventeenth century on a building that I had already passed by several times. Or I would listen to Saint-Remy's church bells sounding the hour. Or I'd watch the ferry arrive from England or spend time gazing at the afternoon sun playing across the trees and the waterfall in the park between City Hall and the train station. A new email would pop up from a reader of my book about Jeanne, commenting on her or, less frequently, his experience reading my book. Or one of my new friends would call to go for a walk or to have a cup of coffee. Or I would have a quick telephone conversation with family in the States.

Or I would think about Jeanne. I wondered how she managed to adapt to all the new experiences, new living conditions, new neighbors speaking different dialects, and the challenges of raising children in her new home in a frontier village in Quebec. Imagining her fortitude always provided a new perspective on my experiences during this adventure in France. I knew that at least I had the option to return to the States if I wanted to. I could also call members of my family using my landline or connect with them over the Internet. Jeanne, once she began her life in Quebec, probably never thought about any options for a different future or had any easy way to connect with family and friends back in France, three hundred years before telephones and the Internet.

In addition to these thoughts of Jeanne, I would also remember that every day brought something new — new people, new experiences, new learning — forcing me to think about what I was doing or what I was going to say. To help deal with some of the uncertainty I was facing, I tried to impose some discipline on my life, setting project deadlines, for example, with or without short- or long-term objectives. I also continued to create checklists of action items. Crossing off those tasks I had accomplished always gave me a feeling of control over my life. Often, if I had done something during the day that was not on a list, I would add it purely for the enjoyment of crossing it off!

Besides having all those action items, I was also spurred on by considering the alternatives. At that point in early 2018, I didn't know what else I might want to do or where else I would want to live. But I knew I needed to stay engaged. I agreed with the Welsh poet Dylan Thomas: I did not want to "go gentle into that good night."

TEN

STOPPING TO SMELL THE ROSES

There was a bird that sang while perched on the roof of the house across from the garden of the cottage. I could sometimes hear it, or others like it, singing during the day as well. It doubtless wasn't always the same bird, although I couldn't and most likely never would be able to tell the difference in their voices. Nevertheless, it was lovely, cheerful music that caused me to frequently stop and listen – something I didn't remember doing very often in Hartford or in Boston.

Nor did I remember ever taking much time to listen to the sound of the wind swishing through the trees, or to watch flowers grow, or to let my hands get dirty pulling weeds. My beautiful Arts and Crafts style home in Hartford had hedges along the sidewalk in the front, big old trees in the back yard, and lilac bushes along one side of the house. I had a deck built so I could spend more time outside, but I don't think I made much use of it. It turned out I wasn't someone who could simply sit and stare at the flowers in the garden or watch Quincie sleep. "Watch paint dry" was what one friend might suggest. I always had to be busy doing something.

In Dieppe, on the other hand, as I sat in the little cottage and tried to write, I would find myself not infrequently choosing instead to watch the pink camellia bush put forth new blossoms or wait patiently for the lilies of the valley to appear along with early roses, stalks of rhubarb, and those berries that my French tutor liked to pick so that she could make jam. At that point in the spring of 2018, a few months into my second year in Dieppe, the hollyhocks that seemed to grow everywhere were not quite ready to blossom. Even so, their shoots were providing great meals for the snails that loved the garden. The silk tree next to the camellia bush would not bloom until months later.

Growing up in the small town of Nashua, I didn't pay much attention to what could be called the "finer things in life." While I had lessons in piano and in ballet, tap, and ballroom dancing, the arts were never my strong suit. My family didn't go to symphony concerts or visit museums. Excursions were usually limited to shopping in Boston, although we did see a couple of musicals in New York City.

In high school, my focus was math and science. That was where my interests and skills seemed to lie. I was a living example of what I would one day discover was a personality trait called "extraverted thinking." I was logical, organized, rational, analytical, and structured. The position of the sun and several planets supposedly even intensified those traits, as I later learned when I had my astrological chart done. In business school, I concentrated on finance and technology. In my professional career, I tended to emphasize those qualities, sometimes to the detriment of personal relationships.

Outside work, I didn't pay much attention to aesthetics, the way my sisters did. In their roles later in life, along with their careers, they cared more about creating a comfortable and pleasing home for their children and surrounded themselves with nice things, like our mother did. Their Christmas presents were always specially selected and wrapped and birthday cards carefully chosen. My feeble attempts to imitate them usually failed. Even now, thinking about how they had made their homes so warm and welcoming and so reflective of their personal choices and about how many of my new French friends, with or without children, had done the same, I wondered how I managed to miss out on that aesthetic gene.

Maybe it had something to do with that extraverted-thinking preference of mine. I knew about this proclivity because, in a prior chapter of my life some twenty-odd years ago, I wrote a book about creativity that combined my research on the topic with the theory of personality preferences, developed by Swiss psychologist Carl Jung.[5] When I began

---

5. See Appendix II for more information regarding Jung's preferences and creativity.

to clear out my condo in Boston, I went through my bookshelves and put all the books about Jung and about creativity in the many boxes I planned to give away, thinking I would never need them again. As I was writing this sequel to Jeanne's story, I found myself wishing I had not done so. Fortunately, they were still available for purchase on the Internet, but it was interesting to see how all that work was playing out in my life.

According to Jung, we have certain normally strong preferences for receiving and acting on information, preferences that are formed early in life. As we mature, we tend to move through different stages of personal growth and development. Jung believed that this progression followed a somewhat predictable pattern that took us from our early preferred strengths to the lesser developed sides of our personality later in life.

Applying that model to my journey so far meant that I should have at some point started to move away from that *extraverted thinking* where I viewed the world around me through the lens of logic and careful analysis and where I also used my *introverted intuition* to look far ahead and create long-term plans and strategies. I was then supposed to progress to a more freewheeling, fun-loving preference for adventure and travel and for relishing the five senses of smell, sight, sound, touch, and taste. In the final stage that Jung called "mid-life" (which to him, writing a century ago, was around the age of thirty-five years), I was supposed to start reaching inside to tap into the least preferred side of my particular personality profile, the "softer," "gentler," more caring side. I guess that could explain, on some level, my search for roots, community, and beauty.

Reflecting on the last several decades, I could certainly see this pattern starting to evolve in my life and slight signals of change beginning to emerge, although not in that disciplined order. And I was still waiting for the promised laid-back, fancy-free, adventurous side of me to appear!

On a Saturday in the spring of my second year in France, I attended a writing workshop entitled "Making the Invisible Visible." It was designed to help writers explore the world around them and see those things not normally seen or to be able to see them differently. As I entered one of Dieppe's small local bookstores in a rather antiquated building not far from the church of Saint-Jacques, I realized that I didn't know what the workshop was about or why exactly I had decided to come. At the top of a narrow wooden staircase, I entered a mansard-roofed seminar room that was crowded with a large, well-used table, odd chairs, lamps, and a mishmash of other storage items.

The workshop turned out to be most enjoyable for several reasons, not the least of which was that I could understand a good bit of the conversation and was able to communicate somewhat with other members of the class. In addition, I came to see that I hadn't been living my everyday life consciously using all those five senses, nor had I apparently wanted to until now. And most importantly, the workshop helped to deepen my understanding of some of my recent experiences in the northern part of France.

Living in this region did make me feel more connected to and engaged with nature. I wasn't sure why. One explanation could be Jung's model, but others could be the amazing light or the cleaner air or the proximity to the English Channel or simply the natural beauty of Dieppe and its surrounding areas. Whenever I would drive along the coast, high on the cliffs above the channel, I would see a sky that was ever so vast and a landscape full of streaks of bright yellow from colza growing in the fields in May, followed by the bands of lavender linen flowers in late June. Soon there would be stretches of green from the wheat, oats, sugar beets, and corn planted there. In late fall and winter, brown fields were left after the harvest; although here in Normandy, with all its rain, the brown didn't normally last long. The clouds, the endless horizon, the cliffs, the ever-abundant flowers, and even the peeling and fading blue paint on the garage door, all seemed different: sharper, clearer, deeper, and more vibrant, yet still inexplicably softer.

A couple of months after that workshop, I rented a car to drive to the city of Le Havre, an hour away, for another workshop, this one on ancient French spelling. I had finally decided that I was going to have to be able to read original sources in my research, given the frequent absence of transcribed versions of historical documents in France. I had wanted to have a car since I had no idea how to use mass transportation to find my way to those archives in Fort de Tourneville that I had visited in 2016. I had also wanted some flexibility in case the workshop turned out to be significantly above my level of comprehension.

Instead, the afternoon workshop proved to be very helpful in my research, even though I must admit it was not terribly easy to understand. I learned that there was no consistency in written French until the eighteenth century. An *s,* for example, could appear in many different forms in a register of birth or other documents. The choice was up to the notary until standards were universally accepted throughout France. That was an "aha" moment that explained some of the problems I had had reading archival records.

I eventually returned to Le Havre for subsequent workshops on the first Saturday of the month for the rest of the year, usually taking the train instead of driving in order to enjoy more of the countryside. That first time, though, as I was returning to Dieppe, I caught sight of a most spectacular sunset in the rear view mirror. The sky with its bands of pink, blue, and yellow clouds was worthy of a Turner landscape or one by Monet.

The sense of awe and serenity didn't last very long after I arrived back at the cottage that evening when I was caught up in the busyness of my life. However, it did make me realize how much I could miss if I didn't slow down or didn't bother to look.

In Dieppe at yet another workshop held once again in that crowded seminar room on the top floor of the local bookstore, we discussed the idea of beauty. In a summary, I wrote: "Beauty for me is a sound, an image, colors, sights, an emotion felt, a memory remembered in an unhurried moment when I am rested, when I take time to reflect." While it wasn't terribly poetic or original, it wasn't something I would have thought to write a few years ago.

Where those five senses were concerned, at least until more recently, it had always been sounds that I was most sensitive and attuned to, not visual beauty. My brothers and sisters would say "overly sensitive," but my discomfort had usually been as a reaction to perturbing sounds like noisy chewing on gum or on ice, overly loud conversations or music, or the annoying backfires of motorcycles. The sounds of Dieppe, in contrast, were different. I liked them. They didn't usually upset me (except for the loud retorts of motorcycles or scooters without mufflers!). The songs of all those little birds near the cottage. The swoosh of the water rushing across the pebbles on the beach. The cooing of pigeons. Even the calls of the seagulls, which most people found rather annoying.

Although Boston and my neighborhood of Charlestown were also located on the water, the sounds there were not the same. In Dieppe, they mingled with the church bells ringing on the quarter hour and with the rustle of leaves on the six tall cypress trees that stood in front of the high school located across the road from the garage with the blue door.

Was this how Jeanne's life might have been? Living in essence, as we would say today, off the grid, with few links to the rest of the world? Instead, her contacts with the world around her would have been more intimate — the music and vista of the St. Lawrence River, the light of the moon and stars, the smells of the earth and the fields, the changes in the weather, and even the silence.

Until my time in France, I've never really stopped to smell the roses. Nor had I had any intimate contacts with the world around me. In the past, I'd spent too much time thinking about tomorrow, next week, or next year. I was still thinking about the future, but "long range" was becoming not so long range anymore.

To be sure, my affinity for the past and for things that kept me in touch with some fond memories was somewhat at odds with that focus on the future. That dichotomy could explain why I had kept scrapbooks, photos, newspaper clippings, maps, and brochures, as well as many of the dishes and other things that our parents didn't take with them when they moved to Arizona and that no one else wanted. This love of the past, the joy of researching and digging up new stories, could possibly be one of the reasons why I called myself a historian. It also explained my obsession with Jeanne's story and the life she lived well over three centuries ago and my appreciation for life in France and all its history.

A week after I had written those reflections in the workshop and while I was trying to balance future and past, Mother Nature sent a message to focus on the present. A terrible storm of torrential wind and rain moved through Dieppe. Although it was not as intense as Tempête Egon, I was thoroughly soaked as I ran for the bus after returning a car I had rented. The wind blew most of the camellias off the bush so now I would have to wait for the other flowers to bloom. Fortunately, the lilies of the valley, those sweet-smelling symbols of luck and love here in France, would blossom very soon, right in time for sharing with family and friends to celebrate the first of May.

Lilies of the Valley

Part Three

EXPLORING NEW HORIZONS

ELEVEN

The Language

When I first met Tatiana, our connection was instantaneous, although we might not have known it exactly at that moment. Tatiana, who had left her native Russia in 1986, had just moved to Dieppe with her husband after living for thirty-plus years in Paris. A psychotherapist by training and a political refugee, she had arrived in France with English as her second language and speaking no French. Her story of how she managed to find support to learn computer skills, master the French language, go on to a successful career in banking, and then return to her psychotherapy practice demonstrated the fortitude, resilience, and perseverance that I came to so admire about her.

Eager to get involved in her new community within a couple of months after arriving in Dieppe, Tatiana came to the June 2018 meeting of the Café Littéraire where we met for the first time. Tall, slim, and elegant, she made quite an impression. While some people said she had a slight accent, I never noticed. I always found her French superb.

Tatiana would eventually come to play a very important role in my life as we gradually became better acquainted. Not long after that initial meeting, we ran into each other twice: at an English class I was leading as a temporary replacement for their teacher and then at a bridge course we both decided to take. Our friendship grew over time based on similar personalities, characteristics, and our mutual interests in bridge, life in Dieppe, our pets, and things Russian.

Early in our friendship, we met for a cup of coffee and ended up having the first of many long conversations about our three different languages. Our first conversation went something like this: "Why did you learn Russian?" she asked. "And then why did you decide to give it up and relearn French?"

"My decision to relearn French came much later in life," I explained. After telling her the story about the limited exposure I had had to my French-Canadian roots when I was growing up, I went on: "Upon graduation from high school, my long-term goal was to finish college and then teach for a couple of years before finding, marrying, and having a family with 'Mr. Right.' I decided, therefore, that in college I needed to find a subject to teach that would be in high demand after graduation. I chose to study a new, more 'exotic' language since four years of high-school French was not going to be enough to find a job in what I expected to be a very competitive market teaching French, particularly in New England. It was also possible that an unconscious bias against my French-Quebecois heritage played a role, but I'll never know for sure."

After explaining the rather romantic American concept of Mr. Right, I went on to give my reasons for choosing Russian. "Partly, I did so because it was different. Since Russian space flights had recently been hot items in the news, I assumed that there would be a great demand for teachers of that language. That was not, of course, a very politically correct decision in the middle of the cold war. Eventually, during my four years of college study, I also fell in love with the language, as well as with Russian history and culture."

I continued, "When I finished college, I spent nine weeks studying in the then Soviet Union, first in Moscow and then afterwards in a sports camp near Kiev. I returned to the United States to teach Russian and Russian history for two years in Tulsa, Oklahoma. In between those two years, I attended a summer language school, immersing myself in the Russian language. I then returned to the Soviet Union, this time for six weeks of study in Leningrad [now St. Petersburg] and then three more weeks traveling. After all that learning, I was able to speak Russian so well that I was once mistaken by a Moscow cab driver as being from Poland!"

"Do you ever regret those years?" Tatiana asked. "Oh no," I responded. "Absolutely not! I had some amazing adventures learning Russian. At the same time, the fact that Russian is now firmly rooted in the language section of my brain is another reason, I believe, for my struggle with French. Too often, the first foreign word that comes to mind is Russian, not French.

"Nevertheless and despite the fact that I might actually have a little Russian DNA in me, I was firmly committed to relearning French. It was goal #6 on a list of things I wanted to do before I died that I wrote in a travel journal from 2002."

"So, is that why you decided to spend all this time in France?" she wanted to know.

"Yes. After I visited Dieppe in 2013 in search of information about my ancestor, I decided to take action to significantly improve my French. I spent the next three years taking weekly French classes at an adult learning center in Boston, but I grew impatient. The classes weren't working quickly enough. I felt I needed to be in France if I was going to learn to speak French fluently enough to not be recognized as an American. And since my ancestor had left France from Dieppe, I thought her spirit might help with my learning!"

After that first coffee, we got to know each other better as we continued to share experiences in Dieppe, as well as memories of our times in the Soviet Union. For the first year of our friendship, I was living in the little cottage on the cliff near the chateau, and she lived in the center of town. So we would see each other once or twice a week, on Tuesdays for bridge and not infrequently on Saturday mornings at the market. Sometimes alone or sometimes with our expanding circle of mutual friends, I enjoyed coffees, lunches, and dinners with Tatiana and her husband Xavier in their apartment filled with beautiful pieces of art and with a collection of books that far exceeded anything I had ever had. Tatiana's broad set of interests combined with her incredibly original and quirky sense of humor and her caring nature made spending time together totally delightful.

As our friendship deepened, I came to appreciate her even more.

Her attention to detail and to the needs of others and her training as a psychologist gave her a very different perspective on situations and people. That and her concerns for what I might call the softer, more personal facets of a decision or judgement helped me begin to move beyond my very and frequently too logical approach. Her wide-ranging knowledge was remarkable. She could talk with ease about anything from the two types of intelligence to the latest art exhibition in Paris to the correct bridge opening of two diamonds. At one point, we offered to make a presentation to our book club about the cold war from our different points of view as a Russian and an American growing up during that time. I was totally impressed by her understanding of the worldwide ramifications of those years and of the historical events that I never knew, never considered, or had forgotten.

We went on to have many more conversations alone, with Xavier, or with other friends on a broad set of topics, including the French language. I was sometimes asked what I liked and didn't like about my adopted language. I would start by explaining my frustrations, which continued to plague me over the months I stayed in France.

"Besides the rather intimidating challenges of correct pronunciation and intonation and words like "nickel" that are spelled the same but pronounced differently, I have been challenged by all those *faux amis* [false friends], that I learned about in high school — similar looking words that mean one thing in English but have a very different meaning in French. They have often turned into enemies, tripping me up in conversations. *Assumer* doesn't mean assume except in the sense of taking on. *Supposer* does mean assume in the sense of thinking that something is true or probable, but it does not mean needing to do something, as in 'I am supposed to be there.' That's another verb. *Demander* is not as strong a word as it is in English and means 'to ask' or, in the reflexive voice, 'to wonder.' *Assister* is translated as 'to attend' and *attendre* means 'to wait.' And the list of these false friends continues to grow."

I went on and said to anyone who was still listening, "Then there are all those words with multiple, different meanings. *Regretter* can mean feeling sorry about something that occurred as well as missing something that happened. The translation of *taille* provides at least four choices: 'waist,' 'size,' 'height,' and 'pruning.' And *contrôler* has several different definitions: 'check,' 'verify,' 'audit,' 'supervise,' or 'master'!"

I then explained, "Bill Bryson, an American author and researcher, believes that invading populations, such as the Saxons, French, Scandinavians, and Germans, brought new words that added more precision to the English language.[6] Somehow, the French managed to keep themselves relatively isolated from those invaders and their vocabularies. According to Bryson and others, there are thus fewer words in French than in English, one half or a third fewer, some have said. To them, that difference explains why a single French word often has to play many roles and why, I've been told, its meaning can depend on whether it is found in the beginning, in the middle, or the end of a sentence or can depend on the context in which the word is used.

"I wonder if the need to surround a word with context accounts for the fact that French books tend to be longer than their English counterparts. There is, for instance, a ten-page difference in the English and French versions of my book on Jeanne. It's also possible that the French tendency to be extremely polite, based on centuries of French diplomatic prowess, adds words. I've learned that when I want to end a formal letter in French, for example, the correct version of 'sincerely yours' can take up to ten additional words."

My comments often went on to include, "What can also be very frustrating and at times overwhelming is that the French language structure works differently from English — at least from my understanding. You put adverbs and phrases in different places. It takes two words to make a negative. When you begin a sentence with 'perhaps' or 'hardly,' you have to invert the verb structure. You make adverbs out of practically every word. You don't use the future tense with 'if.' But you do with 'when.' It's the opposite in English."

In addition to listing my frustrations, I usually mentioned my struggles analyzing and understanding the reasons for a particular

---

6. Bill Bryson, *The Mother Tongue: English and How It Got That Way* (New York: Harper Perennial, 2001), 52 ff.

grammatical usage. "When I've asked for an explanation, I've been told 'it was a judgment made by the Académie Française in the seventeenth century [the language of Voltaire and Molière] that has continued to today without changes,' or 'it's the music,' or 'it's because of the Latin and Greek heritage,' or, not infrequently, 'I have no idea.'"

Some acquaintances have suggested I should stop trying to analyze and instead relish the experience. One evening a couple drove me home from a visit to the Musée de la Résistance et la Déportation in Forges-Les-Eaux, not far from Dieppe. As they listened to my questions asking why a particular verb worked the way it did, they suggested: "Instead of anguishing over why something is expressed the way it is in French versus in English, why don't you simply enjoy the discovery and the new knowledge?" A good question, but I haven't been able to stop the anguish or fully appreciate the experience without the analysis!

Despite voicing these frustrations, I wanted to reassure my French friends that I did indeed love their language, not just because it was the language of my father and my eighth-great-grandmother. "I am fascinated by the nuances and idiosyncrasies of the language and the differences from English. That intrigue, along with the connection with my roots, and the need to manage my life here, probably explains why I have continued the struggle to learn French. Those reasons are much more important to me than a desire to better appreciate French literature about which I have remained poorly educated. Nor do I have much interest in learning French to excel at French cuisine since that has never been a hobby."

I would frequently add that my love affair with the French language included certain French verbs that compacted words in English to only one word in French. I wasn't sure they all understood my passion around verbs like *patienter* (to remain patient), *passionner* (to be passionate about), *lézarder* (to bask in the sun, act like a lizard?), *fragiliser* (to weaken, make more fragile), and épauler (to help or support someone, literally, give them a shoulder, an *épaule*). And then there was *nidifier*, which I had recently learned could be translated as "to build a nest," a *nid!* Their lack of interest in that passion of mine didn't matter to me as I went on to create lists of more of those verbs that I found so charming.

Tatiana generally did not share the same frustrations or passions. But she did complain every once in a while about the gender of many nouns since they often had the opposite gender in Russian. For me, who grew up with nouns without gender, the challenge was different. I had been told that French children grow up learning that everything is male or female, so when they learn a new noun, they learn two words, not one: the noun and its sex. It wasn't just *table*, it was *une table*, and it was *un village* but *une ville* (a masculine village but a feminine city). Okay, I could accept that these were vestiges of the Roman and Greek heritage in the French language, but why then were some US states feminine and others masculine? And why did some words change their meaning when they changed their gender? *Tour*, for example, is a tall tower in its feminine version (*la Tour Eiffel*), but it means a drive, trip, or turn when it's masculine (*le Tour de France!*).

Some of my observations about the French brain did interest Tatiana, I assumed because of her years of training in psychology. We shared conversations about how language could reflect possible psychological differences between the English and French cultures. I, for one, tentatively concluded that the French brain works differently from the English brain, partly because of a different culture and history and the role they played in language development. At that point in time, this was still merely a nonscientific hypothesis on my part, and it deserved more research. But I was coming to believe that the English language had possibly evolved in a way that reflected not only the integration of so many different peoples but also the development of the ego. Did that idea possibly explain why the personal pronoun "I" was capitalized in English, but its equivalent in French was not, unless it began a sentence?

This theory could explain the emphasis in English on the individual person as the actor or agent, in control and being proactive, as opposed to someone being acted upon. In English, we tend to say, "I am hungry" or "I am right." In French, the equivalent is "I have hunger" or "I have reason." The phrase "I am cold" in French translates as "I have cold." I am not thirty or fifty or seventy-five years old; I have (or possess) thirty or fifty or seventy-five years.

Things happen to people in French versus people making things happen in English. When I wanted to say to my sister, "I miss you," I couldn't translate that word for word from English into French. If I did, the meaning was quite different. But I could tell her in French that she was missing to me. Many French phrases, it seemed, suggest an absence of personal ownership. "My head hurts" translates as "I have a pain in the head." That's just one example.

From what I could see, the French tend to use the passive voice and the impersonal much more frequently than is customary in English. The more correct version of "I must" or "I need do something" is often translated in French as "it is necessary for me to do something." Could these examples support my tentative theory that language reflects cultural differences in the development of the ego and the corresponding power of an individual to take action? Or maybe the reverse could also be true and language has some sort of effect on culture? I also questioned whether political structures played a role in the way languages developed. Did the existence of very powerful French kings before the Revolution leave a legacy that affected the progress of individual independence?

Tatiana and I agreed that these ideas deserved more research someday. I did, however, have a particular, more personal and pressing concern. If the French brain did in fact work differently from the American one — or at least that French logic was not my logic — did that mean I would never be able to express myself fluently in the language unless I changed my way of thinking and gave up my desire to always take action? If a language reflected its culture, did that explain the difficulty I faced trying to become fluent in it after the age of seventy-three years?

Whenever I raised this topic in conversations, my French friends didn't exactly know how to respond. I wasn't sure if that was because I hadn't made my ideas clear or whether it was something they had never thought about or whether they basically didn't find the topic very interesting.

Someone once wrote that learning a second language could help simplify your life. "It's as if in your own country you received a hundred channels, and suddenly, you have been reduced to only one or two."[7] I couldn't decide if learning French had simplified or complicated my life, but I did know that I had to concentrate more. I found myself searching for simpler words to express myself when a phrase in French didn't come easily to mind. And I had to slow down, to think before I spoke, not simply to reflect and be less direct, but also to find the right words and use the right grammar and correct pronunciation. That tendency could also disturb the flow of conversation, as Tatiana kept reminding me. "Just talk and stop correcting yourself all the time. It gets in the way of our communicating!"

Two of my nieces who had each spent a few years in France in their early twenties told me that it took them at least three years of living there to be "fluent." At that point in my French adventure, I knew it was undeniably going to take many more. Although I was often complimented on my ability to speak French and new acquaintances would often say, "I wish I could speak English the way you speak French," I couldn't imagine my own goal of "mastering French" being attained any time soon. In the meantime, I decided to set an intermediate goal of making sure I could communicate in everyday settings with merchants, technicians, waiters, and friends. And of speaking more quickly.

I hoped I could continue to be able to laugh with friends when I mixed up words that sounded so much alike but meant something totally different. Once while taking a yoga class on a glorious summer morning on Dieppe's esplanade, I confused the words for "stretching" and "interment." The French words sounded very similar (*étirement* and *enterrement*), at least to me, but my mistake resulted in much laughter on the part of my friend who was stretching in the space beside me and who has frequently reminded me of that episode.

For me, it was the challenge that made the struggles all worthwhile. I had to use my brain. Even though I sometimes felt like a child when

7. Judy Kronenfeld, "Speaking French" in *France, A Love Story: Women Write about the French Experience*, ed. Camille Cusumano (Emeryville, CA: Seal Press, 2004), 281.

I had to speak slowly or needed to be corrected, at least I could laugh at myself and with others, and it generally felt okay. It was, of course, most agreeable when people appreciated my attempts to speak French, as was usually the case. One time I was in a beauty shop looking for some facial cream. I mixed up the French word for skin (*peau*) and bucket (*seau*). I didn't know why but perhaps because they sounded similar. The clerk was kind enough to smile and help me anyway, especially when I pointed to my face. At least, I told myself to avoid being embarrassed, I was not bored. I also tried not to be insulted when I discovered that my friends intentionally tried to speak more slowly than they normally would when I was around.

More than 1,200 years ago, Charlemagne, the first French king to be crowned Holy Roman Emperor, supposedly said, "Learning a second language is gaining a second soul." I still haven't figured out what that means, but I did know that I needed to use different parts of my body, particularly my mouth, when I spoke French, and was frequently reminded to do so. According to Camille Cusumano, writing about her discovery of French at age thirteen:

> Speaking French was sexy. It made me sit up and use my body in startling ways. It meant a voyage to new places in my lips, tongue, nasal passage, and abdomen. My whole body resonated with the discovery of challenging vowels, consonants, and diphthongs. The new sounds ignited enough visual imagery to sustain a budding romantic.[8]

I hadn't really thought about feeling sexy while trying to speak French, but I did know that it was indeed **my** head that hurt!

---

8. Camille Cusumano, "Introduction," *France, A Love Story*, xi.

TWELVE

The Culture

While I had spent many months and years studying the French language, I hadn't applied the same effort to understanding the culture. Before coming to France for my sabbatical year, if I had done more of that research, particularly about life in small towns outside of Paris and other large cities, I might not have been so surprised to discover that so many stores were closed at noon or shortly thereafter for two-hour lunch breaks or that banks and many other stores were closed on Monday, or at least Monday morning. Nor would I have been rather shocked to sit through long, nonstop, well-attended lectures on esoteric topics, such as "Abbeys and Churches in Fourteenth Century Normandy" or "Heraldic Symbols of the Twelfth Century," lectures that began at eight-thirty in the evening and often ended two hours later with hardly anyone leaving before the final applause.

I probably would not, however, have learned about the preference to use keys instead of drawer pulls in most older furniture, keys that invariably got lost and for whom duplicates were almost impossible to find. And, even if I had done the research, I doubt that I would have been prepared for the visits that occurred right before the Christmas holidays at the end of my first year in Dieppe. On one dark and not very stormy night, a man knocked on my door. He said he was from the town's trash collecting service. I was somewhat afraid to open the door because I didn't know if anyone would hear me if I screamed for help, living as I did on that quiet and rather isolated lane. But I did open the door. He asked if I was having any problems with collections. I answered no, thanked him, and closed the door. The next night, it was two men from the fire department. This time I received a calendar. As they walked away, I asked them if people normally gave a tip for these visits. Not surprisingly, they answered, "Yes." I, needless to say, obliged.

Later that week I told my friends about these visits. They were a bit embarrassed that they had not warned me to expect them as normal holiday practice, and, yes, I should give them a tip. So I was prepared for the third visit, this time from a representative of the post office.

These visits were only a small example of the many new experiences I had living in a small town in France. Growing up in the United States, its culture had become part of me, primarily in my unconscious. Nevertheless, my tendency to analyze everything, from differences in everyday practices to the larger, more philosophical, even psychological, distinctions made me much more aware of the contrasts, as well as the similarities, between the two cultures. It was the differences that I found the most interesting.

My most vivid initial experiences with the cultural differences involved the rather special relationship the French have with food, not only with the preparation of their meals but also the customs that surround its consumption. This observation would not have been such a revelation for others. But it was for me, who normally had quite limited interest in recipe ingredients or even eating, unlike my acknowledged-foodie brother-in-law David who did take issue with some of my observations!

First, I learned about some of the many differences in cooking nomenclature and usages. A *tarte* (pie), for example, had to have pastry. So even if a dessert arrived in what I called a "pie plate," "No," my friend told me, "it's a cake. It doesn't have a pastry shell." And a cookie? No, what I knew to be a cookie was actually a cake or perhaps a biscuit. Cookies were those things to be found on a computer, apparently.

Names were not the only learning challenge I had across the very broad spectrum of French cuisine. I also needed to learn how to distinguish the many different French mushrooms — over three thousand I read, although hardly any were edible — and French cheeses — over three hundred, I was told, all quite edible as long as the smell of the more aged variety wasn't too bothersome.

Then there was the wine. I hoped that one day I'd be able to find a course in Dieppe in order to become knowledgeable enough about the distinctive varieties of French wines to be able to understand the complexities around ordering and appreciating a good glass of wine. In France, I couldn't walk into a bar and simply order a glass of Pinot Noir as I could in the States. Only a rare bartender would be able to serve me one since they would need to know the geographic region (Côtes du Rhone or Bourgogne, for example) where that particular Pinot Noir grape (*cépage*) was grown and which producer (*propriétaire*) had the right to use it in a very tightly regulated industry. To find a bottle of Pinot Noir for my Thanksgiving turkey, I ended up having to go to a wine store where a knowledgeable salesperson (a *caviste*) could help me find the right wine.

And there were all those special glasses to be used not only for wines but also for beers and cocktails. At the flea market last summer, I noticed several vendors selling every conceivable sort of glass for drinking red wine, white wine, champagne, brandy, beer, and different cocktails and aperitifs, many with brand names imprinted to identify the proper beverage to be imbibed. Apparently, no ordinary wine goblet or beer mug would do!

There were even restrictions on how to talk about food. An ice-cream dessert — loaded with whipped cream, chocolate sauce, and a cherry — could not be described as "sinful." It could be "too good," but nothing edible could ever be "sinful," I was told. Similarly, a dish couldn't be "very delicious." Simply "delicious" would do.

My friends seemed to take cooking very seriously. In their kitchens, there was almost always a scale to ensure that the proportions of ingredients conformed to the recipe. The first time I saw one was in Joël's kitchen. I even had to ask what it was and how he used it. For me, who tended to read a recipe when I did cook but who rarely religiously followed it and instead tended to throw things together, it was curious, to say the least.

During a meal, the most important topic of conversation was usually food. Frequently I would hear comments about the best vendor in the market for cheese, vegetables, or fruit. "Oh, did you see that the vendor with the sheep's milk yoghurt has returned?" Or, "Try the black bread at the merchant at the corner." Or a friend would rave about the latest cookbook she had purchased. There was almost always a conversation regarding the recipes for each dish served, the details of where the ingredients were purchased, and how the dish was prepared and cooked. The highest compliment to a host was a request for the recipe. Politics and religion were rarely brought up as topics too disturbing to discuss during a meal except with me since many people were eager to hear how we Americans could possibly have elected the man who was residing in the White House at the time.

I've heard a saying that whereas Americans eat to live, the French live to eat. My experiences seemed to confirm its validity. But the saying was more than about merely eating. The company of friends and the time spent together were as important as the food, if not more so. In a conversation once with some friends while enjoying the four-course meal prepared by one of them, they described the concept of "savoir faire" to me. In their version, which I heard also called *"savoir vivre,"* or knowing how to live and closely related to the French well-known *joie de vivre,* the term had to do more with knowing how to enjoy life and relishing good food, good friends, and good conversations than the typical definition of "know-how," practical knowledge, or street smarts.

At the same time, those conversations over dinner when they did expand into other topics beyond food were also a bit of a surprise. The discussions could turn loud and quite animated, and at times it felt as if there wasn't much listening. Guests often seemed more intent on hearing themselves speak, sometimes repeating what another guest had said a minute ago, rather than engaging in an exchange of ideas, at least as far as I was able to understand. They frequently talked with much emotion that appeared to me as threatening. "Don't worry," a friend counselled one time. "They were not attacking you, even though you might feel as if they were. It's totally the French way."

I experienced "the French way" or the French culture not only around sharing meals but also around French history and tradition. In early June, 2017, my new friend Sylvie introduced me to Thursday afternoon hikes with two of her friends. One cool Thursday in August, the four of us took a walk in the Arques Forest that covers a broad expanse of terrain not far from Dieppe. It was raining, but that didn't stop our hike. As we walked along the dirt paths under the beech trees, hardwoods, and evergreens, they chattered away on topics I sometimes understood and at least tried to absorb. As I looked around, I noticed very large holes — almost craters — among the trees.

"Those are what's left from World War II bombs," they explained. "From locations near this forest, the Germans were launching U2 rockets that were aimed at London since this area was the closest line of attack to that city. The Allies were trying to destroy those rocket launching pads with bombs that often landed here in the forest. The bombs are gone, but the craters remain." Indeed, at a nearby chateau, one of those launching pads had been preserved as another reminder of the tragedy of war in France.

That experience was not my first introduction to the importance of history in French culture. In 2013, at the *Fête de la Mer* (seafood festival) in Granville, a French man about my age overheard me talking and asked — in French — if I was an American. After I replied, "*Oui*," he thanked me on behalf of the French people for what the United States had done for France during World War II. I thought that a bit odd, so I asked him, "Why?"

His answer: "Without the sacrifice of so many of your young American men, France would have become German."

His comment and other similar ones that I heard later began my introduction to the more recent history of France. Memorials to the American Revolution, to the Civil War (in the South, anyway), and to war dead exist in the States, but they could not compare to the ever-present reminders of war in France. Around Dieppe, for example, remnants of German bunkers could be seen in backyards (sometimes serving as patios), along the coast and sometimes even on the beaches where they had fallen because of the erosion of the cliffs. Bombs were still being discovered in the English Channel. Museums to war efforts, the resistance, and deportation activities could be found in a great number of towns, beyond the beaches of lower Normandy. Cemeteries filled with American, French, British, and even German war dead could be visited throughout northern France. In almost every major town and the surrounding villages, at least in Normandy, there were plaques and monuments dedicated to preserving the memory of soldiers killed in battles that occurred not only in World War II, but also in World War I and the 1870 war with Prussia.

Besides the prevalence of physical reminders of the perils of war, there were also annual ceremonies. In August of my sabbatical year, the commemoration of the seventy-fifth anniversary of the disastrous August 19, 1942, raid on Dieppe took place over the course of several days. I hadn't truly understood the severity of that raid before then, but I definitely gained a much greater appreciation of it after those few days.

First, I joined others to walk twenty-six kilometers as part of a guided tour of some of the eight hundred German bunkers, built during World War II with mostly French forced labor to defend German positions around Dieppe. The next afternoon at a nearby cemetery, I participated in the reading of names of those lost during that battle, including that of Jean-Jacques Lévesque, although I wouldn't learn about our familial connection until later.

The next morning, I rode in one of three buses going to the various locations where the fighting took place or where soldiers were buried. The buses carried French officials; Canadian government representatives; the mayor of Dieppe in New Brunswick, Canada; mayors of towns on the English coast; veterans and their families; Canadian, Belgian, and English visitors; and other participants and observers. At each stop, we listened to speeches and witnessed the laying of wreaths by politicians, by leaders of all sorts of civic associations, and by children to remind us all of the horrors that war can inflict. We sang the Canadian, American, British, and French national anthems and enjoyed hors d'oeuvres and glasses of champagne.

I learned later that slightly modified versions of these commemorations — usually without the champagne stop — were carried out annually in Dieppe on May 8 for the end of World War II in Europe, on September 1 for the liberation of the town in 1944, and on November 11 for the end of World War I. I also discovered that history was kept alive not only by monuments, ceremonies, and museums, but also by conferences on the histories of nearby chateaux and the people who lived there in addition to the ones that I attended on Dieppe during the war of 1870, the reasons for the World War I, and De Gaulle and Quebec.

Family memories also helped preserve the more recent history. Many of my friends shared stories of family members involved in the resistance, conscripted into the German army or workforce after France capitulated in 1940, or finally joining up with the Allied forces to bring the war to an end. Other acquaintances remembered sharing ration cards or being sent to the countryside for safety. One friend's father was sent to Germany as a conscripted worker. When his dad came home, he had lost more than fifty pounds. After the war was finally over, the family then lived through the reconstruction of their town that had been destroyed in 1940 by the Germans as a "lesson" to France. A retired doctor I met one day showed me pictures of her father who had served in both the French provisional government of Phillipe Pétain and the resistance at the same time, only to be rounded up by the Gestapo and sent off to die in a German concentration camp.

In the United States, we learned about wars, usually from stories of events that happened elsewhere. Except for the American Revolution and the Civil War, most large-scale hostilities and horrible casualties took place on foreign shores — at least up until September 11, 2001. In France, war had been lived for centuries and reminders continued to be ever present. Fortunately, the need to remember the horrors of war or the past has not yet been accompanied by the American addiction to guns.

This focus on history, from what I could tell, went well beyond wars. In addition to a street or boulevard named after General Charles de Gaulle or called the "Avenue of the Republic" or "Avenue of the

Liberation" that could be found in almost every town, there was usually a park, bridge, or school honoring famous and not-so-famous writers, painters, politicians, and other local celebrities. I was astonished when I read about the amount of money and effort spent to repair, renovate, and preserve French cultural heritage from its ancient past and the thousands-of-years-old caves of Lascaux and Pech Merle to the standing stones at Carnac and megaliths in Corsica to so many centuries-old churches.

While I, as a history lover, greatly appreciated this preservation of heritage and the incredible availability of local, departmental, regional, and national archives, I sometimes wondered if the focus on the past didn't have some negative consequences as well. From my experience, there was something about the French psyche that made it resistant to change — a trait not necessarily limited to the French these days. I regularly heard comments about how the traditional reliance on the government, the lack of personal responsibility and initiative, and the desire to preserve the past were restricting economic growth in the country. Could it possibly be that this appreciation of both the past and the present conflicted with the need for a more entrepreneurial attitude about the future?

After several months in France, I also noticed other important differences in approaches to life, not the least of which was the experience with my English group that Dana and I had regarding the idea of "good enough." There were others. The US motto is "life, liberty, and the pursuit of happiness." At its best, for privileged American citizens and residents, that meant an innovative spirit, an incredible optimism, and a "can-do attitude," focusing on finding solutions to problems. At its worst, it could be displayed in selfish, boorish behavior, proliferation of guns and violence, and lack of concern for others (the "lone cowboy" syndrome).

Similar words appeared emblazoned on public buildings in France: "*Liberté, egalité, et fraternité*," but they have somewhat different meanings. At their worst, from my point of view, liberté and egalité occasionally went too far, resulting in frequent worker strikes, often called France's best known "product." These strikes, organized by France's several different labor unions, along with demonstrations and protests against different policies and proposals, sometimes went on for days and caused bus, train, or metro delays or traffic hold-ups. I was told that the strikes normally did not represent the views of the majority of the French population. In addition, friends offered explanations of these strikes and protests as being protected by law and as being rooted in the French history of revolutions and demonstrations, presumably as the preferred method for effecting change and having their voices heard. There were probably other explanations as well.

The impact of these strikes and demonstrations on my life in Dieppe, far away from all the drama in Paris and other large cities, had in truth been minor. Toward the end of 2018, protests by the *Gilets jaunes* (protestors wearing yellow vests) stopped traffic, sometimes by burning tires at road intersections, and caused delays in bus routes in and around Dieppe. My often tightly scheduled days could thus be affected. Bridge classes and a conference in Rouen were canceled because of anticipated disruptions from planned demonstrations. A couple of times, my friends and I had to maneuver around metro troubles in Paris. I once planned to take the train to Rouen to meet a friend for a day-long event. Because of a train strike, we had to drive instead. None of these situations were major inconveniences, and I had to admit that I hadn't given equal consideration to all sides of the problem. Was I — heaven forbid! — becoming more conservative in my old age?

This resistance to change that was often manifested, at least to me, in these strikes and demonstrations could be seen as having negative economic results. At the same time, I had to realize that they could also often reflect a concern for "solidarity" — that is, what was best for the community and a sense of responsibility for others, as opposed to the ever-growing sentiment in the United States of "every man and woman for themselves." At least, that's how it sometimes felt in small-town France and admittedly in one run by members of the French communist party where a great deal of attention was paid to social services and the well-being of residents.

Perhaps the best example of this concern for the well-being of others throughout France was the French healthcare system. While I came to recognize some of its drawbacks, I continued to be astounded not only by its coverage and costs but also by the acceptance of the system as a basic human right. Over a birthday dinner I once held, my friends urged me to apply for healthcare in France. I replied that I wouldn't feel comfortable doing that — I later changed my mind — since I hadn't paid into the system. Their reaction surprised me: "Well, we paid into the system for others as well as for ourselves."

This concern for solidarity and the wellbeing of others could also account for the importance that the French place on family. The number of my French friends who stayed close to their families and visited with them frequently was evidence to me of this family value. Many of them as grandparents devoted significant time and effort to taking care of their grandchildren during school vacations or on weekends, to free up parents and because they really enjoyed having these children around. From what I could tell, the feelings were mutual. I was also amazed at the number of adults accompanying their aging parents — with or without walkers, canes, or wheelchairs — on the boulevards or in town.

For sure, these attachments were made somewhat easier by geographical proximity, France being significantly smaller than the United States. And many families still lived close to one another, although I was told that recent demographic trends could change this situation. Of course, it was perfectly possible I just hadn't noticed these relationships in the States, given perhaps my rather insular life in a Boston neighborhood where most of my single friends didn't have children and where my siblings, with the exception of Dana and his wife Ginna, didn't have young grandchildren. Nor did I have elderly parents or relatives needing care.

Despite those too frequent strikes, demonstrations, and other disruptions, life in France felt more enjoyable than in the States for other reasons besides the healthcare system and the family focus. I couldn't tell if the values of community and family translated into a broader sense of acceptance for others, but it certainly seemed that way. One of my nieces who had lived in France for several years had noticed it as well. In a phone conversation, she once told me: "In France, I found that there was less of an emphasis on your work, or where you go to school, or where you live. Instead, who you are and what you think, believe, and appreciate appeared to be much more important."

Given my time in France to date, I had to agree with her. In the United States, one of the first questions at a cocktail party when meeting someone new was often, "What do you do?" In France, even when the answer was "I am retired," I sensed that I would be probing too much if I asked what someone did before retiring. It wasn't that important to them. Being a doctor or a lawyer in the States was seen as a credential worth mentioning, no matter how discreetly. In contrast, it took me several months to learn that a new French friend had retired from a medical practice.

While there were many different explanations for that sort of response (perhaps she didn't want to be constantly asked to treat an ache or pain), there did seem to be less of a need to prove oneself, at least in the social circles I found myself in. Job titles weren't mentioned nor were the names of employers or the colleges or universities attended. The importance of one's achievements in life or in a career was much less evident. Making money was not something everyone believed was good. All of this worked for me, as I have grown older, but not necessarily for the French economy.

At the same time, this sense of acceptance could explain what I have observed is a widespread tolerance for what might be called poor customer service. Although my views could reflect the American preference to be direct and much less accepting, I wondered if this attitude demonstrated a lack of desire to rock the boat or a long heritage of diplomacy among the French. Or was it their unconscious acceptance of "that's just life in France?" — an unexplained paradox with all those protests and demonstrations!

Instead of complaining or demonstrating, I tended to take action. I often had to be assertive when asking for service in stores or when I needed access to particular archival records and met with some resistance because the assistant at the desk insisted, incorrectly it turned out, that I didn't have the necessary approvals. And I fought the first traffic ticket I received and won, although it took over a year for me to get a satisfactory response.

All of these experiences with French culture meant that, despite resisting to some extent, I was forced to learn acceptance and exercise more patience than ever before. I learned to use the words *on verra* (we'll see), another version of *que sera, sera* (what will be, will be), more frequently than I was used to, to accept what could happen instead of making it happen. It took a lot of self-control on my part to sit through meetings with no agenda that ended without agreement on next steps and through long conferences full of details and little interaction. On more than one occasion, I was quite surprised by a group's failure to pay attention to the agenda or the hours — evening meetings tended to start at eight o'clock, a bit late for this early riser — by the lack of focus on a topic, by distracting side conversations, and by the tendency of attendees to talk over one another. One friend explained that at the root of these rambling conversations was the French preference for expressing ideas over taking action, which most surely was the exact opposite of my favored course of operation. The seriousness with which the French took such intellectual discussions was another explanation.

Whether these observations were true or not, I usually chose not to push too hard. To be honest, sometimes the real reason I bit my tongue and didn't speak up said less about an increase in patience on my part and more about my lack of facility with the language. Perhaps my inability or reluctance to push back was actually the correct response in those situations. Did an American have any right to try to change long-entrenched French attitudes and customs?

On a walk in the woods with a new group of acquaintances, I met a woman who was born in France but who had spent enough years in the States to qualify for American citizenship and to carry both passports. I asked her what she liked about Americans. "Their optimism, their friendliness, and positive attitude" was her response. "The

French can be so pessimistic, always complaining about problems, and rarely looking for solutions." And what was it that she didn't like about Americans? "Their superficiality," she replied — something I also heard from others.

My friend Joël would in all likelihood have agreed with her comments about Americans, in any case. During one of our weekly language exchanges, he was expounding about the horrors of communism, which he had learned from a book about the topic. After thirty minutes of listening to his recounting the legacy of the disastrous massacres perpetrated by Lenin, Stalin, and others, I exclaimed, "It's a beautiful morning. Let's talk about something more pleasant."

To which he responded, "How American of you!"

THIRTEEN

REFLECTIONS ON HOME

August 5, 2018, was a very hot and humid Sunday in Rivière-Ouelle, Quebec, much too hot for the Fille-du-Roi costume I was wearing, with its ankle-length, voluminous skirt and long-sleeved cotton blouse, covered with a heavy linen tunic laced together with ribbons. To help celebrate the Lévesque Association's twentieth anniversary, I had been invited to assume Jeanne's identity, participate in the readings during the Mass, and then give a short speech as part of the ceremony in the cemetery. Right as I walked out of the church into the blazing sun on my way to the cemetery, I saw my brother Dana and his family drive into the parking lot of the church. They had finally arrived!

Earlier in the week, Dana and his wife Ginna had driven from Vermont to Quebec City in their truck and huge new camper to spend a couple of days with me there. They then planned to pick up their son, daughter-in-law, and three-year-old granddaughter Lexie at the airport in Quebec City before heading to Rivière-Ouelle to join me for the celebration dinner on Saturday evening. But major complications caused by flight delays, bus schedules, and nonexistent (for all of us) phone connections had kept them from arriving on Saturday as planned. I wasn't certain they were going to make it to any part of the event.

My arrival in Quebec had been much easier, although it did feel odd to be making a roundtrip flight from France to North America, rather than the other way around. The flight had turned out to be much longer than the Boston-Paris flights I was used to since Dieppe is located about three hours farther from the airport than Boston is, and

I'd had to make a plane change in Montreal to reach Quebec City. In any event, I made it, and after leaving Dieppe something like eighteen hours earlier, I was overjoyed to see Patricia my host (and friend) waiting for me at the arrival gate to pick me up for another stay in her studio apartment.

The next day, I had donned my carefully packed Fille-du-Roi costume for two days of festivities at the Fête de la Nouvelle France where I was informed that the time and money I had spent in Dieppe having it made by a costume designer had been wasted since it wasn't "accurate." It was unquestionably more upscale than the Quebecois version of the outfit that I saw other women wearing. I wore mine anyway to give my brief talks on Jeanne but changed back to regular clothes in order to drive to Rivière-Ouelle for the reunion dinner. I arrived in time and sat with my French friend Nelly and her family all the while worrying that Dana and his family might not even make the Sunday ceremony since we had had no way to communicate. Neither Dana nor I had figured out how to arrange for phone service in Quebec and instead had decided, not too wisely, to rely on WIFI connections wherever we could find them.

But they had finally arrived — and not a minute too late. After a huge sigh of relief and quick hugs, we joined the group gathered around the monument to our ancestors Robert Lévesque and Jeanne Chevalier. On behalf of Jeanne, in front of my family and friends from France, Quebec, and the United States, I gave a short speech. Despite my heavy American accent, I hoped they understood her words of appreciation to her descendants for continuing the Lévesque legacy in Rivière-Ouelle, for having the courage to leave home when it was necessary to find new lives elsewhere, and for maintaining the family values of hard work and friendship.

With that task thankfully over and with little time to wait around and listen for any messages of approval from Jeanne, I guided my family over to the Lévesque Association luncheon where they could meet distant relatives. Later, we drove to my favorite brasserie farther along the St. Lawrence River so we could share stories. Unlike my prior, very enjoyable visit there, this time the mosquitos were everywhere, and they cut our time together short. In any event, Dana and his family were eager to start their drive south towards Prince Edward Island. I returned to Quebec City for another few days of shopping and visiting with colleagues, relatives, and new acquaintances before my return flight to France.

When my plane landed in Paris, I didn't know if I felt like I was coming home, but it definitely felt good to be back. After picking Quincie up from the friend's apartment where she had been staying during my trip and after settling in, I then turned to face the decision of what to do with my condo in Charlestown.

In the few months prior to the Quebec trip, I had been busy, arranging for the costume to be made, continuing my lessons with Martine and my conversations with Joël, and giving talks dressed as Jeanne so I could become used to playing that role. I returned to Hautot-Saint-Sulpice for another annual meeting of the Cousins of the New World. With a group from Connect, an association formed so that Anglophones could meet up with Francophones, I visited Amiens and its enormous cathedral. There I tasted the exceptionally delicious *frites* (French fries) in a restaurant overlooking the Somme River and watched local farmers arrive in long boats to deliver their produce for the Sunday market. I made a couple of trips to Paris with friends to visit art exhibits, including an exposition of the work of American artist Mary Cassatt in the very charming Musée Jacquemart-André.

In an attempt to transplant some of my American way of life to France, I had scheduled an appointment to have my teeth cleaned. As a dentist's daughter, I was expecting some version of the forty-five-minute visit with a hygienist in the United States, involving the familiar (at least to me) handscaling and a full mouth polish. Instead, my visit took a mere twenty minutes with a dentist who used laser instruments and hardly any polish. My first French pedicure was also a bit unexpected. A doctor used what appeared to be instruments similar to those at the dentist's office for buffing my feet and toes. To have nail polish applied, I was told I would need to find a manicurist.

In early July, I had started having phone conversations with my nephew Max so he could teach me about European football (soccer). I learned some of the rules as we watched the quarter and semifinals of the World Cup matches together, some five thousand miles apart. For the final match between France and Croatia, my friend Nadine and I viewed the action at a pub near the beach. Outside the pub, an enormous TV screen had been set up on the esplanade lawn for the huge crowds, who wildly cheered each French goal and then went on to celebrate the French victory for long hours afterwards.

In the excitement over the next few days, I bought a World Cup victory shirt for Max. Eager to share the mood of the win, I packaged it up and sent it off to him late one afternoon. When I arrived at the cottage from the post office, I searched for the door keys in my back pack and then in the pockets of my jacket and jeans. No luck. After a few more minutes of panicked searching, I finally realized that I must have mistakenly put them in the package for Max. I rushed down to the post office and arrived five minutes before it closed. I am not sure the agents totally understood my explanation of why I needed to search through the bins for the package, but they kindly allowed this some-what frantic foreigner to grab it since it was fortunately resting on top of the pile. They watched bemusedly as I undid the wrappings and took out my keys, feeling rather foolish and wondering why I hadn't paid better attention to what I was doing!

Indeed, I had been quite busy and a bit stressed. In the midst of all these activities and the preparation for my Quebec trip, I hadn't been writing much nor had I been able to do more research on the remaining questions about Jeanne and her third husband. Instead, I had begun thinking about selling my condo. For some forgotten reason, I had started questioning how much longer I wanted to remain a landlord. I was enjoying my freedom from homeowner responsibilities and my time in France, especially since I had no idea where else I might want to be. I had even gone so far as to sketch out an analysis of the positives and negatives of selling and a list comparing what I would and wouldn't miss about living in Charlestown. I wrote out my reasons for staying on in France for another year or two and the reasons against staying. (There weren't a lot in the second column!) I then began to think about all the things I would need to do and all the decisions I would have to make regarding what to fix in the condo before I could put it up for sale. What did I want to keep or get rid of, and what would I need to store (and where) in the event I did indeed decide to sell without knowing where I would be going next? The thought process was turning out to be quite overwhelming despite the many long baths I took to try to relax.

As I worked through some of my anxieties on the phone with Chris, my real estate agent in Boston, he suggested that I concentrate on the decision to sell my condo and worry about the logistics later. Great suggestion! But how to decide?

During the two days that Dana and Ginna were in Quebec City, I had had a chance to talk about the decision I was facing. Sitting on the deck of the restaurant in their campground the first night of their visit, we spent some time tossing around the pros and cons that I had come up with. Their advice: "Don't sell! You need to keep a home base." "What would you call 'home' if you sell?" "Real estate is one of the best investments!"

I shared with them the competing advice of some friends who had told me: "Sell! Renting gives you more options and freedom." "You will be free of responsibilities; you'll be more financially secure."

And Dana had, in fact, agreed that selling could make life easier for those left behind after I died. That would be particularly true if I could get rid of a lot of my stuff in the process so that they would not have the unpleasant chore of cleaning up after me, as he and the rest of us had had to do after our parents died.

While we agreed that selling didn't necessarily mean I would have to make any short-term changes in my life, the long-term planner voice inside me wouldn't stay quiet. *If I sell, where will I live? Where will my home be?* I thought.

I had at one point toyed with the idea of living in Quebec City. It would be closer to the States and to brothers, sisters, nephews, and nieces. There were several archives located in the city and a good university library. During my several visits there, I had found a comfortable yoga studio and had learned my way around. I already had a couple of friends and even some relatives living there. It would make moving, staying connected to family, and transitioning to a new culture a lot easier. Yet, the prospect of being shut indoors during six months of snow and ice and, I have to admit, the lingering prejudice against Quebecois French made that possibility less appealing. If I wanted to learn "real" French — said my mother's voice in my head — I needed to stay in France.

All these conversations and thoughts raised questions for me about belonging and roots — both physical and psychological. Nashua, New Hampshire could be considered my "hometown," since that's where I grew up and spent eighteen years and several more summers. Yet I didn't have any friends who lived in Nashua anymore. I only had memories that were more vague than vivid, despite the two scrapbooks that my mother had made. But I had never lived anywhere else long enough to call it "home" other than Boston, which is what I tended to answer when people frequently asked, "Where are you from?"

Like Jeanne, I was now living thousands of miles away from what might be called home, or "the place where I was born." But if I sold my condo, I wouldn't have a physical home base. I wouldn't have ties to any place in any state, except Seattle where Carla lived and where I've spent several Christmases over the past thirty years.

I had to admit that I found the whole concept of "home" somewhat perplexing. In the past, it had been relatively easy for me to gather up my belongings and set them down somewhere else when I grew bored, perhaps too quickly, with locations. That sentiment partially accounted for the seventeen moves of residences in five different states in the fifty years since I graduated from college and officially moved out of the family home in Nashua. I moved first to Oklahoma, then to New Jersey, on to California, then to Connecticut, and finally to Massachusetts. My twenty years in the Charlestown condo would be the longest time I had ever lived in the same place since leaving Nashua so I wasn't sure I could accurately describe what a home or roots really meant!

In all honesty, it wasn't always boredom that precipitated those moves. Each time, there had been other, more legitimate reasons for the decision, whether it was for a new job, to go back to school, to take up a new residence after a relationship ended, or to find a better place to live. Personal or family ties were never the first priority. I was always able to rather easily make new friends, keep some of the old ones, and maintain long-distance relationships with my family.

So where were my roots? Where was my home? If I was ever to find my roots, would I then want to plant them deep and never pull them up again? In the book I wrote about creativity twenty years ago, I wove in a theme about the Dutch seafaring explorers of the sixteenth century. It was an idea left over from my graduate-school days even further back in time. The theme connected well with my feelings of constantly being in a state of becoming, always preferring to reach beyond the current horizon and then to start thinking of where I was going to be next, of what ocean I then wanted to explore. Perhaps, at the base of my being, I was a constant searcher, an adventurer, and would forever remain at sea and rootless. Why did some people stay and others need to go? How did those who moved on find an anchor, or how did they learn to live without one?

At a holiday dinner held a year or so before my departure for my sabbatical year in France, my family and I had watched a video that my sister Laurie had made out of films she discovered among some of our mother's things. There is a scene in it of me about the age of four or five, walking around with a suitcase, kissing my parents and siblings goodbye, and pretending to walk away. My sisters believed this was portending my life as a constant traveler, never to settle down.

Had the time come to begin thinking about settling down? From a logical point of view, the decision to sell at that point made perfect sense. The market was most favorable for sellers, and I knew I should lighten the load of my belongings. I did indeed need to downsize so that those who survived me wouldn't be burdened with cleaning out my things. In addition, my ties to Charlestown had already been weakening. I had limited connections left there: members of my church, work and community colleagues, doctors, dentist, and Quincie's vet. I would be leaving behind very few people I could call close friends: Carol, whom I've known for over forty years, and her husband Arthur; Seta, who accompanied me to the hospital and waited with me for over three hours for a diagnosis after a car accident; and Helaine, who loved to take care of Quincie. But my siblings and their children lived elsewhere. Many of my other friends were also flung far across the United States and beyond. So it was probably true that the roots I had in Boston would not be very difficult to pull up and set down somewhere else after all. Or it might be that roots for me were not necessarily permanent structures in my life but were bonds that I could take with me wherever I went.

In truth, in the summer of 2018, if I sold the condo, I didn't need to decide immediately where I would live or even where I would want to be living in five years. I also had to face the possibility that I really was a seafaring adventurer who genuinely didn't need a home or roots or an anchor, and I never had. I had been living in France without a real home for well over a year and a half. Although I had added a few personal touches to the cottage and had rearranged some things to make room for my books and other belongings, it didn't really feel like "home," whatever that meant. I hadn't added plants or tried to hang any pictures of my own, and I was doing fine so far, living like a visitor. The cottage would do for another year or longer until I decided if I needed something more permanent. Or I could travel to all the places I had never seen.

By selling the condo, I would free myself of homeownership responsibilities. I wouldn't have to worry anymore about who would shovel snow, clean the stairway carpet, or deal with the minutes of our condo association meetings. Nor would I have to worry if there were leaks in the bathroom or peeling paint in the office.

I could do whatever I wanted to do. The options for where to move next were many, but they were not ones I needed to address at that moment. Maybe I could try for once to live in the present and not have a detailed plan for the future. I would not be "homeless," as my friend Carol pointed out when we had this conversation. "You have friends. You have your sister in Seattle!" So, was home where you go for Christmas?

Despite the logic of this move, the decision wasn't an easy one. I was helped in the process by some photos of my Charlestown apartment that I happened to find after my return from Quebec. They reminded me of the good times I had had there and how comfortable, though not particularly elegant, the place was. At the same time, I also knew that the view of downtown Boston from my kitchen window was becoming less charming as the tree in the neighbor's yard continued to grow and hide much of that skyline. There was also no garden or green space, something I was becoming a bit attached to in Dieppe as the months went by. Whether I was able to spend time out there or not, it had been so very nice to wake up to grass, trees, flowers, and some open space. To be able to open the windows and not be hit with dust from the traffic below was definitely a treat.

So logic and sentiment were teaming up on me! I finally had to ask myself, *Does it matter that you don't know where you will go after another year or two in Dieppe? Why not listen to what a friend advised? "Cross that bridge when you come to it. Why can't you totally enjoy the moments there?"*

Perhaps I could simply plan to stay in France until I became bored. And after a recent visit to Paris and thinking about the rest of France and Europe, I realized that such a milestone could take a very long time to reach. Besides, I didn't feel as if I was done doing what I needed to do in France. And I still couldn't answer the question so often asked of me, "When will your second book, the saga of your journey to discover Jeanne's story, be done?" Maybe by staying in France for a while longer, I could put off facing some of those decisions about my next few years and, instead, wait and see where this adventure was taking me.

I was at some sort of crossroads with all these decisions to make. Strangely, those were the words our minister used in a sermon a couple of weeks after my return from Quebec. The subject was "Signs,

Symbols, and Crossroads." He urged us to consider whether it was time to make changes in the direction of our lives! Coincidence or some sort of signal from the universe?

During our conversation in Quebec City, Dana and Ginna had insisted that I had already made up my mind, but I truthfully hadn't then. However, at the end of the month, having turned seventy-four and despite a dream about losing the keys to my home, I decided to move forward with the sale — particularly after my niece Zoe offered to help, exactly as she had done when I moved out of my place in Hartford twenty-two years ago! I started making lists.

FOURTEEN

SEARCHING FOR AN ANCHOR

"Okay, Chris…. I am ready to sign the contract!"

Since my return to France from Quebec, I had exchanged a few emails with my real estate agent about some remaining questions around the sale of my condo. After mulling over the decision to sell and over my plans for the coming year, I finally made up my mind. Letting Chris know I was ready was at the top of my action-items list.

There were other items on that list, but most could wait since there was a more important item I needed to address before I could really settle back into my life in Dieppe. Quincie had fleas, a problem that I had apparently failed to notice before I left for Quebec since she had never let me comb or brush her and because I hadn't seen her scratching herself. Upon my return, I finally started paying attention to her new choice of sleeping on the kitchen counter and the black dust that she left behind in the morning. I realized at last that the black dust was not dirt but was caused by fleas and that I needed to do something. After unsuccessful attempts at remedies that would avoid the trauma of trying to give her a pill, which had always been difficult, I gave in and somehow managed to give her one from the box I bought at the local pharmacy. She might have been worn out by the discomfort of the fleas, or I was somehow able to convince her that she needed to try this solution.

The pill apparently worked and worked rather quickly. Two nights later, after a day of some rather frantic behavior on her part that had been predicted by the instructions on the box of medicine, Quincie resumed sleeping in my bedroom for the first time in the six weeks since I had returned to Dieppe.

After that rather disturbing episode, for which I profusely apologized to her, and with the end of the summer break, life resumed. This was the second *Rentrée* (Return) I had experienced in France. In the States, activity planning, budgets, and life in general, at least in my experience, tended to follow the annual calendar, ending in December and beginning on the first of January. In France, life's annual rhythm seemed to revolve around the school calendar, not only for students but for adults and bus schedules as well. I also learned that August in essence was a vacation month for a large part of the population. This schedule meant that gym classes and monthly book-group gatherings, along with other social activities, ended with the closure of schools in early July to be enthusiastically restarted in September with the reopening of school.

With the Rentrée, instead of basically picking up where the rest of my life had left off in July, I decided to make some changes in my weekly routines. I wanted to continue my grammar lessons and conversation exchanges. At the same time I knew I needed to increase my level of physical activity. The Hatha yoga classes weren't doing enough for me. So I signed up for new yoga classes and weekly workouts.

My first new exercise class in the basketball gym at one of Dieppe's sports complexes was a bit unexpected. Once again, I had walked there — it wasn't far from the cottage —and was already dressed in my gym clothes, unlike a friend who changed out of street clothes before the class and back into them afterward, even though she had also come from home minutes before and would return there. Patricia, the instructor, arrived — in workout clothes — and energetically led the session. Her instructions and counting were in French, naturally, but she played American rock-and-roll tunes from the sixties as background music. It felt very surreal as I stretched to touch my toes, listening to "un, deux, trois...." and at the same time to the Archies singing "Sugar, Sugar!"

In addition to those new gym classes, I decided to add weekly bridge lessons to my routines. I had always enjoyed playing bridge since first being introduced to it in college over fifty years ago. I thought bridge lessons would be a fun way to meet new people and improve my French, but when I signed up, I had no idea how many new words for face cards, suits, and bidding I was going to have to learn. Little did I know as well that there are an incredible number of different rules that the French insist on following. I went ahead anyway and started lessons for beginners with a local organization and eventually learned that the rules for bridge had changed internationally, and I was many years behind the times. And it was only later that I learned about all the worldwide federations of bridge, the tournaments, and all the different levels of expertise to be acquired, in France, the United States and beyond.

Bridge would become a significant part of my life in Dieppe, especially with Tatiana as my frequent partner. I would, though, continue to be struck by how seriously the French play what for me had always been a pleasant pastime. With my friends in the States, we played, caught each other up on the latest news, had a glass of wine, and munched on snacks. In France, we would play for two hours, focusing on the rules and sometimes replaying a hand to learn from our mistakes. Chatter and snacking were replaced with thoughtful attention to bidding. Any drinks, food, and gossip had to wait until we were done playing.

In the midst of adapting to these new activities and getting wrapped up in all the details regarding the sale of my condo, I did my best to maintain a somewhat normal life. Ann, a friend from my banking days in Hartford, and her husband arrived in Dieppe to spend a few days with me. I played tour guide and showed them around Dieppe and Varengeville, where we visited the sixteenth century Manoir d'Ango and marveled at this "jewel of the Italian Renaissance" and its well-preserved dovecote, one of the largest in France. We picnicked on bread, wine, and cheese at that little church in danger of falling into the sea. I also organized a party, this time at a local pub, so they could meet my French friends.

Their visit was followed by several more from very distant Lévesque cousins from Quebec who had arrived first in Hautot-Saint-Sulpice in search of their ancestral roots and then, at Nelly's suggestion, decided to come to Dieppe. After a couple of such visits, I developed my own walking tour. It included a stop in the Canadian chapel in Saint-Jacques church to see the plaque in Jeanne's honor and then another one at the Porte des Tourelles, the last remaining tower from Dieppe's fortifications, to view the plaque for the Filles du Roi who had left France from Dieppe. We'd take a brief tour around the Canadian Square, and then I sometimes included a hike up to the castle for a view of Dieppe or a break for beer at the Bar-o-Mètre at the end of the beach or at the usually quite crowded Café des Tribunaux in the center of town.

My tours for visitors, showing off the history of Dieppe and describing Jeanne's story, all reinforced my decision to sell my condo and extend my stay in France for another year, although I still didn't have any real long-term plans beyond that. So, I needed to renew my visa yet again. This time, I was prepared with all the right documents. I once again had a long wait before seeing an agent and obtaining the proof of my application that would be valid until I returned in January to pick up the long-stay visa good for another year.

Sporadically, I tried to find more information about Jeanne's third husband, Jean-Baptiste Deschamps — primarily his certificate of baptism. I also made some attempts at writing my promised second book. Life was too busy with the visits, lessons, and other distractions, especially once I offered to give a presentation to my book group on Mary Cassatt. In one of our meetings earlier in the year, I had described my recent visit to the exposition of her work in Paris. Once I realized how little the group knew about this American artist's work, I offered to give a presentation on her life. That offer required research since I actually knew little about her or her art. For more information, I made two visits to the Terra Foundation Library of American Art in Paris. Walking along the Avenue des Champs-Elysées, seeing all the stores boarded up, and then later chatting with café owners, I witnessed firsthand the impact on the economic life of Paris of the destructive demonstrations of the Gilets jaunes and those who chose to take advantage of the movement.

All these new activities in addition to my old routines, plus planning for another year in Dieppe, and rarely finding time to write or do more research finally caused me to start feeling very much out of sorts. No doubt living in a foreign country, far from family and essentially alone with my lovely but ornery cat, and struggling to communicate in French, especially over the telephone, while well on my way through my seventies were all contributing to my distress. The imminent sale of my condo without a real plan for the future was a bit overwhelming, as was the thought of sorting through, discarding, and packing up all my things there. I started second guessing my decisions. Maybe I did in fact need a home base to tie me down — something to keep me on an even keel, despite my ambiguity about needing roots and my history of so many moves, most decidedly when I was a lot younger and more flexible than now.

I found a quote about uncharted waters written by American jurist Oliver Wendell Holmes in the book I had written about creativity:

> I find the great thing in this world is not so much where we stand, as in what direction we are moving: To reach the port of heaven, we must sail sometimes with the wind and sometimes against it — but we must sail, and not drift, nor lie at anchor.

I wasn't sure I agreed. What if we wanted to avoid drifting and instead wanted the stability of an anchor every now and then?

Long hot baths, yoga classes, and Sunday church services helped me relax, but sometimes even they didn't help. One cool rainy evening later that fall, Tatiana and I were walking home after another bridge lesson. I happened to mention that I was feeling a bit anxious lately, in all probability because of all the things going on and especially the pending sale of my condo. We stopped before parting ways at the fountain in front of the Café des Tribunaux, Tatiana to her home two blocks away and me to the cottage up the cliff. As we were saying goodbye, I voiced the idea that my angst might be because I wouldn't have an anchor. "But you do have an anchor," she observed. "All your French ancestors!"

As I climbed the cliff, I had to admit that she was right, although I was not totally convinced that they were the anchor I was seeking. I had never thought of them that way, in any event, but I figured they would have to do, at least for the moment. And to be fair, they were not insignificant. Through one of Jeanne's grandsons, I could trace my family tree to Philippe Auguste, that long-reigning French king who not only was victorious over the English king Richard the Lionheart, but also initiated the construction of the Louvre and substantially extended the walls around Paris. Then through Philippe Auguste, I could even find a link to Charlemagne.

Many French people could surely claim that same ancestry, but not everyone would be as astounded as I was when I discovered that King Henry I of France, one of those ancestors, had married the Russian princess Anne of Kiev. Could that connection possibly be the reason I spent so many years in college and then several years after graduation learning Russian?

These bonds could certainly be considered heartwarming, but I wasn't persuaded that my ancestors provided the anchor — the feeling of rootedness and belonging — that I was starting to feel I needed. Did knowing that my ancestors were from France all the way back to Charlemagne or even that my eighth-great-grandmother had been a Fille du Roi have a real impact on my life? Would that knowledge satisfy this longing for whatever it was that I was longing for? Or instead, as a new friend once advised me, "Why not forget the past and move on?" Could we ever really move on? Could I? Did I want to?

Back in February, shortly after Dana had left, I had found myself sitting next to an English woman during a break in a conference at the Protestant church in Rouen. We struck up a conversation about how we had come to attend the meeting and then about our different origins. "So, who are you?" she had asked.

"That's a good question," I had answered. "I am not sure."

And the longer I stayed in France, the more confusing that question had become.

When my cousin Peter was visiting in September 2017, we had stopped for coffee at Joël's home. During our conversation, I had replied to a similar question, "I am half French." Peter, who is 100 percent French-Canadian origin, had said most affirmatively, "Well, I am an American."

Okay, I had had to admit that I was American first before being French, although by descent I was in reality 50 percent French, or French Canadian. And of course there was the other 50 percent mixture of Swedish, Scots-Irish, and English ancestry from my mother's side.

The questioner in Rouen, who was carrying dual passports, reflected about my response and her own situation and added, "Well, we both are possibly somewhere in between, don't you think?"

Although I didn't really know what that meant, I agreed.

I had at one point referred to this journey that I was on as an "identity quest." After some research, I decided that such a description was much too complicated and most likely inaccurate. Other than trying to discover more about my French roots, I wasn't really trying to sort out my identity, the essence of who I had become. So what was it that I needed to figure out so I could have more easily answered that woman in Rouen?

Upon reflection, I realized that it had more to do with who I was becoming in a different culture. Despite my mixed origins and my initial response to Peter's comment, I knew I was most decidedly an American. As Joël once remarked, it came out loudly all over me. I wondered, though, if my enthusiasm and high energy (tiring at times, he added) were more pronounced in a different culture. Did I appear more adventurous, inquisitive, and assertive in a country where those attributes were generally not the norm? Did I seem even more serious because France was a country where people valued leisure and good times more than I apparently did? Were my questions more challenging and too direct and not diplomatic enough? Did my independence and courage stand out in a country where many women, at least those of my generation, appeared to me to still be playing a more traditional role?

And then, what happened to this person called "Lynne" when she couldn't communicate as easily or as efficiently as she did in English? How much did my true essence still come through when I stumbled, stuttered, and mispronounced words in French? My siblings and close friends would probably say, "No, Lynne, don't worry. They'll know who you genuinely are, wherever you are."

But I had my doubts. How immutable were the attributes that made up who I was? Did they become more nuanced or more pronounced in a new and different culture? And as importantly, how much would I, should I, or could I change the longer I remained in France? Like Jeanne and my great-grandparents who found themselves in cultures decidedly different from the ones in which they grew up, I was going to have to choose how much to adopt, adapt or give up, in order to fit in. Should I even try to lose my accent and the music of my native language so that I was not instantly recognized as English or American? How French could I ever become, even with my French nose and all that heritage?

Would I ever be able to find a nice, distinguishing balance between two cultures as I believed Tatiana had? Despite living in France for over thirty years, she had found a way over time to keep her ties to her Russian origins, although she no longer held a Russian passport. She still spoke her native language frequently with friends and relatives and liked to buy her favorite foods from a Russian vendor in the Saturday market so she could cook Russian dishes for herself and her friends. Would I ever be able to do the same with my American roots?

Once, when I was having lunch with my friend Isabelle, I noticed that I had unconsciously kept my practice of eating with the fork in my right hand, holding it upright, and switching hands briefly to use my knife only when I needed to cut something up. My niece Raina, after living in France for three years, had adopted the French way of eating with the fork in her left hand, tines downward, and actively using the knife in her right hand to guide food onto the fork. I hadn't been able to make that change, or, more truthfully, I didn't want to.

Was this some sort of unconscious last stand, a rather small and insignificant one to be sure, that I was taking to preserve some part of the American side of me? I had also managed, so far, to maintain my eating routines and had not yet taken up having a more substantial meal around noon, nor had I fallen in love with olives. On the other hand, I had given up my long-held preference for tea over coffee. I not infrequently found myself looking forward to a cup of fairly strong coffee alone or with friends — even though I hadn't yet learned to drink it black!

Maybe in fact my essence was made up of multiple facets, a repertoire of characteristics that could be called "identities." With age, maybe I was simply adding more sides to who I really was. Or maybe some were expanding, softening, or even hardening around the edges of a largely central and stable core. I wondered if there were people who had been able to put all the pieces of their lives together, all the different roles they had played and lives they've led — whether in their home culture or in a new one — people who knew consistently who they were and where they belonged, no matter where they found themselves.

It was indeed quite possible that one of my key identifying characteristics was that constant quest for challenge, for something more — another question, another answer. In fact, I was slowly coming to realize that this journey was less about defining who I was in a different culture or how much to adapt, although those questions would almost certainly remain with me forever. It was more about finding a place where I belonged — that harbor, that anchor — where I could be nurtured and feel comfortable totally being me, whoever that turned out to be. What a rather strange discovery to be making right as I was about to decide to sell my home of twenty years without knowing where I would be living in five years!

FIFTEEN

DECISIONS, DECISIONS

We met on November 7, 2018, at the giant fern in the Rouen train station. I'd just applied for a renewal of my long-stay visa for another year at the Prefecture, and Paula, my college roommate, was in Paris for a week-long visit. We had decided to get together in Rouen for lunch and an afternoon together to catch up on our lives.

I arrived a few minutes early and soon saw her coming up the stairs, looking as jaunty and stylish as ever: a fashionable cloche hat, leather coat and boots, and her unforgettable broad smile. I couldn't believe it had been over fifty years since our first meeting as freshmen at Mount Holyoke College.

After many years of exchanging emails and Christmas cards, after spending a couple of vacations together — one in Scotland and one in Ecuador — and after several visits to her home in North Carolina and one to my place in California, we still had a lot of stories to tell each other. I had forgotten how much fun Paula could be with her amazingly different perspectives on life and her ability to focus on the present. I remembered her comment made in jest during a winery visit in Napa Valley years ago. Amid a group of visitors trying to learn more about the subtleties and the sophisticated language of wine-tasting, she had remarked, "It has a bouquet of…. popcorn. It pops in your mouth!" I also remembered how penetrating her questions could be.

From the train station, we walked down the hill past the Jeanne d'Arc tower and the Alexander Calder sculpture in front of the Musée des Beaux Arts. Over lunch, seated in the balcony inside one of the restaurants next to the Rouen Cathedral, we chatted and shared stories of the most significant recent events in our lives.

I mentioned that I'd seen a quote from a Mount Holyoke commencement that the writer Anna Quindlen had given several years ago. In it, she quoted George Eliot, who had once said: "It is never too late to be what you might have been."

Then Quindlen had added: "It is never too early, either. And it will make all the difference in the world."[9]

Paula and I started to chat about what we had become and what we might have been, but the arrival of our lunch interrupted our conversation.

After brief visits to the cathedral — so well-known from Monet's many different paintings in the changing light — then on to the rather macabre Aître Saint-Maclou, and finally to Jeanne d'Arc's church with its magnificent stained-glass windows, we stopped for a drink at the historic Hotel Bourgtheroulde. In the two-story cocktail lounge with its odd mix of pop art and sixteenth-century elegance, we settled into the soft leather armchairs and returned to our conversation about Quindlen's speech. Over a glass of wine before we made the climb back up the hill to the train station, Paula asked in her inimitable way, "Why did our lives take the turns they did? How is it, for example, that we decided to go to business school [Paula to Harvard in 1971 and me to Berkeley four years later] when we didn't have any role models to guide us?"

Our mothers had not been role models for us since both were essentially homemakers, although mine had been very active in local politics. Theirs were most assuredly not the paths that either Paula or I had wanted or chosen. I didn't recall having any real role models for my future, except my "spinster" Latin teacher Miss Barnes or my rather matronly doctor whose single passion in life outside of work seemed to be golf.

I remembered Paula commenting once about another classmate who had chosen the homemaker route. Paula believed that Linda was

---

9. Anna Quindlen, Commencement Address, Mount Holyoke College, South Hadley, MA, May 23, 1999.

lucky. At the end of her day, after a well-cooked meal and with children in bed in a freshly cleaned home, she could say to herself: "Well done!"

Without a role model for a different life, we had no standard to hold ourselves to at the end of our days and be able to say, "Well done!" It wasn't always comforting, this forging new paths, being our own role models as women with careers and without children.

"Why," Paula wondered, "have things turned out the way they have for each of us? Was it destiny, DNA, or simply happenstance?"

Paula's questions reminded me of a conversation I had had with Joël one Wednesday morning about his experience with a deadly disease and the course of his recovery. He had questioned how much control we genuinely had over the decisions we make. Whether it was choosing to go to business school at a time when most women were very much in the minority, or choosing a marriage partner, or deciding on a next career or life path, or managing to recover from a bout with cancer, did we have as much real control over these decisions as we'd like to think? Was someone else in charge or playing a major role? What part did Jeanne or other "guardian angels" play in my life, for example? Or was "by chance" a plausible explanation?

Joël believed that a higher power played a significant role in our major decisions. Paula and I never got to finish our discussion or come to any conclusions before our trains took us back to Paris and Dieppe, respectively. But our conversation and Joël's comments started me thinking about my journey to discover Jeanne's story and to come to France, as well as my life before then. How had I made any of the key decisions in my past and how had I made these more recent, rather life-changing decisions? How many times did I control what was happening versus some other force (Jeanne's spirit, perhaps?) pushing me in a new direction?

Many of my major decisions had been easy, some more complicated, and some had some rather significant consequences. On a few occasions, someone else made the decision for me. When Stanford Business School, for example, decided not to admit me, the choice to go to Berkeley became straightforward. I had to turn down an exciting job offer in Detroit after business school because my then husband refused to leave California.

At other times, a friend's comment made me see the situation in a new light. I vividly remembered the advice of a respected colleague in whom I had confided about the deteriorating state of my marriage. She asked me a question that possibly reflected her principles of personal responsibility, accountability, and possibility: "Do you need a man in your life to make you happy, to give you the things you need and want?"

After some thought, I realized that I didn't (at least not that particular man!), and shortly thereafter I divorced my husband.

Not all my decisions had been that dramatic. Instead, sometimes they were made easier because of synchronicities, like looking for a house in Hartford, Connecticut. I knew precisely what I wanted: one exactly like the one that Helle, a friend from long ago, owned, and I wanted it in her neighborhood. Shortly after I arrived in Hartford from California in early 1987, an Arts-and-Crafts-style home exactly like hers and up the street was set to go on the market. I was able to buy it before anyone else even knew it was for sale. And what about finding the cottage in Dieppe three days before I was scheduled to leave France or connecting with the Deschamps family without an exact address to find them?

It was true that at times there was a hint of a choice that required more effort on my part, like leaving the winery in Quebec to visit the Letarte family or finding my way to the Maison de Mes Aïeux on the Île d'Orléans. Sometimes I had to ask the right question or make the right comment, and others would help. At a presentation I was giving on Jeanne to the Cousins of the New World in Hautot-Saint-Sulpice in 2016, I mentioned that I had still not been able to find on any map the location of the village of Mont Levêque that had belonged to the family of Jeanne's third husband. A gentleman in the audience had the answer and provided me with directions. I am not sure what I was expecting when I drove there, but it was no longer a village. I was rather disappointed to find not even a manor house but, instead, an old farm building and a large, parked trailer truck.

It was also true that I had frequently used very rational models to make, or at least justify, certain decisions, such as weighing the pros and cons, as I did with the decision to sell my condo. Even then, I had to admit, there was often something else involved. Both Paula and I are generally organized, analytical, and good at numbers, preferring to make our decisions using logic and careful study. Nonetheless, we would probably agree that many of our choices were not strictly logical. Family history and even our hearts played a small role, at least one or two times. My decision to move back east from California, for example, was in part driven by a desire to be closer to family there.

Most of the time, however, I had used fortitude and an independent resolve to move forward, relying on my "unconquerable soul" and my rational thinking. I remembered the ending of a poem from a speech I gave in high school that became my enduring principle, although at the time I could not have known how my life was going to turn out: "I am the master of my fate; I am the captain of my soul."[10]

And what about the choices that Jeanne had to make in her life and their consequences? Even though she might have been strongly encouraged, she did leave France and sail off to Quebec. While we will never know the reasons why she made that decision or how she chose her three husbands, only the first marriage did not turn out well. When that husband disappeared and left her destitute seven years after their marriage, she apparently learned or had the good luck to make a better choice with the second, Robert Lévesque, with whom she eventually had a quite comfortable life over their twenty years of marriage. And it could be said that her third marriage to the nobleman Jean-Baptiste François Deschamps de la Bouteillerie brought a somewhat fairy-tale ending to her married life.

Like Jeanne, I left the place where I grew up, at roughly the same age, when I married and moved to California. Unlike Jeanne, I did not have children. That was a clear choice on my part. My mother one time commented on the fact that I didn't have children. She felt it was a

---

10. William Ernest Henley, "Invictus," eds. Poetry House, *150 Most Famous Poems*, (Springville, Utah, USA: Vervante, 2020), 123.

reaction to her as a role model. I didn't think so. I knew I wasn't suited to having children or being a good mother.

Nor had I had three husbands like Jeanne. And I had not found a Prince Charming. After my divorce, I never really tried to find a partner with whom to share my life. Instead of waiting or searching for Prince Charming or a knight in shining armor, I had, in all probability, pushed away any man who wanted to take care of me or showed any signs thereof. I must have told myself that I didn't need a man to protect me or define me, as my colleague had reminded me during the months my marriage was in trouble. Instead, I believed that I could be tough and take care of myself — financially, materially, and presumably emotionally.

Whether consciously or not, I had succeeded in living my life to date in that belief. This stance of independence and strength these days often played out with women friends as well as men. I didn't need any coddling or cuddling, although that was no doubt a bit of an exaggeration. I had had to reach out and rely on friends more in France than I ever did in the States, and I had a greater appreciation for friendship and concerns for my well-being than I had ever had before my time in France. Nevertheless, I knew I would probably have a difficult time making significant changes in my belief in self-reliance at my age. I questioned sometimes if this was the path I was meant to be on as my destiny or one I had deliberately chosen.

Few of these and other decisions I had made had caused remorse, even though I had to admit that I might have made them with a too rational, cool-headed approach and too quickly. I didn't think I would have any second thoughts about selling my condo in Charlestown, just as I had not regretted the decisions regarding the other two places I had sold. I did have some warm memories of friend and family gatherings and visits in each place I had lived, but I had needed to move on from California and then from Hartford. And I was in no way disappointed in my decision to spend so much time in France, so far.

In fact, I didn't have any real regrets regarding the many tradeoffs I had made as a result of my decisions to date. I was reminded of one of those tradeoffs several months after Paula's visit. For some odd reason, I was in touch with an old flame from high school and college. Over the fifty-plus years since our parting, we'd never had a conversation about what had happened to end our relationship. I only knew that he had chosen someone else over me. Before he had made that decision, the two of us had never actually talked about marriage. I had moved to Oklahoma to teach Russian and Russian History, and he had traveled to another country for graduate school. We had somehow managed to stay connected. I don't remember how we did that in those days before the Internet, but we did. Eventually, we drifted apart and wound up with different partners. To this day, I couldn't remember feeling distraught or suffering from a broken heart when we parted.

While we ultimately ended up living in the same city with both of us married to someone else, we rarely crossed paths. In time, I divorced and returned to the East Coast. He and his wife remained in the city, set down deep roots, and had a family. At some point over the years, we started sharing birthday wishes and Christmas cards so we stayed updated on each other's lives.

In a recent email exchange, presumably around his birthday, we were reminiscing about an almost disastrous mountain-climbing trip we had taken not long after graduating from college. That memory then led to the subject of what had happened to us. In our choices of other partners, were there regrets over how things had turned out or over what might have been? My response was quick: our lives — or at least mine — would have worked out very differently, and I was, at least 99 percent of the time, extraordinarily happy and content with the way mine had turned out. His reply was in essence the same.

Reflecting afterwards on "what might have been," I concluded that I potentially would have missed out on many memorable experiences if we had married: business school, my career in banking, multiple trips to the former Soviet Union, my doctorate in creativity, my travels as a tourist and consultant, my times with my nieces and nephews as they were growing up, and then my adventure in France. It was also quite possible that Jeanne might not have found me and pushed me to write her story; I might not have spent so much time in France to relearn my father's maternal language; and I might not have had the opportunity to enjoy the interactions with so many new friends and come to better appreciate the ones I had in the States and elsewhere.

Instead, assuming we had remained married — clearly not a sure thing given my relationship-challenged personality — I would probably have experienced motherhood, parenting, and grandparenting. There might have been some other joys along the way, but I couldn't imagine what married life with him (or with anyone else) would have been like. At the time and since then, I had chosen not to dwell on the subject anymore.

Many years ago, I had a conversation with a business-school colleague. For some reason, as we explored the boutiques in a shopping center in Palo Alto, California, we reflected on the choices we had made. We decided, "Life is a series of tradeoffs. We probably cannot have it all."

And that brought me to one of my favorite poems, "The Road Not Taken," by American poet Robert Frost:[11]

> Two roads diverged in a yellow wood,
> And sorry I could not travel both.
> ......
> And both that morning equally lay
> In leaves no step had trodden black.
> Oh, I kept the first for another day!
> Yet knowing how way leads on to way,
> I doubted if I should ever come back.
>
> I shall be telling this with a sigh
> Somewhere ages and ages hence:
> Two roads diverged in a wood, and I —
> I took the one less traveled by,
> And that has made all the difference.

---

11. Robert Frost, "The Road Not Taken," *150 Most Famous Poems*, 107.

Thinking of my old flame and thinking of all the other decisions I had made over the years, I found it interesting to follow how my life had evolved. Not one of the decisions or choices I'd made was forced on me or was taken under truly dire circumstances. I chose to divorce; I chose to move to so many different places. I had chosen how to respond in all these situations. I had chosen the path I was on. And I had chosen to pursue my obsession with Jeanne, no matter where it might eventually lead me.

Way does lead on to way. It's true.

Part Four

NAVIGATING THE EBBS AND FLOWS

SIXTEEN

FACING FORWARD

"The return to France this time was almost catastrophic. I was totally surprised we made it."

I was sitting and writing at my desk in the cottage's second bedroom, also known as my office, at the top of the narrow wooden staircase on what is called the first floor in France. Quincie was back in the sunroom, lying spread out on the cabinet in the afternoon sun of that late February day in 2019. And I was trying to finally absorb what had happened during our whirlwind visit to Boston.

For the prior two trips to France in 2017 and 2018, I had had help, first from Carla and then the next year from Dana. But this time it had been just Quincie and me.

We arrived in Boston on Saturday, January 5. I had splurged on a three-hour taxi ride from Dieppe to the Paris airport instead of trying to negotiate my luggage and Quincie in her carrier on the bus or the train. I was glad I had done so since Quincie was not her usual self during the ride, despite the calming pill I had given her in order to put on her harness. Somehow, she had managed to work her way out of the harness while we were fortunately still in the taxi and she was still in her carrier. It was a rather disturbing moment, threatening an easy passage through security. I called Isabelle who had helped me with the harness earlier and asked her to call the vet for me to see what I should do. On their advice, I managed to give Quincie another pill and got her back into the harness, all before we arrived at De Gaulle airport. We made it through security without any more problems.

Our flight to Boston went without further incident, but that was not the case upon our arrival. We had a quite long, unexplained wait for our luggage, then a difficult exchange with the inspection agent who insisted on confiscating the extra supply of Quincie's food I had brought to ease her into an American diet. "Banned goods for the port of Boston," the agent told us. "You can keep a couple of days' worth, but the rest has to go."

I was not happy to see a week's worth of her special, rather expensive kibble being dumped into the trash bin. *Oh, well,* I thought. *She will have to adapt. I'm sure she'll eat when she gets hungry.*

It was freezing cold in Boston when we finally were able to leave the airport. Fortunately, despite the long delay, Helaine, my friend and Quincie's "godmother," had waited patiently in a nearby parking lot. She picked us up and dropped us off at my place in Charlestown but not before we agreed to get together for dinner.

After settling us back into the condo, I checked to see what the renters might have left behind and was amazed at how different the place looked with the fresh paint on the walls and the new Venetian blinds that my real estate agent Chris had arranged in my absence. I then almost immediately began to tackle the action items on my list. Quincie wandered around, first snarling at long forgotten spaces, then making herself comfortable in a very short time. And, yes, she did adapt and soon started eating the American food that I bought for her the next day.

I spent the next few days and nights busily cleaning, moving furniture around, and making the place presentable for the open houses to show the apartment for sale that Chris had planned to begin on Thursday. Miraculously, I received an offer for the condo the very next day. With a bit of negotiation on Saturday, the offer was finalized in time to cancel the remaining open-house events. I now no longer had to keep the place "show ready" and could relax. I had expected my place to sell quickly but honestly not that quickly!

With the very important step of a firm signed offer out of the way, I could now begin to tackle the work required to move out and to decide what to store, give away, or discard. I knew I didn't have the energy, desire, or need to try to sell items. Therefore, my rarely used bike and cross-country skis and poles, heavily used office shelves and bookcases, dozens of picture frames, piles of hangars, several plants, two brass planters, a rug, kitchen stools, two armoires, two upholstered chairs, an oak bureau, a pine chest, and other things I didn't want to keep all found good homes — thanks to the Internet-recycling platforms of Craigslist and Freecycle. For the most part, I didn't have any regrets at the time about giving away most of the stuff and didn't feel too much anxiety seeing so much of my life of so many past years being taken away. Some of the new owners even sent thank-you notes!

My niece Zoe and her husband Kyle arrived from Vermont to take away furniture, rugs, kitchen items, and other things that they wanted for their new home. We had lunch, and thanks to the relatively mild winter weather in Boston that day, were able to take a walk around Charlestown before they left with their now-totally-loaded truck. I then returned to the tasks of packing up.

In between appointments with doctors and Quincie's vet and dinners with friends, I spent most of my hours sorting through books and putting them in twelve cartons to be hauled away by an organization that would resell them. In spite of the weather that had turned bitterly cold again, I ventured out of my apartment on four different occasions to pick up a rental car which I would then load up with clothes and miscellaneous items to drop off at collection centers and at a women's shelter. I didn't realize until later, however, that I had been a bit rash and hadn't paid a lot of attention in deciding which books and other possessions to give away.

I had a party to empty my liquor cabinet. What we didn't consume during the evening as we shared memories of good times together or what my friends didn't take with them, I ended up eventually sharing with neighbors or throwing out. (Some bottles had come with me from California over thirty years ago!)

I packed up several containers of clothes, pots and pans, dishes, and office items that I knew I wanted to save. And every week, I made several trips downstairs to the trash barrels to recycle papers and files, leftover from former chapters of my life.

I had said my goodbyes to friends, had lunch with my minister, made a quick trip to New York City to visit a cousin, and drove up to New Hampshire to see another one. I stopped in Nashua on my way back to Boston to visit my parents' grave and say goodbye since I didn't know when or whether I would ever return to that town.

Despite some last minute issues with the buyer, we finally signed the contract for the sale of my condo. All the financial matters for the condo association were put in order and the necessary documentation filed. I managed to dig out the information about the remodels and repairs to the condo made during the twenty years I had lived there so that I could file the necessary tax returns. The process made me stop for several hours and recall memories of my life over those years, but I soon resumed the work I needed to complete since I didn't have time for too much reflection.

In addition to organizing my personal financial affairs, I signed a new will and estate plan. Like Jeanne who had arranged to have her will written and executed by a notary four years before she died, I wanted to make certain bequests. Unlike Jeanne, however, I did not leave money for masses to be said at eight different churches. Both of us, rather synchronously over the span of three centuries, stated we were of sound mind and did make our wishes known about funeral arrangements "at the least possible expense."

On Friday morning, February 8, five enormously busy and stressful weeks after our arrival in Boston, three men from the moving company arrived to pack up the belongings that remained from my sorting and that I had not been able to pack by myself. All the boxes and furniture were to be moved out of the apartment on Monday and then put in storage until I could decide what I wanted to do with them, as well as what I wanted to do with my life. After the men left, I took the subway out to the airport to pick up another rental car.

With a signed contract for the sale of my condo in hand, I had our last few days in Boston rather tightly organized with a long list of things remaining to be done before our anticipated flight back to France the following Tuesday evening. I spent Saturday disposing of more last-minute items at places that were willing to take my final discards. On Sunday I drove over to a friend's apartment nearby to drop off my suitcases and a sleeping bag as part of my arrangements for the Monday night before our flight the next day, since my bed would have been moved out earlier on Monday morning. I even put a frozen turkey pie in their freezer for my last night's dinner. I then returned to my condo, called Helaine to confirm her availability to drive us to the airport on Tuesday, finished packing, and made sure everything was in order for the move the next morning. As I looked around at all the cartons and containers filled with the stuff of my life to date, I tried to reassure Quincie and myself that it was all going to be okay. I was now ready to enjoy my Sunday evening, the last one in my home of twenty years.

In the middle of what was supposed to be a relaxing bath, I received an urgent message from my travel agent. Air France was strongly recommending I move my flight up one day because of an impending storm that would endanger our Tuesday evening flight. Since I had not been paying any attention to the weather forecast, this was all news to me. Staying in Boston was not a good option because the agent couldn't arrange a similar flight until Friday.

At that point, I had no desire to extend my stay in Boston since I was more than ready to leave. Besides, I would not have any furniture to sit or sleep on! I quickly finished my bath, got dressed, and frantically rearranged my Paris rental car reservation. I called Helaine to see if she could change her plans and come over the next day to help put Quincie into her travelling harness and carrier. I dried my hair. I got back into the rental car and quickly returned to my friend's place to retrieve my suitcases, the sleeping bag, and the frozen turkey pie, all the while thinking something about the best-laid plans often going awry.

The next morning, I rose early to give Quincie the sedative she needed to get ready for the flight, but not before she sank her teeth into my thumb. The movers returned at 8:30 a.m. to empty my apartment of the remaining furniture and all the boxes that either they or I had packed. They also had to crane out my sofa, sideboard, and two armoires since those items wouldn't make it down the narrow stairway out of my condo. In between watching them move and checking on Quincie, by now slightly sedated and hiding out in a closet away from all the action, I got in the car and drove to the local high school to drop off my printer and other computer equipment and returned my modem and cable box to my Internet provider.

After the moving trucks drove away, I somehow managed to complete all the remaining tasks on my list and do a final walk-through of my now-empty apartment with Chris. I didn't have any time to reflect on the twenty years I had spent there or on what I had done or on the fact that I truthfully didn't know what I was going to do after returning to France for another year. Dealing with those emotions would have to wait until later!

Helaine arrived, and we got the now slightly more docile Quincie into her harness and carrier. I gave Helaine a bag of unused cat litter, a few remaining cat items, and the still frozen turkey pie. I then finished packing up the car with our luggage and Quincie and drove to the airport to return the rental car and check us into our flight. There were some incredibly awkward and frustrating moments as I extracted two enormously heavy suitcases, a carry-on bag, a backpack with my laptop, and Quincie in her carrier out of the car. Since there appeared to be no one around to help, I managed to find a cart to use for the luggage. Then, not very gracefully, I juggled all my stuff onto the cart to transport us from the car to the bus that would take us to the international terminal. I ignored all the weird looks I received as a seventy-five-year-old woman struggling to keep all my stuff and Quincie's carrier from falling off the cart, trying to avoid crying, and wondering why I had chosen to do this all by myself.

Fortunately, the Air France agent took pity on us and offered to check all the luggage, except for Quincie and my backpack. We then settled into our seats in the waiting area at the gate. Before boarding the flight, I sent messages to Helaine, Carla, and my other siblings, letting them know about our progress. After a pleasant dinner, three movies, a brief nap, and kind attention by the flight attendants to my still throbbing thumb, we arrived in Paris. But not before we shared a laugh when I confused their concern for my thumb *(pouce)* with a question as to whether Quincie had fleas *(puces)*!

The saga was not over since my tired brain and body led us to the wrong customs line, the wrong luggage pickup, the wrong location for the rental car, and finally several wrong turns on the road back to Dieppe. (In my hurry to leave the airport, I had failed to correctly program the car's GPS system.) But we made it — finally.

Quincie appeared glad to be back in our cottage. There was no snarling or hissing before she quickly got resettled. I felt good as well. The weather was pleasantly mild; the fields and the little lawn were green; there was a hint that the cherry tree in the neighbor's yard was getting ready to bloom — all promising that spring was on its way in Normandy. I unpacked so we could quickly return to our daily routines. Two weeks later, the sale of my condo in Charlestown was completed, and I was now free of that responsibility and officially without a home.

This was the second time a plan for the flight to France had gone awry, and, like the first one, it eventually worked out. We were now safely back in our little cottage on the lane beside the ever-peeling blue garage door and ready to begin another year in France, significantly less burdened with material possessions and without any definite plans for the coming year.

SEVENTEEN

LOOKING BACK

On Easter Sunday, April 21, 2019, a few weeks after my return to France and the sale of my condo, I was up before dawn. It was still not quite light as I walked down the cliff to meet a friend. Together, we made the twenty-minute drive to what would be my third Easter sunrise service at the magnificent Moutiers estate, located on the edge of the English Channel in the nearby village of Varengeville-sur-Mer.

Drive to Varengeville

The prior year, we had met in one of the estate's formal gardens, directly in front of the lovely Arts and Crafts manor house of the family who had owned the estate for a century. This year, over fifty of us, members and friends of my church, gathered down the hill from the home, in a sheltered grove, encircled by almost-ready-to-bloom rhododendrons. As I remember the morning, it was cool but not very damp. We read scripture, prayed, sang Easter hymns, and breathed in the fresh sea air and the scent of the foliage around us. It was a moment of utter tranquility.

Too soon afterward, however, I was back in the cottage and online, reading the news from the States. After all, it was the day after Pete Buttigieg had announced his candidacy for president. If I had ever thought that coming to France was going to radically change me, I would have been badly mistaken — for at least a couple of reasons. First, I obviously had not been able to shake my interest, or perhaps obsession, with politics. And second, as the five-plus weeks in Boston had proven, I was still forever wedded to meticulously planning out my days, weeks, and months.

After carefully executing the plan that I had worked on for at least six months before my trip to Boston, I was now back in France and thinking about what I had left behind — besides the comfort of being able to communicate clearly and easily with others. Some losses would prove to be permanent, some would be temporary, and some still needed to be tested. My condo, my homebase for twenty years, had been sold, and many of my belongings were now gone. Most items could, without a doubt, be replaced if needed. My US voting address and driving license were no longer valid. Gone as well, though not forgotten, was a life in Charlestown as a local activist and as a member of St. John's church.

I had left behind — hopefully temporarily — family and friends. With all the latest technology, I could continue to stay in touch, something that I had had to learn to do over the years since I had moved so many times in my life. So far, distance had not proven to be a real problem in maintaining connections, or so it seemed to me at least.

I had also left behind — presumably temporarily — ninety-eight items in a storage unit at a Gentle Giant Moving Company facility not far from Boston, where the cartons and containers of belongings and a few pieces of furniture filled up three vaults. A safe deposit box in a Charlestown bank held my jewelry and important papers, and my niece Zoe was guarding some books and my silverware in Vermont. I didn't know if I would ever return to Charlestown for more than a quick visit to the bank.

The memories of my life to date, my friendships and all our special moments from birthday parties, holiday celebrations, and family gatherings, I would carry with me, hopefully forever. All the photos in albums and boxes would help keep those memories alive.

I had also left behind the level of understanding politics that I had achieved in the States. While I had been able to follow Macron and his presidency, I still didn't have a solid grasp of organizational structures, voting parties, and the major issues facing France. I was also not sure how much I frankly needed to delve into those questions at that moment in my life.

Then there were the things I needed to abandon, one of the major ones being my hope of "mastering French," of becoming fluent, and of losing my accent. That goal had continued to be daunting and depressing. As I had written in my journal back in April 2015 after almost four weeks in France, including three weeks at a French language school in Rouen: "I am frustrated. The language of Voltaire and Molière, as my landlord Michel calls it, continues to elude me."

In the spring of 2019, more than four years later, I continued to be frustrated and perplexed. Thanks to my high-school French teacher Miss Milan (I kept the notebook from her twelfth-grade course) and also to Miss Barnes who taught me Latin, I could find my way through the grammar for the most part, although I still managed to get tangled up all too frequently. The challenges of learning a new vocabulary, the correct pronunciation, the intonation and music, and all those idiosyncratic French phrases and constructions remained almost overwhelming. Very minor things could throw me off, like trying to type on a different computer keyboard that mixed up *a* and *q*, *z* and *w*, and other letters as well. When writing a check, I still had to remember to use commas instead of decimal points in numbers, to put the date before the month — not after it — and to not capitalize the first letter of the month. Oh, and I always had to make sure I wrote my name as "Levesque Lynne," not the other way around!

My weekly lessons with my tutor Martine had positively helped, as had the sessions with Joël, frequent chats with friends, and all my social activities. Sometimes conversations would flow, but at other times I would stumble. I struggled to say what I wanted to say, and I always wanted to make sure my friends understood me. My aging brain, my knowledge of Russian, my proclivity to analyze everything, and my perfectionism wouldn't stop getting in the way!

It was possible that my endeavors to express difficult ideas and my deepest thoughts rather than merely a simple sentence in a language not my own also played a role. Martine once told me she thought I was learning at an advanced level of French. I had to agree with her, especially when I thought about the conversations that occurred in a certain church group. In our semi-monthly meetings to edit a book on the theology of a British philosopher attempting to combine a belief in God with Newtonian physics, I had trouble keeping up with ideas that I might not have been able to understand in English!

Despite these frustrations, I felt extraordinarily fortunate about my life. Most everything that I had left behind or decided to abandon, whether temporarily or permanently, had been replaced by an incredible number of exceptional experiences, new friends, and a heightened sensitivity to nature, for sure. I knew a lot more about my faith and the Bible. I still had Quincie to keep me company. In addition to my sessions with Martine and Joël, I was still taking the yoga, bridge, and gym classes that I had added the previous fall, and I had started working with children and some adults in their English classes. With Martine's help, I had prepared a proposal to give a twenty-minute presentation on my ancestor Jeanne's life at a historical congress to be held in Dieppe in October later that year. I had lightened my load of material goods and responsibilities and had more financial security. And my love and appreciation for life in France, particularly Dieppe, had kept on growing. I could say, in fact, that I was starting to set down roots! My decision to spend another year in France — what would be my third year — had been made, not because I had no other options of somewhere better to go, but because I was finding it a welcoming and delightful place that I was in no way ready to leave.

Along with those feelings about life in France, my brain had certainly expanded. I was not, however, sure about the condition of my body. My hip had not yet fully recovered from carrying so many items up and down the stairs of my condo, and my level of energy had faded a bit — perhaps because of the change of seasons, the new stress resulting from the challenges of obtaining a French driver's license, or simply the realization of what I had done to myself (and Quincie) over the past three years.

So what is my plan for moving forward, I asked myself. *Can I live without one? Can I take some time to absorb my recent experiences, or will I give in to my usual habit to immediately keep right on moving along?*

That's what I had done at other critical moments in the past. For example, in 1987 after I had left my life of fifteen years in California to move back East, I immediately went to work unpacking and beginning a new life and new job in Hartford without taking any time to celebrate the move or to absorb the change in residences and lifestyles.

That was also what I did when the closest friend I had in Hartford was kidnapped out of the parking garage of the division's headquarters and tragically murdered. Instead of pausing to mourn her death, I had covered up any personal feelings, telling myself that after a mere two years, Diane and I hadn't been all that close. *She was only a work colleague*, I said to myself. I had quickly assumed my role as a member of the division's senior management team and taken on the responsibilities for managing the impact of her death on our colleagues and for dealing with the security failures in the building.

A few days after she died, however, I began to realize that Diane had indeed been a dear friend. We had taken yoga classes together, shared dinners, played bridge, and gone antiques hunting and gallery shopping. We had talked about our goals and had had conversations about future plans. Diane had always wanted to move to Hawaii and start a new career there. Her death was a close and personal reminder of the fragility of life.

The sudden loss of my friend had also made me think about my own vulnerability. I had always believed that my height would protect me from danger, but, in reality, Diane was two inches taller than me. I realized then that height might not be as much of a "weapon" as I had thought. I needed to be more careful. Equally as important, I vowed to treasure friendships more and focus on good times in the here and now.

I'm not sure how much I fulfilled those promises to myself or whether her death caused me to be more in touch with my feelings. In fact, in

1994, five years after her death, the pattern was repeated. My parents died within two months of each other, deaths that occurred right before and after my fiftieth birthday and not long after I had left my banking career and had unexpectedly ended a business partnership with a colleague. Without allowing myself any moments to grieve for any of those events, I chose to basically keep on living the life I had been living.

Back in Hartford in 1989, I stoically attended Diane's funeral as a member of the management team. Afterwards, I drove over to the Honda dealership to pick up the new car I had ordered. I moved on with my life, although not before making some notes about our times together and the feelings I did have. Similarly, with the death of my parents and the end of my business partnership, I chose to return full-time to my doctoral studies instead of spending any time mourning. While I would visit my parents' graves whenever I was in Nashua, I hadn't thought too much about Diane until I ran across her name as I was leafing through my files and found those notes.

So now the pattern played out again in France. Even after all the changes I had put myself through over the prior few months, it hadn't been too difficult to tell myself, *There is no time to reflect now, just as there wasn't back then. Take action. Create a plan.*

Without a plan, how could I answer questions about what I was doing in France and whether I was actually moving to France? "Not sure yet" had been my uncomfortable response to any questions about my future.

"Are you an ex-pat now?" my brother asked after my return to France in February.

"I am not certain I know what that means," I had replied.

There definitely were complications that had to be sorted out, including the observation that Joël had made in one of our conversation exchanges about all my activities in Dieppe: "You are getting so integrated here. The longer you stay, the harder it will be to go back to the States."

And that was probably quite true, but I wasn't doing anything to stop that movement forward in France. I was still trying to resolve issues about health insurance, address changes with the US Internal Revenue Service and with credit cards, and the list went on. This transition had not been straightforward or easy, this idea about spending a sabbatical year and then another one or two or perhaps more in France. Clearly, one of the things I had left behind was the simplicity of living a life I had always lived in a place where I had always lived. But then, given all the moves I'd made, did I ever have or want that simplicity?

Meanwhile, I had continued to develop my ability to adapt to new surroundings and to living in someone else's space. I was helped by my accommodations: the charming cottage with its warm spirit, wooden beams, fireplace, and garden and by its view of flowers and trees with old homes in the distance — as opposed to the view of the parking lot from my window in Boston.

My German friend Peter once said that he admired my ability to reach beyond my comfort level. I sometimes questioned whether leaving Boston had been all that wise a choice, but fortunately I didn't do that questioning very often. That was probably because I felt deep inside, at the time at least, that the positives of life in Dieppe outweighed the negatives, or the things that I found too challenging.

I had also realized that returning to the States might not be a desirable option. If I moved to Seattle to be near Carla, what would I do with my time? What sort of life would I have? Although my connections with different members of my family had grown closer over recent years, I questioned when or how those relationships could or should change. They were all settled in their own lives. What role would I play if I were to live closer to any of them? How would I resume my life with the friends I did have in the States, get re-engaged, and build that community that I craved?

EIGHTEEN

CONNECTIONS

"You need all sorts of different friends in your life," my therapist in Boston once told me.

And that advice had proven to be true. Like love, I had learned that friends come in many different shapes and sizes. In my life to date, I'd been able to quickly connect with work colleagues, companions, pleasant acquaintances, and kindred spirits — some of whom evolved into friends who inspired me, helped me learn, and became confidants and family. "Friends for a reason, a season, or a lifetime," someone once wrote.

Something felt special, however, about my connections with so many different and interesting people that I had met since beginning this search for the story of my ancestor Jeanne Chevalier almost a decade ago. In fact, I had originally planned to write this sequel to show my appreciation for all the outstanding people I had met during my years of research. And since the publication of my book on Jeanne, that number had continued to grow especially during my time in Dieppe.

Despite all those relationships I had made over the years, genuinely close friends in my life, other than Carla, had been rare — until I came to Dieppe and met Tatiana. Our friendship grew stronger for a variety of reasons that included our almost daily contact, although our common interests and personalities also undoubtedly played a role. We would spend so much time together that people regularly mixed up our names!

Tatiana was not the only friend who made Dieppe such a special place for me. I did meet many other individuals, who were much more than mere acquaintances and with whom I ended up forging solid bonds. They all seemed to have many other friends, activities, hobbies, and relatives to keep them busy. Despite those responsibilities, all of these friends were always available and willing to help and support me in unexpected ways, often putting their own needs aside to take care of mine.

One of the first friends that I had made in Dieppe was Nadine, whom I met during my second visit in 2015 as a result of that suggestion from my homestay hosts in Rouen during my three weeks of studying French there. The next year, Nadine and I exchanged homes. Then in January of 2017, at the start of my first year-long stay in Dieppe, she helped me settle in and continued to check in with me regularly. In the next few months after my arrival, she spent several days helping me with the translation of my book into French. Over the years I was in Dieppe, she would frequently invite me and visiting members of my American family to dine in her home. I once asked her if she could pick Quincie and me up from the vet's office after an appointment. We had taken a bus to the vet, but a return bus was not easily available. I could have called a taxi, but I asked Nadine instead. When I wanted to be sure she was not inconvenienced by my request, she was almost affronted and replied, "I would have been extremely upset to learn you had called a taxi instead of me!"

A year before meeting Nadine, I had connected via the Internet with Nelly as a result of my contact with the mayor's office in Rivière-Ouelle back in 2014. As the secretary of the Cousins of the New World, Nelly had become the point of contact for Canadian and American visitors in Hautot-Saint-Sulpice.

She became much more than that to me since we first met in person during the same 2015 visit when I connected with Nadine. In fact, I came to refer to Nelly and her family as my French family. She also could be called my agent. She once organized a lunch and then later a conference so I could spread the word about Jeanne in that village. She made sure that the banner being created for the Levesque family reunion in 2017 included mention of Jeanne. During each of the visits to France that Carla, Dana, and my nephew Cyrus, his wife and daughter had made, we would drive down to Hautot-Saint-Sulpice where Nelly arranged for us to visit the church that was usually locked.

After participating in the translation of Jeanne's story into French, she came to my book signing in August 2017. Despite the hour-long drive from their home, she and her husband attended several parties that I held for visiting friends and relatives. When my nephew Max visited in 2017, we met up with Nelly and her family at the Rouen Christmas market. Two years later, my niece Maron and I joined them there for another Christmas celebration where they were exceptionally helpful in dealing with the theft of my mobile phone. And Nelly, also known to many as "Madame Kodak," frequently managed to keep in touch through her delightful photos and creative cards.

Isabelle, whom I met in the summer of 2018 through a mutual friend, was also a prolific sender of photos whenever she traveled. Having grown up not far from Dieppe and having worked in the area, she still had very close ties and obligations with her siblings, nephews, and nieces, as well as with friends from her past. Yet, besides remembering me with photos, she would frequently take the time to help me with everything from choosing and then planting flowers to handling all the details regarding obtaining a French healthcare card and social security number, to dealing with a traffic citation. She would drive me to appointments and wait until I was finished. We would take many long walks together along the cliffs or in the nearby forests and have the most interesting conversations. When she planned to shop at a hardware store, she remembered that I needed a stepstool. Together we explored Mary Cassatt's chateau and village. And Isabelle drove me back there three months later to give a talk on Cassatt's life in the salon of her chateau.

Joëlle, another delightful new friend, frequently organized extended hikes in the woods or along the beach at low tide. She always included me in her invitations for these walks, as well as shorter ones. She loved to cook with her new Thermomix, said to be "the world's most powerful blender that also cooked and stirred" and that could replace almost every other kitchen appliance. With it, she made some of the most amazing dishes, resulting in delicious meals and lively conversations in her home. Joëlle took care of Quincie during my time in Quebec in 2018. She invited me to give my presentation on Mary Cassatt to her artist friends and later, with her daughter, surprised me by attending that same presentation at Cassatt's chateau. We spent one New Year's Eve together when she taught me to play French scrabble. The next day we met up with Isabelle for a long hike on the cliffs, a hike that became a New Year's Day tradition.

I met Yann at the seafood festival in Granville during my 2013 trip, just by sitting down at the table opposite him and his sister. We struck up a conversation that led to an invitation to join him shortly thereafter at his home and, over the years since then, to several other visits, once even with Quincie. As a retired English teacher, he also helped in the translation of my book shortly before its publication in June 2017 and then introduced me to that other author of a book on the Filles du Roi. In January of the next year, when Dana and I made the trip with Joël from Dieppe to see the Normandy beaches, Yann drove over to meet us for lunch. And in June 2019, he joined Tatiana and me for dinner when we were in Granville for a conference. Later that year, he spent a day leading Carla, her husband David, and me on an incredibly detailed guided tour of Mont St. Michel.

My conversation buddy Joël, as a relatively new friend from church, called to find out if I needed anything when he heard that I was sick in bed with a cold. Later, he helped me deal with my first traffic fine through long discussions about the appropriate strategy. Over the next few years after our first language exchange, we continued to meet weekly to discuss history, politics, and other sometimes controversial subjects, half in English and half in French. Surprisingly, our sometimes-heated discussions never seemed to disturb our growing friendship.

Besides our weekly meetings, Joël and I would make regular shopping trips to Dieppe's health food store. He never had a problem waiting for me if I had to run an additional errand. If it rained on Sunday morning, he would stop without being asked to pick me up on the way to church. Together we attended several conferences on a variety of subjects, and he showed up to lend support at book signings or whenever I gave local talks about my book.

Like Joël, Martine went far beyond her role as "helper" with my French language learning. As we worked on the French translation of Jeanne's story, on grammar lessons, on blog articles, or on emails, she was always encouraging, positive and engaged in my struggles not only to learn French but to adapt to French culture. Her patience, dedication, and concern for my progress showed me yet another marker on what could be called the spectrum of friendship.

When my friends Patricia and Pierre were residing in their home near Paris instead of their place in Dieppe, they would check in via emails and phone calls and were always eager to arrange bridge games or lunches when they were local. It was Patricia and Pierre who suggested I sign up for French health insurance during my birthday dinner one August.

I first met my German friend Peter years ago, when I still had my apartment in Boston, after he had reached out over email with questions about my book on creativity and Jung. Not long after his first email, our unforgettable face-to-face meeting for coffee and visiting museums in Paris in 2002 eventually led to a friendship of over fifteen years. During that time, we managed to meet in cities in the United States as well as in London, Paris, Brussels, and Amsterdam. In frequent phone or Internet conversations, we would continue to encourage one another in our professional and personal endeavors. Since my arrival in France, he always made sure that his family vacations included a stop in Dieppe.

Although Sylvie was in my life very briefly, she added so much with her humor, patience, and friendship. Other friends whom I had known for just a short time were part of the team who worked on the translation of my book. Many showed up at my book signing in August of the first year I was in Dieppe. Then there were all the friends from church with whom I had so many shared experiences as well as the companions with whom I played bridge, took gym classes, went hiking, and attended conferences. And all the other people whom I met as these contacts multiplied into new ones on this journey to discover more about Jeanne, her husbands, and her life in New France.

In the past in the many places where I had lived, worked, and travelled most of the connections I had been able to so easily make, with a few exceptions, were what I would more accurately call acquaintances or possibly kindred spirits. People whom I could consider close friends had been rare until my time in France. I had kept very few friends from high school, from my years at different universities (my roommate Paula being a notable exception), and from my various careers. From my travels, I had remained in annual contact with two friends in Australia. From my years in banking in San Francisco and then in Hartford, colleagues with whom I was still in contact were limited, mostly around birthdays or holidays, except for Ann who once came to visit me in Dieppe with her husband and with whom check-ins tended to be more frequent.

In fairness, because I had moved so often, I clearly hadn't had the opportunity to nurture many true friendships in the same location. Proximity and frequent contact, I've come to believe, played a vital role in helping friends to stay in touch, to learn personal preferences and idiosyncrasies in order to provide mutual support, and to deepen the bond. At the same time, I was beginning to realize that I had never learned what it meant to be a good friend, at least until my months in Dieppe. And it was probably also true that I had not really appreciated those friendships I had and had kept in the States and beyond. Or maybe I had never let myself consciously feel the warmth that the support of friends and family could provide.

Admittedly, some of those past relationships had been problematic, either because of clashing political or personal values, differences in personalities, my absolute unwillingness to accept bad behavior (sometimes over trivial matters, upon reflection), or because of distance, competing activities, and diverging lives that limited our ties. With attempts at professional partnerships during my years as a consultant, I had had even less success for a variety of reasons, mainly as a result of misunderstandings of goals and expectations. I could blame the time of my birth since my astrological chart revealed all those challenges in the house of relationships. My natural preferences for logical analysis over contextual decision-making and my propensity for prioritizing goals and objectives over maintaining personal rapport could also be blamed. Or did these challenges speak to my independence and relative lack of recognized need for others in my professional and personal lives to date? Or to my ability to move on quickly when something wasn't working? Or to my unwillingness to respond to offers of care and support? Or, worse, to my lack of concern for others (hopefully not!)?

Whatever the reasons of the past, this adventure to discover Jeanne's story made me realize how fortunate I'd been with all the different people — friends, colleagues, as well as brief acquaintances, staff and volunteers — I had met along the way. In addition to helping me with my research, they all taught me countless lessons about the many different shapes and sizes of friendship.

To be sure, I had not always been so fortunate. There were still holes in Jeanne's story that I had not been able to fill. Nevertheless, all these unexpected experiences more than made up for the frustrations of dead ends in my research. From all of these people I learned important lessons about friendship, one of those gifts in life that "give value to survival," according to author and theologian C.S. Lewis.

How did that all happen? I couldn't remember ever putting "connecting with others" on any list of action items or objectives, but somehow it made its way to prominence on my list. What had brought about all these and other delightful and helpful connections in my journey? My loud voice? My American accent? My interesting research? My passion for my ancestor's story? Was Jeanne at work in my life again?

Skeptics would say I simply happened to be in the right place at the right time. Instead, I wondered, *Are they signs from the universe that I am on the right track in my search for Jeanne, her story, and my French roots? Are they messages of encouragement from Jeanne? Or are they proof of the significant number of good and generous people in the world?*

Or perhaps there was something else going on. I had always heard that solid friendships became more difficult to create as we aged.

That didn't seem to be the case, as I was learning in France. Perhaps I was becoming more open to the give-and-take of relationships, more accepting and more willing to ask for help. Or perhaps I was consciously or unconsciously taking more time to nurture the connections I had made because I recognized — finally — that I did indeed need support. It was equally possible that I was also more engaged in different activities, rather than solely focused on my career and business, and more eager to nurture new friendships as I had grown older.

It was equally possible that the French culture was more nurturing of friendships. I was so often impressed at how my friends in France helped each other out, knew so much about each other, and stayed so connected, and how they were always so wonderfully gracious and patient with me and willing to help me in so many unexpected ways. A conversation with a French woman whom I met in Boston during my last visit there started me thinking about this role of culture. After five years in the States, she was looking forward to returning to France for several reasons, one of which was a different attitude about friendship. "In the United States, I find friendships are seen as an exchange. In France, you are friends because friendship is important."

My friend Isabelle and I took a walk once on the Avenue Verte, the walking and biking greenway that connected Dieppe with Paris along what had been part of the Chasse-Marée, the road that fishermen had used for centuries to make daily deliveries of their products to Paris. On that fine sunny March day, we continued a conversation about friendship that we had begun three months earlier on another walk. This time, she observed that people in France possibly had more hours, in both their personal and working lives, to devote to nurturing loving relationships. With longer vacations and fewer worries about healthcare, they were able to concentrate on spending quality time with family and friends and on creating special gifts for them, like the photo albums that she and Nelly had created for me.

Another friend offered a different perspective, suggesting that perhaps jealousy, conscious or unconscious, played a role in limiting personal ties in the US: "Could it be that the priority Americans place on business and financial success affects the depth of friendships? It may be that we French are less status-conscious and treasure mutual interests in art, literature, nature, history and music — rather than personal achievements."

It could also be that there was something about Dieppe that made it fairly easy to develop friendships with so many wonderful people, kindred spirits with similar values and a broad range of interests. As an adult, I had never lived in a place the size of Dieppe. Maybe its size contributed to the feeling of neighborliness that I never felt in the big-city cultures in both San Francisco and Boston where it was difficult to establish lasting friendships — for me anyway.

At some point, I came to realize that it was time to stop trying to analyze the reasons or to determine Jeanne's role or Dieppe's or France's in all these new experiences. Instead I needed to enjoy our times together, simply being ourselves, and treasuring the human connections, the differences and the similarities across the cultures, that we shared. To learn how to be a better friend in France and to cherish my American friends and family more as well!

Once I had observed the care with which Nadine and others were surrounding a friend who had cancer. I wondered if I would ever have that closeness in my life. After not quite three years in France, I didn't need to wonder any more.

NINETEEN

BRAVERY OR BRAVADO?

"Brave…."

There was that word again. In June 2019, the president of our book club was commenting to the club members on the presentation that I had just given on the American painter Mary Cassatt. To her comments, she had added her observation on how brave I was to have come to France on my own. I had heard something similar from a woman whom I had met on the train in Cornwall in the south of England over three decades ago when she learned I was traveling alone: "Oh, how very brave of you!"

My friends saw me as courageous. Tatiana called it "risk-taking." Of course, I didn't see it as anything other than merely living the way I usually did. Except for the ten years I was married, I had lived alone — well, not exactly, because I usually had a cat or a dog to keep me company. After a most unenjoyable trip with my then husband and a couple of rather unpleasant experiences traveling with now ex-friends and after some quite delightful journeys alone to Quebec, Germany, and Scotland, I had determined that I also preferred to travel by myself.

So was coming to France to spend a year there (or two or three?) all that brave? While it may have seemed that way to many, perhaps they hadn't seen the careful steps and considerations that had gone into the decision. I had been to Dieppe three times before deciding to spend a year there. I was therefore somewhat familiar with the town. I had made acquaintances during those visits, people with whom I had stayed in touch and who helped me settle in. My commitment to being an active Christian had led me to a caring community of new friends and many exceptional memories. My interests in history, things French, bridge, and staying fit as well as my insatiable curiosity had done the same.

Because I could easily stay in touch with my family in the States and because they continued to be healthy, as far as I knew, and had spouses, significant others, and relatives close by, there was no apparent need for me to be more present in their lives. For the most part, my homes in the States had been hundreds and thousands of miles away from them. Besides, they seemed to enjoy visiting me in France. I was in good health and had no problems climbing up and down the cliffs to do my shopping and get back and forth to activities and, in general, no problems walking wherever I needed to go. Sufficient financial resources and the relatively inexpensive cost of living in Dieppe also helped, for sure. And finally and quite significantly, I had and would continue to have at least one driving reason for being here: I had undoubtedly been pushed by my ancestor to take this step.

And how brave or courageous were my adventures compared to the risks that Jeanne and the other eighteen Filles du Roi on my father's side of the family took when they agreed to leave France for a new life in Quebec? My mother's family certainly had had its share of pioneers as well. Her mother, Abbie Lorton, who had pre-Revolutionary War ancestors, described her own "true grit" in a story she wrote about her train trip of several days in 1904 from Shell City, Missouri, to start a teaching job in Idaho. My mother's paternal grandmother Eva Wallein moved from Uppsala, Sweden, to the United States in 1872. In all probability, I could find other young women with European roots in my maternal family tree who had moved from Kentucky and Missouri west to Utah and Idaho, some alone, in search of a new life like so many other non-native Americans. Maybe all those women who made up my heritage had provided me with some sort of unconscious role models or helpful companions.

Whatever the source of my support and guidance, I had never thought of myself as particularly brave. However, when the instructor with the Château Auto-École (whose mother was younger than me at the time) used that same word a few months after a couple of driving lessons, I began to think that maybe it wasn't about bravery or courage. There was probably an element of naïveté or ignorance or even some masochism involved in my not totally understanding the consequences of some of the choices I had made, as I was to learn when it came to driving in France.

Near the end of my second year in France in November 2018, I realized that, along with renewing my visa for another year, it might make sense to check into whether I could continue to use my US driver's license when renting cars. I went to the appropriate office in Dieppe to figure out what I needed to do to drive legally in France. There, I learned that after a year of living in France, the law required a "visitor" to have a French driver's license, a legality I had somehow failed to discover. I was told that there were two ways to obtain such a license. Within the first year of a long-stay visa, a US driver's license could be exchanged for a French one. That process required assembling a significant number of documents, including an officially translated copy of a US birth certificate and of a US driving record clearance, as well as the surrender of the US license. The second way was to study with a French driving school, an *auto-école*, to pass a written test on the French code first and then a road test. Auto-école programs could cost over 1,000 euros and required several hours of study and practice, but the schools controlled the process and obviously the market. That path was something I hoped to avoid, so I asked for the list of documents required for an exchange, even though I realized I might have exceeded the legal time limits.

While in Boston in early 2019, in addition to getting my condo ready for sale, I carefully put together all those documents and arranged for the translation of the most important ones. In March, not long after my return to France that year, I took the train once again to Rouen and walked over to the Prefecture. I passed through security, took a number, and sat down in the waiting room until my number came up on the overhead screen. When I was finally called, I proceeded to the appropriate desk, sat down, and handed over the documents. The agent, after reviewing my file, said, "Madam, you are not eligible for an exchange of licenses. You've been in France too long."

I had indeed missed the deadline and was in fact several months beyond the limit of fifteen months. Instead, the agent told me I would need to start from scratch to obtain a French license. Those were not the words I had hoped to hear!

In retrospect, the first option would not have been all that wise anyway. In order to drive safely in France, understanding the signage and the rules made sense. Until studying the code, for example, I had mistakenly believed that a road sign with a crossed arrow was signaling an approach to a railroad crossing (which never seemed to appear,

Temporary Change in Priority

but I never wondered why). I also had no idea that in France, unless otherwise indicated, "Drivers must always yield to cars coming on the right," known in France as the "Priority is always on the right." That's true, even on major roads — except when there are signs that say it's not (like the sign above!). So, despite the cost and several months of stress, I was quite glad that I took the second option.

As importantly, if I had given up my US driver's license, I would have had to start all over again to secure a new one if I were to decide to permanently return to the United States. As it happened, I had until August 2020 to exchange my Massachusetts driver's license for one in another state in order to avoid having to take a written and a driving test in the United States.

Realizing that I now had no choice, I looked for an auto-école, not a difficult task since there were several in Dieppe. I signed up with one that was located near the cottage. After paying the initial registration fee, I was handed a manual and instructions for the online tutorial in order to be able to work at home.

I then devoted several weeks intensively studying the code via written materials, online tutorials, simulations, practice exams, and question-and-answer sessions with the folks at the school. I created long lists of new-to-me French words related to road signs, the various internal and external parts of cars, environmental and safety rules, fines, alcohol limits, what to do in case of an accident (be sure to put on your yellow vest, or *gilet jaune,* before exiting the car), and various good driving techniques. I carefully studied and tried to memorize the words and phrases on bus rides to the supermarket or to the school where I was volunteering to help teach English to eight- and nine-year-old children. I repeated the terms to myself on any walks I took. I attacked the exam the same way I had always studied — with great detail, meticulous memorization, long hours, and with too many questions, or so the folks at the auto-école told me. Finally, I was ready.

The test was scheduled for the morning of June 6, my personal D-Day. I had planned to walk the four kilometers over to the exam site, but Isabelle insisted on driving me there and waiting for me to finish. I entered the waiting room and discovered, not unexpectedly, that I was the oldest student by far. We were ushered into another room with individual tables, tablets, and headsets. On the tablets, we had to pass through several layers of security before accessing the test. We were given thirty minutes to answer the forty interactive multiple-choice questions, each within a set amount of time. The time passed ever so quickly.

Afterwards on the ride back to the cottage, I was relieved, but I could not give Isabelle any idea as to whether I had passed. I waited anxiously that day for the call from the driving school. Right before dinner, I learned I had passed, correctly answering one more than the required thirty-five questions!

The ordeal was not over. The written exam was followed by several weeks of lessons to learn how to apply the code to driving. After almost sixty years of driving in the United States, Great Britain, and Australia with a single driving ticket, this task should not have been a major challenge for me. It did, however, prove to be one since the rules and the roads in France were different enough. Or perhaps the rules had changed in the States, and I had not kept current. Or perhaps the rules were simply more stringent — although not necessarily more strictly observed — in France.

Most of the time, I worked with the same instructor who had her own set of hand controls in the car to stop me from making mistakes and who was prolific in the corrections to my driving practices, naturally all in French. "Slow down. The priority is on the right."

How to tell? "Look for markings on the pavement or for a stop sign."

I found that a bit difficult to do while trying to pay attention to the road ahead, as well as to the speed limit. "Speed up. The limit is fifty kilometers here."

But since the government had recently changed the speed limit on country roads, it wasn't always easy to know what speed to keep. "Put the left turn signal on. You are in a rotary and taking the last exit." Or "There's an obstacle in the road, and you need to let the drivers behind you know about it, so put your blinker on."

Fortunately, the instructor was usually kind and patient and let me know she thought I was rather "brave" to be trying to obtain my French driving license — at my age — and using a manual transmission at that. In any event, by mid-September after eight driving lessons and after paying several hundred euros more, I was ready for the road test. I passed, although not exactly with flying colors since I had failed to put my blinker on before an obstacle in the road.

In the months after obtaining my license, although I had forgotten most of the vocabulary, I was much more careful when driving. I did lose one point for speeding but regained the point after six months of "clean" driving. I had, unfortunately, become a bit of an annoyance with friends whenever I would point out the need for them to use their turn signals in rotaries or when they were exceeding the speed limit.

Luckily I had remembered most of the lessons. Once while driving back to Dieppe with Tatiana after our visit in Granville, I heard a strange noise in the rear of the car. I pulled the car over to the emergency lane, turned on the emergency lights, put on the yellow vest, and carefully exited the car to try to find the source of the problem, only to discover that we had simply left the back windows open. And despite my studying the importance of using the right fuel in filling up a gas tank, I almost made a near-tragic mistake when I started to fill up Tatiana's car with gasoline instead of diesel fuel. Right before it was too late, I noticed I was using the wrong-colored nozzle. I had learned enough about the possible dire consequences to immediately stop fueling and call roadside assistance.

Looking back on all of my experiences during this journey, I realized that, while courage had often been required, I had mostly been extremely fortunate. I had had a great deal of help from others, including Jeanne, along the way — both in my research and in general during my time in France. I hadn't suffered much from any of those undertakings, although I had been somewhat naïve and had significantly underestimated the effort involved in learning a new language and new rules and adapting to a new culture in my seventies.

These decisions, these choices, had started me on different roads in life, unexpected ones. Some steps led to other ones, like the first year I spent that segued into two and then to three. Way truly did lead on to way. Life did just happen, sometimes without a plan. Despite my predisposition for long-term planning, lists, and goals, I realized that I had, on a couple of occasions at least, jumped without much thought to what I would do next. I had left my banking career without much preparation and had somehow landed on a path that led to new opportunities as a writer and consultant in creativity and leadership development in arenas I could never have imagined. Then I had given that all up to pursue the research into the story of my ancestor, which then brought me to France where I had to deal with daily challenges of communicating in the language of my father, in a language other than the one in which I still thought and dreamed. Indeed, my journey and the people I had met along the way had been remarkable, had given me significant new perspectives, and had added new dimensions to my life. Brave or not, I had certainly come to enjoy the adventure of it all!

TWENTY

RECKONING

"It's not anything to worry about," said my friend, a former doctor.

I had awakened that morning in the middle of July during my third year in France with a locked jaw, something I had never experienced before. I couldn't open my mouth wide enough to put a cherry in it! My friend suggested I stop worrying and instead join her on the long walk she had planned for that day. I followed her advice but asked her to stop on the way home for some pistachio ice cream. Several bowls of that ice cream and a heating pad seemed to cure the problem which disappeared the next day.

I was thus able to keep my plans for a trip to Paris to renew my US passport at the American embassy and to see a lawyer to discuss my residency status in France. I wanted to be sure I was now following all the rules since I had missed the regulation about obtaining a driver's license. After taking care of those tasks and despite the heat wave that struck Paris and northern France that day, I joined friends from Dieppe to visit the Berthe Morisot exhibit at the Musée d'Orsay. Upon our return to Dieppe where the heat wave had weakened, I was ever-so glad to be living by the English Channel and its cooling breezes.

Unfortunately, the locked-jaw problem returned less than three weeks later. This time, no matter how much pistachio ice cream I ate, several weeks passed before the problem went away. I never was able to figure out the cause. I knew I was indeed using different muscles in my mouth when speaking French. And perhaps the anxiety caused by those driving lessons, which at the time were still underway, was a bit too much to handle. Additional stress as a result of news from Paula, my college roommate, could also have been a significant factor. Via an email and telephone exchange not long after her birthday, I learned that she had had a stroke the prior April. She was doing well, but it was a major scare.

Paula's brush with death was not the sole rude awakening I had recently experienced. A year earlier, Sylvie, the friend who had helped me discover all the stairways in Dieppe and had introduced me to walks in the Arques Forest with her friends, had died barely seven months after learning she had advanced-stage ovarian cancer. She had always been so full of life with funny stories about her cat Harry. She had been most tolerant of my attempts to speak French and always helpful. It was Sylvie who taught me the French-nuanced equivalent of "loves me, loves me not": *Il m'aime un peu, beaucoup, passionnément, à la folie, pas du tout.* (He loves me a little, a lot, passionately, madly, not at all.) I had had a hard time expressing my feelings to her near the end of her life. My limited fluency in French was part of the problem, but I also didn't know what to say to someone who was dying — and not just in French.

Over the following months, I had had to deal with death several more times. There was the death — this one relatively peaceful — of the husband of the couple I had met long ago in Hautot-Saint-Sulpice. A few months later, I learned that the professor with whom I had worked closely at Harvard Business School for five and a half years, a man several years younger than me, had died. Then came the news of the somewhat expected death of a dear friend of more than fifty years.

The most painful, however, had been the tragic death of Xavier, Tatiana's husband, in mid-October of my third year in France. We had had lunch just two days before at their new apartment, surrounded by all their many still unopened boxes. When Tatiana called me early Sunday morning with the news of his fatal heart attack, I rushed down to their place and did what I could to offer her my support in the first few hours after the tragedy. Fortunately, her daughters and other friends arrived to surround her with their care during the next couple of days and weeks since a planned visit with Carla and her husband David kept me from being by Tatiana's side and from attending the funeral ceremony. I was able to join other friends a month later for the spreading of Xavier's ashes in the channel. The forlorn sound of the ship's horn as we circled the spot would forever be engraved in my memory.

It was a very, very sad time — a dark time — particularly for Tatiana but also for all of us who had known and appreciated Xavier so much. Tatiana's natural resilience, aided by her beloved dog Pioss, her recently adopted kitten Kiska, the support of all her many friends, and the ongoing challenges of life enabled her to move slowly on with the next chapters of her life.

These recent losses of people so near and dear to me, while clearly not a surprise given our age group, were all too many reminders of the fragility of life. Of course, I had had to deal in the past with the deaths of my parents, Diane, other friends, and a dear cousin. Nevertheless, these latest deaths were more distressing since they were decidedly closer to home. And then came Paula's news about her stroke, another disturbing reminder that at my age, death was not that far away.

The end of August in any year was never a particularly good time for me to be facing those gloomy thoughts. A former therapist once called my mood at the end of the summer "anniversary depression" since my birthday happened to be the same day as that of my wedding, Diane's funeral, and the birthdays of my father and one former, now deceased, boyfriend. And more recently, the same day as the death of my last living aunt.

But facing these realities was necessary, whether at the end of August or sometime later. In our phone call, Paula said she was ready to die — might even welcome it — so long as it was quick and she didn't linger. I responded to her reflections on our lives to date: "Yes, I agree. We have both lived good and full lives, but I, for one, am not ready to die, despite my ever-increasing number of wrinkles and strange aches and pains." Then I added, "There is too much left for me to learn, too many places to explore, people to meet, nieces and nephews to watch continuing to grow up, and now there is another generation for me to know as well."

No, I thought, *I am not ready to die, so long as I can keep my wits about me.*

When my Aunt Estelle had died, our family had held a celebration of her life. Those present were asked to share memories about her. What was the story that I wanted my family to tell about me? That was most likely one of the reasons why I had written Jeanne's story and was writing its sequel. I wanted my relatives to remember certain things about our family, especially about Jeanne and our French roots. I also thought it was important for them to recognize the legacy of independent women in our family history — women who emigrated without husbands or other family and those who moved away from home to find a better, or at least a different, future.

Whenever I would meet people in France, they would often ask about my family, perhaps wondering how and why I was able to simply pick up and spend so much time in France, so far away from them. I would usually respond, somewhat lightly, "Oh, I am single and don't have children, but I do have a cat!" Then I would add, "I do have family back in the States — two brothers and two sisters, four nieces and two nephews, and now a grandniece and two grandnephews, but they live in many different locations in the States, far from one another. I love them all, and we regularly stay in touch."

My decision to come to France and stay for several years could indeed say something about the sort of connections we did have, particularly as far as people in France were concerned, most of whom had closer ties — both physical and emotional — with family members. In one of my scrapbooks, I once found a Christmas picture of the five of us siblings as young children in pajamas, posing and smiling on the stairway in our home in Nashua. I had memories of us playing together during the summer and recollections of Sunday dinners at the dining room table. Yet I also remembered fights, both physical and verbal, and a lot of teasing that could be biting and not genuinely good-humored. We didn't share a lot of childish laughter, giggles, silly games, hugs, or other signs of affection. My godmother once observed that I seemed to be smiling more at the age of fifty than I did as a child growing up.

In those respects, I am not sure how different we were from other families growing up in the 50's and 60s except perhaps for the absence of an extended family. In all likelihood, other families shared the same issues of old stereotypes that refused to die, sibling rivalries and somewhat painful memories like the one of my brother Marc, who knew I was deathly afraid of spiders, pasting a giant black plastic one to the ceiling above my bed and then laughing hysterically at my screams when I climbed into bed.

After our parents sold the one place on Taft Street that could have been called our family home, they soon moved to Arizona to get away from the cold winters. So, unlike Jeanne whose descendants remained in or around one village for at least five generations and many of whom still lived there, none of us had the same sense of belonging to any one home or one town.

Nevertheless, we all managed to survive our childhoods and live relatively healthy and prosperous lives. As we grew older, we celebrated holidays together until marriages and geographical moves made getting together more difficult and less frequent. I moved to California with my then husband, and Carla moved to Seattle. The others stayed in New England. Eventually, I moved back to the East Coast, alone. Carla married David and stayed in Seattle. Later my brother Marc moved with his wife Susan to New Mexico. Dana and his wife Ginna established a second home close to them there, but they still lived part of the year at their place in Vermont. Only my sister Laurie remained in New Hampshire.

Over the years, our relationships have had their ups and downs, but we have remained a family. We all attended the memorial service for our parents in December 1994. My sisters and I took my four nieces to France a few years later, and there was one memorable family reunion in Quebec in 2004. There were other get-togethers at graduations, weddings, birthdays, and holidays. With a few exceptions, it was usually a combination of the five siblings — usually with spouses, significant others, and offspring. Rarely did our gatherings involve anyone else other than a couple of cousins.

Based on some notes that I recently found from 1994, the year my parents died, I had at some point wanted to improve my relations with my family — at least then. In that blue travel journal, written eight years later in 2002, however, I had one single item relating to family: "Live long enough to see my nieces and nephews reach the age of fifty." Fortunately, I still had a few years to go on that item since Max, the youngest, just turned twenty-five in October 2019. And if I added grand-nephews and a grand-niece into the mix, I could live to be well over 100!

While my relationships with my siblings had ebbed and flowed over the years, my role as "Auntie Lynne" with my nieces and nephews had grown stronger. I wasn't sure that being an aunt and a great-aunt (or sister even!) had always been my highest priority, although I did play a fairly involved role in helping to raise my twin nieces through their time in college and beyond. And, because of our age differences, I could say that I had become a substitute grandmother for Carla's children, Max and Riley, who grew up without grandparents.

As my role evolved, I had never become that free spirited "Auntie Mame" of movie fame but I was for sure the aunt who had never settled in any one place for long, except for those twenty years in Boston. I was also the aunt who, as my nieces and nephews became adults, had hosted "meet-ups" in various cities in Europe. The cottage in Dieppe had already provided occasions for visits. I knew that my nieces Riley, Raina, and Zoe were all eager to visit me and that Max, Maron, and Cyrus were looking forward to returning as well.

And despite the distance separating us, my siblings have responded willingly when I have reached out to them for support. Carla and Dana helped me in my trips to France in 2017 and 2018. Carla assumed responsibility for managing my mail and we talk frequently, not just about the mail. And Marc has remained the executor of my estate. In general, however, it's safe to say that because of the distance that separated our homes in the States for decades and perhaps because of my independent spirit, my years in France had not significantly altered our sibling bonds.

Because we were spread out all over the United States, I had usually tried to create a family wherever I lived. That's what I imagined Jeanne did when she arrived in Quebec without any apparent familial connections and when she found herself in need of friendship and support. I built my family of friends through joining church congregations, developing ties with colleagues at work, and by finding friends who shared joint interests, such as politics, hiking, bridge, dream work, and yoga. In California, particularly after my divorce, I held Thanksgiving dinners and celebrated other holidays with the family I had created. And that tradition had continued in France, as I constantly searched for the ingredients to make a real American Thanksgiving dinner.

When Carla and David were in Dieppe for a visit in October 2019, we didn't talk much about family or my plans for the future. They had arrived from London via the ferry on a rather rough crossing. We took the Varengeville walk, actually completing it this time, had dinner with Nadine, took a couple of days to visit the landing beaches in lower Normandy, and then met up with Yann for that awesome tour of Mont-Saint-Michel. We were able to spend brief moments with Tatiana before we left to play tourists in Amiens on the way to Calais to see them off, back to England with a smoother ride on the Eurostar train. It had been a great visit, and we probably hadn't wanted to color it with too many deep and dark thoughts or any conversation about the future. And although I did have an appointment to renew my visa for what would be my fourth year in France, I hadn't made any definite decisions regarding any long-term plans beyond that.

After they left, however, I began to think that I honestly did want to stay on in France for at least a couple more years. I had had so much fun with them showing off the French countryside and visiting with my French friends. There continued to be too many nascent friendships to deepen, and too much still to learn, see and discover. I knew I wasn't ready to return to the States, especially since I no longer had a home there — in any event, not a physical one.

At the same time, I was starting to feel the need to have my own things around me — my three vaults of belongings and the other paraphernalia scattered among relatives and at the bank. I had lived long enough in a rental cottage with someone else's pots and pans and furniture. And although I had bought my own linens and had added a few kitchen utensils, some dishes that a friend had given me, and plenty of books and papers, it still didn't feel like home, no matter what I did.

Seriously contemplating that the life and community I had been building in France was worth keeping, at least for a few more years, I began the search for a new place to live in Dieppe. It was becoming clear to me that I did in fact need some sort of anchor in my life. The little town on the English Channel was indeed becoming home, just not the cottage on the lane beside the blue garage door!

Still, I had reservations about finding another place to live since a more permanent move to France could possibly bring complications. If I found the right place, I would have to sign a lease. Buying real estate as a seventy-something-year-old American would bring too many financial and logistical problems if I happened to die in France. Besides, the financial counselor at my French bank said I was too old to get a mortgage! Signing a lease would mean a commitment to stay on, presumably for another year and possibly more. Not an insignificant decision.

That pending decision brought me to the subject of selfishness, in the sense of thinking only about myself. Would extending my adventure in France thousands of miles away from my family for a few more years mean that I was being selfish, or at least inconsiderate, or — worse yet — irresponsible?

I hadn't thought so until I started reflecting on the situation. What would I do if something happened to one of my siblings, nieces, or nephews? Fortunately, they all had family nearby, so my physical presence would not be necessary, but how would I be able to say goodbye? Equally as important, what would happen if I needed help? Or what would happen if I died an ocean away?

My sudden death could be a problem that needed to be discussed. After all, I knew Carla's husband David had had to address this situation when his brother died unexpectedly and alone. In order to manage many loose ends and close out his estate, David and his sister had had to make several trips to and from his brother's home on the other side of the United States.

My demise in any unexpected way in France could cause similar and even more complications. It would require international flights at great expense and significant time commitment and would force my heirs to deal with the details of death in a foreign country and language.

Despite these potential problems, I also knew that any move back to the States would require me to start over building a community of friends and set of activities. I would be forced to find a new set of challenges to keep busy. I wasn't sure I had the energy or the desire to do that without a driving reason.

Why did I need to go back to the States? I wondered. *How should I weigh possible problems for my family against enjoying my life in France?* I did need to ensure that they all knew that a decision to stay on in France did not mean that I didn't love them. I hoped that they wouldn't see me as abandoning them, rather that I would be pursuing another life.

I had tried my best to foresee potential problems and to simplify my life with careful estate and financial planning. I'd executed a will, although I couldn't make the same living arrangements that Jeanne had made with her sons. I had contacted a notary in France to create the documents needed to avoid any additional complications dealing with my French bank accounts and other possessions. But the reality of needing to make these arrangements was certainly something to consider and not take lightly.

A few weeks after Carla and David returned to the States, we talked on the phone. I raised the possibility of staying in France and shared my concerns that my death a continent away could raise problems. Her reply was quite philosophical: "Well, if something happened to you there, we would have to sort it all out and close out your life there, not an easy thing to do at any distance. But I've already talked with Raina about that possibility. We would do what we needed to do."

And when I asked Carla if she thought I was being selfish, she responded sweetly as only she could do, "Yes, you are indeed being selfish and irresponsible, but so what?"

Part Five

CASTING ANCHOR

TWENTY-ONE

SAYING GOODBYE

I was once told that there is no exact translation in French for the word "discombobulating." Perhaps *très, très perturbant* or *déstabilisant* would do. It's something like feeling as if the world had been turned upside down. That was definitely what the months had been like since November 2019 through the end of the year. And, as it turned out, that was how the new year could be described as well.

It had all started in November after Carla and David's visit when I began to seriously consider the idea of staying in France more permanently – even if it could or would be seen as selfish! After three years in France and after the third renewal of my visa, it was time to make a decision. I needed to be able to finally answer my brother Marc's question, "Are you an ex-pat now?"

I could still see many reasons in favor of staying in France and hadn't found many to leave, and right when I didn't think I was looking, I found the apartment of my dreams. Well, it wasn't perfect, but it had many advantages and one single real drawback – no bathtub.

A casual inquiry to a colleague about any availability of apartments in her building, which was well located and quite desirable, had connected me to a real estate agent who then led me to a possible rental in an even more desirable building, the most impressive in Dieppe, in my opinion. Despite being a bit shabby with age, Castel Royal A offered incredible views of the English Channel. Built in 1901, it sits imposingly on the boulevard facing the channel. None of the other buildings along the beach could match its height of six stories, and only one could be considered equal to its elegance. I had often noticed it on my walks along

Stairway in Castel Royal

the esplanade and wondered what it would be like to live there.

A former hotel, it had a truly amazing, two-story-high entry hall with twelve gigantic columns, an intricate mosaic floor, exquisitely carved moldings, floor-to-ceiling mirrors, and a most spectacular marble stairway that curled gracefully up the six flights of stairs.

The current building, I discovered, was the second on the site, replacing a hotel built around 1838 during the time when Dieppe was becoming so fashionable as a resort for both Parisians and English visitors. In 1888, Mary Cassatt's brother spent a month with his family in the hotel presumably enjoying time with artists Edgar Degas and Jacques-Émile Blanche, who had homes nearby, and with Mary, who was summering in a neighboring town.

In 1900, the building had been sold to a British group who demolished it and in less than nine months built a grand hotel on the former foundation. Advertised in British newspapers as one of the finest hotels in France, Hotel Royal offered fabulous views of the channel, renowned cuisine, stylish dining facilities, grand banquet rooms, a reading room on the ground floor, and smoking and billiard rooms on the lower floors. With proximity to a golf course and the very popular casino, it attracted visits from the British upper class, American Hollywood actors, and European royalty.

During World War I, the hotel served as a hospital and was subsequently reopened to guests in 1921 after much restoration. Unfortunately, the hotel's owners could not retain its profitability during the following years, given economic troubles in Europe and rivalry with the more fashionable resorts of Deauville and Honfleur. It was sold in 1938 and turned into apartments. Its name was changed to

Castel Royal, but the former hotel's initials remained in the mosaic on the floor at the front entry.

With the fall of France nine months after the start of World War II, the hotel served as one of the headquarters for the occupying German army. Supposedly traces of their presence had been found in the lower level, which was later converted into storage rooms. Along with many other buildings in Dieppe, the hotel suffered significant damage during the war. Beginning in 1947, the French state offered concessions to individuals wishing to renovate the roughly fifty apartments which were then sold off as condominiums, or *copropriétés*. The courtyard in the rear was eventually turned into a parking area, as was the circular entrance in the front. The restaurant was replaced in 1980 with a rather unsightly addition to the front of the building.

Among the first to accept the government's offers were the parents of the current owner of the soon-to-be-available apartment. They purchased the copropriété with its four rooms, plus a kitchen and bath, on the fourth floor — the only floor where the stained-glass windows in the stairwell landing had been retained. The new owners slightly lowered the ceilings to save energy, added many fine touches, and turned the place into a real home. Their two children were born in the apartment. They subsequently moved to a large family home near the castle, rented out the apartment for several decades, and then returned to live out the rest of their years, looking out over the English Channel. When the surviving parent died in 2017, the heirs took some time before deciding to keep the apartment and offer it for rent.

For my first visit to see the place, I came with a list of "needs" and "wants" and three friends. Tatiana was one of them, and, though she had recently moved into Castel Royal B — the annex around the corner — she was initially able to be quite objective. My list was slightly different from the one I had made over three years ago, but it still began with "cats accepted" and "calm." This time, I also wanted charm, as well as a view opening onto green space, privacy (no facing building), a balcony or terrace, a top floor location, a bathtub, wood floors, and good closet space. Most of all, I wanted it to feel like a home, a cozy and permanent setting, not merely a temporary stop or vacation cottage on my way to somewhere else.

As we walked through the living room, dining room, office, and bedroom — all with wonderful unobstructed views over the channel — then through the small library nook, into the very large bathroom, and then into the kitchen, all tucked away behind the main rooms, I saw clearly that many of my needs could be met but not all. It was certainly charming, offered privacy, and accepted cats. However, in some respects, it was actually a bit too large to be cozy; the bathtub that had been there had unfortunately been recently replaced by a very large shower; and it was not located on the top floor of the building.

All three friends convinced me that I could make do and that the channel views, the light from the floor-to-ceiling French doors in every one of the main rooms, the high ceilings with moldings, the solid wood-paneled doors, the amazing amount of closet and storage space, and a front door that opened onto the windowed stairwell instead of a dark corridor all more than compensated for the lack of a bathtub. The apartment came with a parking space of sorts, a first-come-first-served allocation of considerably fewer spaces than the number of residents. There was even storage space, to be shared with the owner, in the rather scary lower level that felt more like a dungeon.

"You need to be closer to town, closer to us, your friends who could help you out in emergencies," they counselled. "You will figure out a way to keep Quincie from jumping off the balcony." "You can learn to live with the shower. It's safer and more environmentally friendly." "We'll help you make it cozy."

"And," the rental agent added, "since many of the apartments are second residences for Parisians, it's a quiet building. There shouldn't be a lot of noise from above. Plus parking is not really a problem given all the free spaces along the esplanade."

There were still several pieces of furniture in the rooms, pictures still hanging on the walls, and items left in closets and cupboards from the former occupants, all waiting to be removed. Nevertheless, I was able to begin envisioning my furniture, or what was left of it, in the space, which was a bit larger than my Charlestown condo. I tried to imagine writing from what would be my office, looking out through the French doors, over the esplanade, and onto the beach and the English Channel. It would be quite a change from the small office in the cottage which could sometimes feel cramped and a bit somber. There was a back hall closet for coats, something I had never had and had always wanted in Charlestown. I would have a kitchen with a full dishwasher and full-sized refrigerator and plenty of drawers and spaces for my own dishes, glasses, silverware, utensils, pots, and pans.

The next several weeks involved return visits with the rental agent and with my friends to continue to get their opinions and help with translations, Tatiana by now much more encouraging and much less objective. I met with the owner, a very gracious and quite accomplished painter of impressionist art, to discuss the terms of the lease. I then had to put together a list of additional issues to be resolved since the apartment had been empty for roughly two years. The time also demanded considerable reflection and analysis on my part: *Can I really live without a bathtub? Will I get tired of the red walls and matching carpeting in the foyer and library area? Are they too much like an entry to a bordello? What will I do with visitors since there is no guest room? What will it be like to live in a large apartment building since I have never done that? Do the financials make sense? What about the noise from the street and from neighbors above, below, and beside me?*

My niece Maron arrived a few days before Christmas. We visited the apartment together. She added her comments to those of my friends, "Oh, Auntie Lynne, you have to live here! It is totally, absolutely awesome!"

We placed the decision about the apartment on hold, took a day trip by bus to Bruges, Belgium, and spent some vacation time together in Dieppe. Despite the theft of my mobile phone, we were able to enjoy our traditional Christmas visit at the Rouen Christmas market with Nelly and her family. Once I had reported the theft to the local gendarmerie and arranged for a replacement phone, we went off to visit Paris for a couple of days before she returned to the States.

After seeing Maron off at the airport, I began to feel the stress of the decision about the apartment on the bus back to Dieppe. My body was telling me something. Tatiana suggested that I was tired from exercising too much, walking up and down the cliffs too many times, and all the rest of my activities.

One evening a couple of days later after dinner with Tatiana, as I climbed the cliff back to my cottage, I started to think that maybe she was right. I asked myself, *Is it just age, too much exercise, or do I need new vitamins?*

But looking back, there was certainly a lot of anxiety mixed in with any other problems. There was too much going on; I was trying to handle too many issues at the same time. There were open items about the apartment, questions about the logistics and costs of moving my belongings from Boston to France, issues about giving notice on the cottage, and plans for my trip to the United States. I had not been able to do any more research on Jeanne's third husband, and I still couldn't answer the question from friends about my second book.

However, ignoring all the stress, I decided to pursue the apartment. As soon as most of my questions about it were satisfactorily resolved, I signed a three-year lease on what might be the last place where I would ever live but what would probably be the most spectacular place, certainly the most elegant. I would deal with the challenges. I would make it my home.

Before I could return to the States, I had a lot to do to arrange for the move. Again, I began preparing lists — this time of things to be done in France, as well as in Boston, in order to tie up the loose ends of my life there and to move on to the next chapter.

After arranging for Quincie's care during my stay in the States, I next needed to set up times with the moving company in Boston where all my worldly goods had been stored since the sale of my condo the year before. Because I hadn't known that I would be moving to France when I sold my place, I needed to go through the boxes and decide what to continue to keep and what to find homes for, primarily electrical items that would not function well in France.

Medical appointments had to be scheduled, as did lunch and dinner dates with family and friends. I also had to put together several sets of documents, including one for the French consulate in Boston, to meet the requirements for moving my belongings to France. Another set was required for establishing fiscal residence in Seattle, where I had decided I would most likely live if I ever decided to return to the States. Fiscal residence was essential for registering to vote and for obtaining a US driver's license before that birthday deadline to avoid having to take another driving test.

I celebrated New Year's Eve with friends and then joined Joëlle for our traditional New Year's Day walk. In late January I went back to Rouen to pick up my visa for the year. Four weeks later, while continuing to work down the items on the lists, I handed over checks for the deposit, the first month's rent, and for my share of the cost of some work to be done on the windows in the apartment. I arranged with Mikhail, a very clever handyman whom Tatiana had found, to remove the faded and antiquated wallpaper in the bedroom and paint the walls during my time away. I took Quincie to the cattery. Isabelle drove me to the bus and waved good-bye as I rode off to de Gaulle airport so I could fly to Boston to settle my affairs there with plans to then fly on to Seattle.

My Charlestown friend Seta met me at the airport in Boston and drove me to the hotel where I planned to stay for the next nine days. During my time in Boston, I managed to check off most of the items on my list and see family and friends. At the storage facility, I winnowed down the ninety-eight items to eighty-nine after finding those appliances and other items to give away.

Over a cup of tea when we met in New Hampshire, halfway between her home and Boston, my sister Laurie asked me, "What is it you miss most about not living in the States?"

"Not much," was my reply, "except, of course, my family, enjoying good times together and watching my nieces and nephews and their children grow up."

I drove further north in order to have lunch with my niece Zoe and her son Quinn. Before we said goodbye, we exchanged the silverware and books that she had been storing in Vermont for some of the things I didn't need in France but which she could use in her new home. I then drove back to Boston to continue to attack my list of action items.

As I later watched my worldly goods being loaded into the container that would take them to France and said goodbye to the city that I had called home for the last two decades of my life, I reflected on my answer. *It is true*, I thought. *I would miss my family but I wasn't going to miss much else!* I would have relatively few regrets not living in the United States. That was perhaps because my family was indeed so spread out across the US and they were all busy with their own lives, but also because there was too much to look forward to in France, including possible visits with them in my new home.

A couple of short trips to Charlestown to pick up the contents of the safe deposit box further convinced me. I was too disengaged from what was going on and except for a few friends, I didn't have many real ties any more to keep me there. Plus, I was getting used to the calm and convenience of living in a small town in France.

Then it was off to Seattle, where word was beginning to spread about a strange new virus. In fact, in the middle of my time in Boston, Tatiana had written, asking me to bring back masks and hand sanitizers since there were none available in Dieppe. In Boston, there were ominous signs in the drug stores everywhere I looked: "Sorry, but we have no masks, no hand sanitizers."

I got the same answer at the airport shops in Dallas during my three-hour layover stop on the way to Seattle. No luck. I then spent the rest of my wait observing a slice of life in the United States. I felt disconnected, the same feeling I had had in Boston. I was an observer, no longer a participant in that life. After three years in France, did I feel "American" or "somewhere in between," as that English woman had remarked at the church conference in Rouen two years earlier?

In Seattle, I spent time over the weekend visiting with Carla, David, Max and Riley and with my niece Raina who had come up from San Francisco to see us. On Monday morning, David drove me to Seattle's Department of Motor Vehicles, where I waited for an hour and a half along with several others who had also arrived early. (Apparently, there are waits in governmental agencies everywhere.) When I was finally called to speak with an agent, I anxiously went through all the documents I had brought with me but learned that she wanted only one of them to prove residency in Seattle. Obtaining my license and becoming a registered voter in the state of Washington turned out to be much easier than expected.

Checking those two critical tasks off the list meant I could now relax and spend more time with Carla and her family. I could also continue to buy the items I had not yet been able to find in France, search in vain for masks for Tatiana, and then start to panic over being able to return to France from the city with one of the first serious outbreaks of the virus in the United States.

On our last night together, Carla, David, and I had dinner with some of their neighborhood friends, most of whom I knew after many visits over the past thirty-eight years, usually at Christmas but not always. The conversation during our meal was primarily about the virus, especially about the outbreaks in nearby senior living facilities. They all seemed to know someone who had had contact with someone else close to the outbreak, further raising my fears about my return. How little we knew then about what was to come and how long it would last.

The next morning, Carla and David drove me to the airport. We said goodbye, not knowing when we would see each other again. As I boarded the Air France flight, I thought, *Will they let me back in? What will I find there when I land?*

TWENTY-TWO

DISCOMBOBULATION

After a long ten-hour flight, I landed back in Paris on March 8, 2020, just in time, it appeared, since the French borders were closed not long afterwards. Although expecting to be challenged at customs about exposure to the virus, I made it through without a question or a request for contact details. *What a contrast*, I said to myself, *to the experience I had had in Australia in 2009 during that other major epidemic.*

Back then, at the airport upon arriving in Perth, I had had to provide all my contact information for my stay in Australia and back in the States as well. A health official had meticulously tracked me down after leaving notes at my B and B and calling my sister in the States to check on me!

On the way back to Dieppe in the car I had rented, I picked Quincie up from the cattery. We returned to the cottage and to an uncertain situation in a world that was beginning to be turned upside down by the coronavirus. *How will I get the apartment cleaned? How will I move? How will the deliveries of a mattress, box springs, and a washing machine be accomplished? What about my shipment from the States?*

The lockdown in France began on March 17, nine days after my return. We didn't know how long it would last. We were ordered to stay at home except for necessary trips for food, medicine, and medical and administrative appointments. We were allowed one hour of exercise outside of our homes but were limited to a one-kilometer radius. We were required to carry a document attesting to our reasons for venturing out and risked a major fine for violation of the new orders. The one time I was stopped by a policeman to check my attestation gave me a sense of what it must have been like in Dieppe under the German occupation during World War II.

Fortunately, life in twenty-first century Dieppe went on to a limited degree. We were able to go about our daily lives since bakeries, groceries, butcher shops, chocolate shops, fish stores, tobacco shops, supermarkets, and pharmacies were all still open. Unlike stories from the United States, there were sufficient supplies of toilet paper available, but pasta shelves were empty. The weekly farmers' markets were closed down as were all nonessential places of business, including hair salons. Buses made limited routes. Schools and universities were closed, and all communal activities were disbanded. Physical contact, kisses on the cheeks, and handshakes with friends or strangers were abandoned. We were going to have to find other ways to reach out and touch each other.

My pending move made the situation even more stressful. As soon as I arrived back in Dieppe and before the lockdown was announced, I had expected to go ahead with the move as soon as the work that needed to be done at the apartment was finished. In the couple of trips I was able to make there to check on progress, I found that workmen were still putting finishing touches on the newly painted walls and were still in the process of installing double-paned glass on the French doors. Because of weather problems, they were behind schedule, and that delay further complicated my plans.

With all of the workmen's equipment there, it was hard to tell exactly what the place was going to look like when they were done. The walls in the living and dining rooms and the office had been cleared of the many paintings that had hung there. Most of the furniture and other articles that had been here before I left for the States were gone, except for those few pieces the landlord had kindly agreed to leave for me because I would not have had anywhere to sit or eat until my shipment arrived from the United States, now projected to be sometime in April.

I started packing up my things in the cottage and began to move a few boxes of items that I had no immediate use for. I used Tatiana's car to transport them over to the apartment and was able to leave them in the bathroom (the large shower space came in handy), out of the way of the workmen. That was all before the total shutdown was announced.

Because of the lockdown and the French system for dealing with the economic impact of it, the real estate agent I had been dealing with was laid off. That meant we did not conduct the normally required final inspection of the condition of the apartment's walls, floors, or appliances. Nor did I receive a listing of the accounts or contact numbers for the utilities or of what the landlord was leaving behind for my use. All that didn't seem a problem at the time, although it would later cause some minor complications.

My new washing machine was delivered and installed because deliveries from small businesses were allowed. I was able to arrange to have the gas that had been turned off the year before turned back on. With the help of my housecleaner, who braved the restrictions, I began to clean the apartment to remove any last traces of the former occupants. I was all set to plan out the next ten days and to figure out how to continue the move with the appropriate attestation for reasons to be out of my home when I learned that the mattress and box springs that I had ordered back in January for my new apartment would not be delivered as scheduled. Luckily, I was able to stay in the cottage for a couple more weeks. I put the actual move on hold, although I continued to sneak things over to the new place. I couldn't wait!

When I received word that the ship with my container would be arriving shortly, I was hopeful. Then I learned that, right as the ship was arriving, new regulations were announced, prohibiting moving companies from completing any moves. My shipment had to be taken to a Paris warehouse until it could be delivered to me in Dieppe. Now, I had to wait.

Things could have been worse, I suppose, but it was all very unsettling. I decided to continue to move as much as I could since I found out I could not easily change the date for the transfer of my Internet service. Besides, I decided it was going to be easier and safer to be in town. Luckily, friends offered me a temporary solution for a bed. Isabelle lent me a blow-up mattress, and Tatiana offered a futon from her guest room to put underneath it so I could avoid sleeping too close to the floor.

I was therefore able to make a cozy nest for myself with the mattresses and a bedframe that Tatiana and I had found before I left for the States and that we had stowed in her storage unit until we could then bring it up to my place. In spite of that little nest and in spite of the fact that I had been dealing with a great deal of uncertainty and change over the past few years and should have been used to that sort of stress, the move to France combined with the confinement was more than I really wanted to handle. I felt I needed additional psychological support. Since our local church services had been suspended and had not yet been made available online, I started listening to Sunday services from a church I had attended in Boston. In one sermon, the senior minister shared her anxiety: "I can't see.... I can't see tomorrow.... I can't see next week. For those of us who live by our calendars that are either written or in our heads, it can be, oh, so hard to cope. But it will pass. There will be a tomorrow. It might be different from what we expected, but it will come. We need to have hope, patience, and creativity in order to deal with the uncertainty."

I tried to keep those thoughts in mind as the days went by, but I could not stop asking myself: *How can the weeks be even more discombobulating now than the weeks before I left?*

They were. So instead of making lists of tasks to be done, I tried to live with the uncertainty of not knowing how much longer the lockdown would last or what tomorrow would look like. I tried to avoid constantly peering around the corner, trying to see a month in advance. To help deal with the stress, I took long walks, sometimes alone and sometimes with friends, but always respecting the time and distance restrictions. I did not, however, have the discipline to watch exercise videos online. Nor could I take any nice long baths.

At the same time, while trying to live day-to-day as much as I could rather than trying to plan ahead, I wanted to bring some sort of order to these bewildering days. That proved to be impossible, no matter how much I tried. As I sat in the living room in the landlord's yellow armchair and gazed out at the channel's waves, I leafed through the creativity book I had written. In it, I had included a quote by Helen Keller, who had overcome her blindness and deafness to live a productive and memorable life:

> Have you ever been at sea in a dense fog, when it seemed as if a tangible white darkness shut you in, and the great ship, tense and anxious, groped her way toward the shore with plummet and sounding-line, and you waited with beating heart for something to happen?

I could answer yes, although for another reason. In Dieppe, the city of four ports, we were all waiting for something to happen — with beating hearts, for sure.

I was somewhat also consoled by thinking of Jeanne and how she must have felt living in such isolation in the Quebec frontier, through the long winter and without neighbors or possible communication with the outside world, and having to deal with the epidemics that brought death to at least three of her children and two of her husbands. Hers had obviously been a much harder life with even more isolation than we were being forced to experience. How had she persevered? We were fortunate enough to be able to talk with friends on the phone or via the Internet and easily get to a nearby grocery store or a hospital. And we had streetlights, heat, and running water. We also had hope that cures and vaccines would be found, that this pandemic would end, and that we could return one day to some sort of normal.

These thoughts about Jeanne put my anguish in better perspective, but it was still tough going in twenty-first century Dieppe. I had another telephone conversation with Theodora, my friend in Australia. We talked about how much change was too much change. Her advice: "First, you need to step back and look at all the changes you have put yourself through in the last few years. Make a list, and then acknowledge them. As you're doing that, you might also think about how you could add more joy and lightness to your life."

After we hung up the phone, I had to admit that the changes had indeed been intense, as well as immense. The lockdown was forcing me to step back and take a breath. I tried to follow her advice, but relaxing and finding pleasure and light-hearted joy in everyday life were not part of my normal operating mode.

Despite the encouragement that Theodora's suggestions and my thoughts of Jeanne provided, I again wondered, *Why am I doing this? Why couldn't I be content to live in the United States near Carla and retire in Seattle?*

"No," Carla said when we talked. "Seattle is a great place to live, even during the pandemic, but it's not France. You'd be bored!"

TWENTY-THREE

MARKINGS

Living through the lockdown and moving to France certainly kept me from being bored, in the short term anyway. I stayed as busy as I could.

During those first few weeks, somehow I had managed, with the aid of Tatiana's car, to make ten or eleven trips to move my things — papers, books, clothes, some dishes and wine glasses I had bought at a flea market, and miscellaneous odds and ends — to the new apartment. I did this miraculously without being stopped by the police and wondering how I had accumulated so much stuff. In each of all the moves I had made in my life, I had usually tried to downsize to get rid of unused items and clothes or other things I felt I really didn't need any more through garage sales and donations. But somehow I continued to accumulate. Could I ever stop trying to surround myself with things that at some point in my life I had considered essential but which really weren't all that important? Apparently not!

Finally, on April 13, 2020, I made one more trip to bring Quincie over to our new apartment. Once we were inside, I unzipped her carrying case to let her out. As usual, she jumped out and quickly started exploring our new home. As she tentatively wandered around the rooms, she rubbed her cheeks against the doors and their frames and the few remaining pieces of furniture. Quincie had not been eating her normal amount of food since I had returned from the States, so I was worried about her health. These movements raised concerns: *Is she developing teeth problems? Is it a sign of something worse?*

When I shared my concerns with two friends, I got similar answers: "Oh, she's only marking her new territory."

They were both correct. As I read on a couple of websites, cats emit pheromones from "many scent glands around their heads: around their mouths, their chins, their cheeks, their necks, and their ears. These scent glands are activated when cats rub up against things. [Leaving pheromones] is their way of marking their territory and claiming ownership of their environment."[12] It's their way of signaling that the objects are safe and familiar.

According to my friend Carol when I described Quincie's behavior: "That's wonderful. That means she's accepted her new home."

I'd had cats as pets for over thirty years. Never in all those years had I ever heard or learned about these *markings*, so I breathed a sigh of relief that Quincie was comfortable here. And as the days went by, she began to reestablish her usual patterns of behavior, so I assumed that she was settling in and that her health was fine.

Reflecting on this new information, I looked around our new apartment and thought, *Now how do I make this place my home? How do I mark it?*

There were still many traces from the prior residents in addition to those pieces of furniture. Flowered drapes that were definitely not to my taste still hung in the living room. In the dining room, the slightly antiquated paper on the walls was coming unglued at the seams in numerous places. Tattered silk curtains hung on the doors to the foyer, and the red drapes on the French doors had been faded by the sun. In the office, there were more faded drapes matching the burnt-orange silk-grass wallpaper; I found a note card left in a desk drawer. Elsewhere, I discovered a random playing card tucked away on a shelf in the coat closet along with a few odd hangars, a photo wedged behind a bookshelf, distinctive scents in long-closed spaces, a ten-volume set of the *Grand Larousse Encyclopédique*, strange arrangements of cabinets, shelves, and cubbyholes in the kitchen, bathrooms, and office, and other unexpected finds. The bathroom and kitchen were in fairly good shape, although the white tiles on the kitchen floor were pock-marked and scratched and would need to be replaced.

---

12. https://www.animalfriends.co.uk/blog/why-does-my-cat-rub-his-face-on-me/, accessed August 16, 2021.

What remained were off-white walls in the salon, tasteful moldings along all the ceilings, lovely wooden floors that showed remarkably little wear, a magnificent walnut Normandy wardrobe and acceptable flowered drapes in the bedroom, two beautiful crystal chandeliers, some marble-topped tables, the red wallpaper and carpet in the foyer, four rooms with breathtaking views of the English Channel, and an abundance of space and light. There would now be plenty of room for my dishes and other kitchen things, my clothes, my vitamin and bathroom supplies, and anything else I wanted to store away. Ample opportunities existed for me to add my own pheromones to the apartment to make it my own, bringing in some of my own personality without losing traces of the French flavor, to make it a home — my home.

It was going to take time, not only because I wanted to be thoughtful about the task, but also because the lockdown and new rules meant that my furniture and other belongings were still residing in a Paris warehouse. Meanwhile, I spent time trying to figure out how to *mark* the apartment for myself. What colors should I add, if any, to the mostly white kitchen? Where could I find hooks to hang up my jeans instead of folding them, "the way it's done in France?" Would the books that remained from my culling fit on the bookshelves along with all those encyclopedia volumes? Where did I want to hang the pictures that would soon arrive from the United States? How would it feel to have the shelves in the office organized with all my files and documents? How was my Arts and Crafts dining room furniture going to look in my new apartment in this "art deco" building with its slightly peeling yellow painted walls, graceful sculptured detail along the ceilings, and the spectacular winding staircase?

I knew I could not add too much since I had never been a collector of lots of knickknacks, photos, pictures, and other mementos, and I had no interest in starting. In the past my markings had been my books, crammed into bookshelves upon bookshelves in the living room and office of my Charlestown apartment. They were reminders of my past, present, and future interests in history, Russia, leadership, management, self-help, religion, spirituality, creativity, Jung, France, Quebec, Australia, and the Filles du Roi. Stacked straight up, side by side, and sometimes on top of each other, they represented my engagement in my work, my studies, my travels, my accomplishments, and my struggles. I had had to have shelves and bookcases built to hold them all. They were my identity or, at least, significant parts of it.

Now most of them were gone. When I had packed them up and given away almost two dozen boxes of them before my final move and a multitude more over the past few years, I probably hadn't realized how important they all were to my life. I thought I was keeping simply those I really cared about or would need or read, but now I wasn't sure. Now I wondered how could I reestablish my identity without them. Had those books and other things that I had one time considered dispensable now somehow become precious? Were they gone forever or could they be replaced? Giving things away, I read somewhere, opened up all sorts of possibilities for filling the holes left behind. I wondered how I would fill that void.

I clearly needed to figure that all out if I wanted the apartment to be a real home. Could it be that without all my books? I decided not to wait until my shipment arrived from the Paris warehouse. Instead, I arranged to have the drapes in the office and dining room cleaned and managed to sneak the ones from the bedroom over to a seamstress to have them lined. I started searching on the web for new drapes for the living room. I rearranged the basement storage unit in anticipation of the arrival of my things. And I started chatting with a colleague who had helped me decorate my place in Charlestown.

One day, during my continued efforts to settle in, I remembered something that the author Thomas Moore had written about "soul of place." I found his email address and sent a message to him with a question about that reference, not knowing if it would ever reach him or whether he would respond. Incredibly it did and he did — that very day, in fact. In his response, Moore recommended a book that I then ordered. In it, I found passages he had written:

The need for home lies deep in the human heart.... Few things are more important than finding a home and working at it constantly to make it resonate with deep memories and fulfill deep longings....

The experience of home is so deep-seated that when we find it in our own houses or in the homes of others, we may feel enchantment thick in the air, and when we lack it in our daily experience, we may be haunted by its elusiveness....

The soul's need for home has to do not only with shelter and a house, but with more subtle forms, like the feeling that one is living in the right place, being around people who offer a sense of belonging, doing work that is truly appropriate, feeling maternally protected and enlivened..., being connected with the place in which we live and being enchanted by the sensation of home the place provides.[13]

According to the author Pico Iyer in a TED Talk he gave in 2013, home is not only physical. "That's a piece of soil, instead of a piece of soul," to borrow his words.

From both Iyer and Moore, I came to appreciate that "home is a work in progress," and I would probably forever be weaving new threads into the tapestry of my life. Home was not "merely the place where you happen to be born, it's the place where you become yourself," counselled Iyer. "And," he added, "it's only by stepping out of your life and the world, that you can see what you most deeply care about and find a home."[14]

Home was also the place, I decided, where I would continue to be nurtured, physically and emotionally, by deep and hopefully long-lasting connections. It was more than purely a residence, no matter

13. Thomas Moore, *The Re-enchantment of Everyday Life* (New York: Harper Perennial, 1997), 42-44.
14. Pico Iyer, TED Talk, "Where is Home?" July 17, 2013. (French version: "C'est où, 'chez soi?'" September 15, 2014.)

how rustic or elegant. It was a haven where friends would protect me and push me to step out of my life to see the world in a different light.

I was becoming more and more convinced that Jeanne's home in Dieppe, for no matter how long she had lived here, was going to be my home and Quincie's. It was as if my ancestor had welcomed me here. I felt Dieppe's magic and spirit. But I still wondered how to make my apartment in Castel Royal, my little castle, a real home — perhaps my last.

I knew it would take more than furnishings. Was I ready to become myself here? What was that going to take? How was I going to make this place a home without all my books? To reflect the old parts of me that I wanted to keep and to showcase the new facets that were becoming part of me? Once the shipment arrived, I would have my furniture, paintings, clothes, and other possessions to fill the rooms. I could find drapes for the living room, add plants, and figure out what to do about the balconies to keep Quincie safe, but what else would it take so that I could welcome my friends over, not simply to ooh and ahh over the view, but also to enjoy the warmth of their American friend's home?

TWENTY-FOUR

ADJUSTMENTS

By April 23, 2020, Quincie and I had been living in our new home for ten days. Actually, "camping" would have been a better word than "living" in that still uncertain world. The mattress and box springs that I had ordered back in January had still not been delivered. I was not convinced that the reason was entirely the lockdown, but it was difficult to get a straight answer because I was dealing with nuanced telephone conversations in a foreign language that I didn't totally understand and because I was receiving confusing, automated email messages from Customer Service representatives. The date for the arrival of my shipment from Boston, now in Paris, was also still unknown, but I was being kept better informed about its progress. Fortunately, my Internet connection had finally been installed, although after an unexplained delay of several days.

And I had that temporary sleeping arrangement, thanks to Tatiana and Isabelle and the bedframe. In the kitchen for cooking and eating, I had the dishes, silverware, pots and pans that I had brought over from the cottage. The appliances, including a microwave, dishwasher, stove, oven, and a washer-dryer, worked in the kitchen. The landlord had left a widescreen TV, somewhat comfortable chairs in the living room, a dining room table, and an old, somewhat classy desk in the office with a functional office chair. I had my computer and access to the web, so I could write, do limited research, and stay connected with family. There was hot water for showers, and I had friends nearby with whom I could share my feelings of distress.

And for some very strange reason, I had no aches and pains, no frozen jaws, no foot problems, and no aching hip. All those aging maladies that had plagued me for the last few years had disappeared. I hadn't had a cold in a couple of years. So, life, while very uncertain and most perturbing, was not primitive or uncomfortable or unhealthy.

Nevertheless, the unknowns of life caused by the pandemic and by the temporary solutions for comfortable living were taking their toll on one of us more than on the other. Quincie wanted me close to her whenever she ate, so I had to move her dish permanently to the dining room from the kitchen where I had had a spot picked out for it. Otherwise, she seemed to have adjusted fairly well, exploring new spaces and taking advantage of the additional spots for sleeping, hiding, and playing with her toys.

As for me, well — it had been a bit more difficult. Certainly, I was totally enjoying the views of the channel, the light all day long from the French doors, the spaciousness of the apartment, and the proximity to my friends and to the center of town. I had forgotten how comforting the sight of water could be. For most of my adult life, except for my years in Oklahoma and New Jersey, I had lived near an ocean or a river. Now, once again, I could enjoy the water. I could sit and watch the channel at high and low tides — sometimes with powerful waves crashing on the shore, sometimes with more gentle white caps, and sometimes with mere ripples and bands of blue. Often I could see fishing boats out on the water. One day I spied what I thought might be a seal swimming out there. They were rare around here but not unknown. I did contact the local aquarium but was not able to confirm whether it was actually a seal or merely a piece of wood floating among the waves.

At given times, I could view the arrival of the ferry or hear the sounding of the horn to signal its departure. And to be sure, at almost any time during the day, I could observe the flight of the seagulls outside my windows. I loved to watch them soar by or float on the wind or dive bomb after something on the esplanade. Sometimes when I would be writing at my desk and listening to music, I was positive that the seagulls flying by were keeping time with the music and were showing off their acrobatic skills.

Frequently, a large flock of them would fly majestically over the esplanade and then gracefully land on the grass in front of the building to perform intricate and what seemed to me to be synchronized dances across the esplanade's lawns. I tried but never could figure out who was the leader, who was orchestrating the configurations. Sometimes, they appeared to break up into groups or go off with a friend to — in my imagination — discuss the plans of the day or search for food.

Despite their entertaining maneuvers, the seagulls could be a nuisance as far as many of the Dieppe residents were concerned, including some of my friends, who disputed the reasons for the birds' protected status. They (the birds, not my friends) squawked and squealed and squabbled with each other. They tore up garbage bags and foraged through open trash bins, searching for food and leaving behind an awful mess. They also seemed to enjoy marking cars and my balconies, and sometimes even my windows, with their droppings.

The birds kept us company all year long as they soared over the channel and the esplanade. During the winter, even without the lockdown, the beach below them was relatively deserted. Only a few pedestrians strolled up and down the boardwalk when weather permitted, and occasionally a group of hardy souls could be seen walking through the water at low tide. The unobstructed view of the water was particularly enchanting, and the days tended to be rather quiet.

As I was settling into the apartment, I found these tranquil moments were, however, often interrupted by signs of life in the building. I was having to adapt to new noises — a door closing, conversations in the hallways, dogs yapping — stale odors in the elevator, and smells from meals being prepared elsewhere — some pleasant and some not. There were new living patterns from neighbors beside, above, and below me and new sounds from outside. The person who lived above me seemed to be perpetually rearranging furniture. In an apartment nearby, a dog barked at odd hours. And outside, there were all those annoying motorcycles and scooters with maladjusted exhaust pipes.

The COVID pandemic of course made things worse. The original end to the lockdown, which had begun on March 17, was originally set to end in fifteen days. That date was extended first to April 30 and then later to May 11, 2020. Throughout those eight long weeks, gym, bridge, and hiking activities were suspended. We cancelled the weekly lessons organized by some friends who were hoping to improve their English language skills. I no longer met with Martine for grammar lessons nor with Joël for our conversation exchanges. Tatiana and I cancelled the trip we had planned for a week in Russia: she had wanted to see her father, stepmother, and friends; and I, to witness the changes in that country since my last visit in 1983. I also abandoned my plans to attend the Democratic National Convention in Milwaukee, Wisconsin. I stopped taking the bus on Fridays to teach English to those delightful children. Restaurants and cafes were closed so we didn't have any place to meet outside our homes. The farmers' markets continued to be banned. While masks would not be mandatory until several months later, we still had to carry those attestations with justifications for being outside.

Some friends were stricter with the rules than others, but generally most communication was by phone or email. Tatiana and I arranged regular Sunday evening chats at six o'clock for cocktails over Skype with our friends Patricia and Pierre, who were confined to their home near Paris, but generally the two of us ignored the rules at home. We would sneak across the courtyard that joined our two buildings to share coffee or even have lunch together to catch up on the latest little bits of our lives, our pets, and new recipes.

We both tried to look at the brighter side of the situation. After watching Andrea Bocelli sing "Amazing Grace" on the piazza of Duomo di Milano against the backdrop of videos of Paris, London, and New York — all dramatically empty of life — I did my best to find some hope. I tried to see this unusual time, not only for all its positives gained from my decision to move, but also as an adventure and a chance to exercise another side of myself, using my creativity with decorating, adapting, resolving little items that annoyed me, and learning new coping skills to deal with strange noises and smells.

Each task was also another lesson in French. I had to call the plumber to start the furnace, figure out the trash and recycling schedule for the building, and make arrangements to have a mailbox assigned and my name added to the calling list at the front door. There had also been many lessons in learning patience and learning to stop, look, and listen in order to appreciate the sound of the waves at high tide swishing on the pebbles, the amazing bands of light on the water, and the streaks of color from the totally glorious sunsets — sunsets no longer seen just from a rearview mirror. On rare occasions, with the proper mix of clouds and light, I could even look to the east and catch the reflected rays of the rising sun. And once, early in the morning, I saw the moon, ablaze as a huge orange ball, as it set into the northwestern horizon.

Nevertheless, all of these challenges had to be managed amid the restrictions caused by the pandemic. There was a long list of things that I needed to do to legally reside in France, but I couldn't get them done because most administrative agencies were closed. There were also more things in the apartment that needed to be fixed or cleaned up, more items to buy to make the apartment a home for us, and generally more challenges after three years of calm, rather sedate living in the cottage. I couldn't tackle any of those tasks because most of the nonessential stores were closed. I did spend time searching the Internet for ideas and could have arranged for delivery of furniture bought there but was reluctant to do so. I wanted to be able to touch fabrics and sit in chairs to ensure they would work for me.

Life was not easy. My days were filled with minor chores and gave me barely any sense of accomplishment. It was difficult to continue my research and my writing since libraries and archives were closed. No matter, since I didn't have much energy — except, it seems, to follow the disturbing political news in the United States via CNN's newscast on television. I felt lucky if I could accomplish one semi-important thing in a day. One day, it was taking the sheets to the laundry, which fortunately was considered essential business and was still open; another was one more attempt to check on the status of my bed delivery; and another, the completion of a wash in my new washing machine. Or for exercise, walking up and down the lovely stairway that turned out to equal about ten flights of stairs because of the height of each of the six floors. Or a phone call with Carla or other family in the States. Or an hour spent outdoors, with or without Tatiana's company during her dog-walking excursions in the morning or afternoon. And even a short shopping trip in her husband's car that she had decided to keep. Since Tatiana didn't drive, I had now assumed the role of chauffeur whenever she needed a ride to the vet because of problems with her cat or dog or whenever we both wanted to stock up on groceries at the supermarket, all short excursions to break up our day.

Was this what retirement would be like? Little routine steps to take, none of which was very significant or too exhausting? Was that why I had resisted the idea? Did I really need to create a daily to-do list full of exciting new things to accomplish in order to stay energized, to feel as if I had purpose, and to avoid being bored?

TWENTY-FIVE

MOVING IN

Five days later, on Tuesday, April 28, 2020, I received one of the phone calls I had been waiting for. The voice on the other end was Jennifer's, my contact with the moving company here in France. "Lynne, I have some really good news for you! We have a crew in Paris who can deliver your shipment to Dieppe. They can arrive this coming Thursday morning. Is that going to work for you? Are you ready?"

After I told her that I would most definitely be ready and hung up the phone, I breathed a huge sigh of relief. I was finally going to be reunited with my belongings from the United States after their twelve months in storage in Boston, a voyage of six weeks on a freighter that took them from Boston through the Caribbean and the Panama Canal all the way to Peru, then back again through the Panama Canal to cross the Atlantic Ocean and to finally arrive in Le Havre, France, only to spend three more weeks of storage in a warehouse in Paris.

Of course, no one could have predicted the coronavirus pandemic, which began to seriously spread into France and the United States as the ship was scheduled to leave Boston. Nor could anyone have foreseen the new governmental restrictions on moving companies just as the ship arrived in Le Havre.

Finally, Jennifer had brilliantly found a way to arrange for the delivery before the end of the lockdown in France. She had worked with a team of three separate moving companies in the States and France and had obtained the special permission required from Dieppe's City Hall. She then coordinated with the building management and made arrangements for an outside lift to my apartment, which we had decided would be more efficient than the limited-capacity elevator to the fourth floor. It was all going to happen and very soon!

Two days later, after receiving a phone call that the crew was on its way, I kept a look out for the truck from Paris and for the man with the lift. I then watched with anticipation as the crew arrived and set up the lift and then started to unload what was left of my American life from the truck onto the lift to be brought up four floors and into my apart-

Moving in

ment through the dining-room French doors. It was quite a scene: box after box, each full of my books, files, dishes, kitchen stuff, and clothes followed by my furniture moving slowly up the lift with Dieppe's fifteenth-century castle, the alabaster cliffs, and the English Channel in the background.

It was a superb sunny day, made even more so by the fact that, after more than three years, I could finally begin to put the scattered pieces of my life together and create a real home for Quincie and me here in France.

After the crew dismantled the lift and drove away, I let Quincie out of the bedroom where she been confined during all the commotions of the move. I then looked at what the crew had left behind. Taking up most of the space in the dining room were my Arts and Crafts table, chairs, sideboard, and desk, all of which the crew had carefully unpacked and reassembled. Crowded into the other rooms were a sofa bed, the plaster-of-paris parrot that I had bought over thirty years ago in Key West, Florida, fifty large and small cartons of dishes and books, two cardboard wardrobes of clothes, two large baskets that my mother had left behind when my parents had moved to Arizona, packing crates with pictures and two large mirrors, several plastic containers of more clothes and office supplies, my ironing board, my father's army trunk, and various other items. We had checked off the eighty-nine items, one by one as they came in through the dining room windows.

I wasted no time in making a list of what I needed to accomplish and counting how many boxes and containers needed to be opened and items to be put away. I then immediately began ripping open boxes and sorting through the packing paper that the crew in Boston had used to wrap dishes, glasses, pots and pans, those purple cups my mother had given me some fifty years ago, and things I had forgotten about. After several hours of work that first day, I crawled into my makeshift bed and tried to sleep without thinking about all the things I wanted to get done the next day.

I was up bright and early the next day and the next few days as well, ready to see how much I could get done. I spent hours that day and the following days unwrapping glasses and dishes and putting the paper into an ever-mounting pile near the living-room windows. After I emptied a box, I would carefully fold it back up and store it beside the couch. Each night, I would meticulously keep count of how many boxes were left and continue to hope that certain items that I now considered to be precious would miraculously appear in one of the still-to-be-opened boxes; most didn't.

I took the pictures out of packing crates and rested them against the living-room walls in order to decide later where they should be hung. My invaluable handy man Mikhail arrived to hang the crystal chandelier that I had taken from my dining room in Hartford and then had had hung in Charlestown. That task turned out to be much more complicated than we first thought because a part was missing.

As I unpacked the wardrobes and crates of clothes, I wondered whether I would ever wear some of them here in France. Everyday clothes in Dieppe were so much more casual, and I had become quite accustomed to wearing comfortable T-shirts, sweaters, and LL Bean black jeans. I hung the fancy dresses I had bought several years ago to wear when giving presentations next to a couple of silk jackets and skirts. I was not sure why I thought I might someday need them here in France.

Five days after my shipment had arrived from Paris, what was left of my American book collection was on the bookshelves, next to those ten volumes of the *Grand Larousse Encyclopédique*. They didn't quite fill up the eleven bookshelves in the library nook, but it was a start. My dishes and glasses were arranged on the kitchen shelves. Several empty plastic crates were now packed away in the cellar storage unit along with my Christmas decorations and my mother's ceramic Christmas tree. The kitchen and bathroom were in reasonable order, and clothes were hung in closets and the armoire. I was left with an enormous mountain of packing paper that resembled a huge dragon, several carefully packed light bulbs — totally unusable because of voltage differences — and fifty empty boxes.

I still didn't have a bed, but there was progress. I continued to try to figure out why I had kept certain things, like four different books of English synonyms and all those dresses, and given away some things that I now wished I had kept, including several cookbooks and a brown treasure box belonging to my mother. I must have been so eager to declutter, in too much of a rush to pack up, that I may have decluttered too much. Admittedly, when I was packing everything up after the sale of my condo, I really didn't have any idea where I was eventually going to end up or apparently what I might later find special and worth saving. I tried to take comfort in the idea that by giving so much away, I was making room for something new.

By the end of the week, I had found a place for most of the rest of my things that had arrived. A week later, my new bed arrived. The ever-clever Mikhail found a solution for the missing piece of the chandelier and managed to get that hung, along with all my pictures and the parrot. I would begin the tedious task of hanging the chandelier's crystals later. I bought adapters for my lamps to correct for the voltage. I had given up hope on those missing items that I would never find but had found someone who wanted the boxes and most of the wrapping paper. I had made several trips to the recycling bins with the rest. Fortunately, the building had that little elevator, so I didn't end up with the same sore hips as I had in my move the year before.

What would turn out to be the first lockdown in France ended eleven days after my furniture arrived. Slowly life returned. When I had visited the apartment in December and January, I had never noticed that the kiosks, those street stalls normally used for selling ice cream cones, crêpes, coffee, French fries, hot dogs, and other summer treats during the months of April through September, had disappeared from the boardwalk during the worst of the pandemic. As had all the beach cabins that people rented for the summer — those wooden sheds that they used for storing beach equipment, swimming gear, portable chairs, towels, even barbeques, and for sitting in front of to soak up the sun, sip wine, beer, and cocktails and watch the sun set. Without the kiosks and cabins, the beach front had been wide open, clear of any signs of summer life. During the lockdown and the delayed opening of the beach, I had been able to watch the waves come crashing onto shore and had had an unobstructed view of the pebbles on the beach and the broad expanse of sand at low tide.

Suddenly, there was lots of activity on the beach front. Sometimes I could watch the trucks and cranes bringing back the kiosks and cabins. Sometimes they would simply appear overnight. The view of the beach was now quite changed. The sight of the waves, sand, and pebbles was disturbed by a long row of white wooden kiosks with blue roofs, some emblazoned with menus. Fifteen wooden cabins also partially blocked the view in front of our building. There were more and more people strolling up and down the boardwalk. Children were playing soccer and flying kites on the esplanade lawn. And more and more frequently, the calm was interrupted by those dreaded motorcycles and scooters.

I stayed busy getting settled. With Isabelle's help, I added planters full of geraniums to the balconies off the living room and office and indoor plants for the rooms in the apartment and at the front door. Tatiana helped me solve the problem of finding suitable drapes for the living room. I put the ones that I finally bought into a suitcase and took them over to the seamstress to add lining. On one sunny day, I brought them back, and Tatiana and I managed to hang them with the rings I had salvaged from the former drapes. While most of the time they remained open, cozy is the best word to describe their effect on the room. The apartment was beginning to feel like home.

When the first lockdown ended in May, gym and yoga classes were resumed until the end of the school year. Restaurants and nonessential stores were reopened with certain occupancy restrictions. Martine and I returned to our French lessons. Joël, on the other hand, preferred to hold off restarting our conversation exchanges until the end of the pandemic. We did have one coffee together and a couple of brief visits in the fall — visits that we had no way of knowing would be our last. Sadly, my dear friend Joël died unexpectedly before the year ended. I didn't realize until much later how much a part of my life he had become and how much I would miss him and our conversations despite his somewhat cantankerous arguments.

The travel ban was lifted. During the lockdown, I had received a call from the gendarmerie in Blangy-sur-Bresle, a town about an hour's drive from Dieppe. My mobile phone that had been stolen during our visit to the Christmas market in Rouen the previous December had been recovered! Tatiana and I, eager to get out of Dieppe, drove over to retrieve it and stopped to have a picnic on the way back. As restaurants opened, we started dining out and found we didn't really mind the new space required between tables but instead enjoyed the relative quiet. With new and old friends, I hosted a Bastille Day party to watch the fireworks from the balcony. I also was able to visit the house that I had once thought about buying. It was now being lovingly restored by a man who was originally from Poland and whom Tatiana had met one Saturday in the market.

During the summer, there were exercise and yoga classes on the esplanade lawn and hikes along the beach at low tide. The farmers' markets resumed, and most people respected the new rules about social distancing and masks. I started getting serious about my life here in France, learning about the many varieties of mushrooms and experimenting with new kinds of cheese. I bought champagne flutes and special glasses for drinking aperitifs.

In September, at the return to the regular schedule after the summer vacation, I signed up again for bridge and gym classes. In October, on the anniversary of Xavier's death, I arranged a visit to the cathedral town of Reims for Tatiana so we could be out of town. We spent two days there, visited the cathedral where two of my ancestors had been crowned king, and took a private tour of two champagne caves and of Hautvilliers, the village known as the "Cradle of Champagne." Two weeks later, we drove Tatiana's grandchildren, who were spending a school vacation week with her, to Jumièges to see the abbey ruin that I had last seen in 2000 with my sisters and nieces. Not much had changed except for the new visitor center and admission charge. I also continued to work on my sequel to Jeanne's story, but I took a writing course halfway through the summer that substantially changed its direction and considerably delayed its publication.

Despite my desire to continue to focus on my French studies and my writing, politics managed to interfere significantly with those activities. The split between my two "homelands" became more pronounced. It was difficult to stay away from the news about the election campaigns in the States. So, over the summer and into the fall, I spent too much time watching reruns of the debates and hearing the news about Kamala Harris's historic nomination. During that time, the Democrats Abroad organization initiated yoga classes on Zoom as a fundraiser for the Biden campaign. Carla and I started taking classes together via Zoom, she at 9:00 a.m. and I at 6:00 p.m. Once, even Riley and Max joined us for a session.

At the end of October 2020, a second lockdown went into effect. Masks were now required, and travel was limited to one hundred kilometers from home. Restaurants and nonessential businesses were closed again, although this time hair salons were considered essential and were allowed to stay open.

Life was full of continued ups and downs, including the drama around the American presidential election. In one of the more positive moments, I was able to vote online for president (and vice-president) in the state of Washington. I started planning with friends how we might watch the election returns. Most were not as eager as I was to get up so very early in the morning after the polls closed in the United States. Some even cautioned me by recalling how positive and enthusiastic I had been about Hillary Clinton's chances when I was visiting in 2016.

As it turned out, I did not have to watch the returns alone. Back in 2017, I had contacted the local TV station for coverage of the installation of the plaque in Jeanne's honor in Saint-Jacques church. Over the years since then, I had stayed in touch with one of the producers at the station. Shortly before the election, she called to see if I would be willing to have a TV crew come to my apartment to film me watching the returns. They arrived at 5:00 a.m. on the morning of November 4. Together we experienced the emotional next few hours.

When they finally left around 8:00 a.m., nothing was certain. I had to spend the next three days glued to the television, anxiously awaiting the results. While recognizing that the drama around the election would probably continue past the declaration that Biden had won, finally on November 7, I decided I could take one small step to show my restored pride in being an American, by hanging the US flag from my balcony: a fitting end to my first four years in France.

TWENTY-SIX

FINDING HOME

If you arrive in Dieppe via the Avenue Gambetta, the route the Canadian Army took on September 1, 1944, to liberate Dieppe from the German Army, you will find yourself at the top of a very steep cliff. From this vantage point, the view will make you catch your breath, at least it does mine. Ahead in the distance, as you look out over the rooftops of the stucco and brick homes and buildings, is the English Channel. Sometimes clouds frame the view, and sometimes there's only the clear blue sky. Sometimes the line of the horizon distinctly separates sky and sea, and sometimes it is blurred by clouds or fog. Depending on the weather and the time of day, you might see fishing boats or sailboats navigating the waves or the ferry arriving from England. And there will no doubt be seagulls cawing their welcome. Whether the sycamore trees with their oddly manicured branches that line the avenue are in full bloom or whether their leaves are long gone, the view of the channel, ribboned in color — sometimes blue, sometimes green, sometimes lavender, sometimes grey — is totally enchanting. When I saw the view for the first time and every time after that, I felt as if I was coming home.

And a home is what we are making of our new place, Quincie and I. The months since the move in April have slipped by, but we have made progress despite the lockdowns and the restrictions caused by the virus. The apartment is slowly becoming more like a comfortable nest for us. My pictures have now been hung on the walls of all four rooms. The Hartford chandelier now lights up my office — with all its crystals added. The chandelier from the front hall of the home where I grew up in Nashua is now suspended from the ceiling in my bedroom. In the living room, the new drapes adorn the windows. A gorgeous new rug covers part of the floor. I have found other pieces of furniture that, along with the flowers at the front door and on the balconies and the plants in the living room, make the spacious rooms cozier. And after breaking several glasses on the ceramic tiles in the kitchen, I had the floor replaced with padded gray tiles.

The apartment is still not done, and I am not sure it will ever be. Nevertheless, the various traces of the prior owners are mostly gone, although I have kept some. The dining room, office, and bedroom drapes that were here when I moved in have been cleaned and rehung. Even though they are a bit faded, I decided that they deserve to stay in their home of so many years before me. They add elegance to the apartment during the day, and at night I can close them, shut out the world and feel snug and warm. In the bedroom, the new bedframe and bed in the alcove and the new cream-colored wallpaper provide a perfect setting for the landlord's majestic armoire.

Although the US presidential election seemed to take forever to be decided, I was able to reduce the amount of political noise in my life by unsubscribing from all those mailing lists belonging to Democratic organizations and by no longer watching CNN at 6 p.m. And I have figured out how to deal with the disturbances from the street with the help of a sound machine, ear plugs, noise-canceling headphones, and a bit more patience. While working at my desk, I can pause to watch the birds and the waves. In the evening, I can stand at the French doors in awe of the ever-spectacular sunsets, for a few moments anyway. The light that comes in through those doors on sunny and not-so-sunny days continues to amaze me. I frequently marvel at the expanse of space in the apartment that, while still considerable, is slowly becoming more comfortable and cozy.

I've learned which vendors at the market are the best for cheese, bread, fruit and vegetables. I am actually beginning to slow down and stroll through the market stalls, like most everyone else. I am not sure why exactly people prefer to stroll. I first suspected it could be because they hadn't made lists of what they wanted to buy. But now I believe they are in no hurry to check out what's fresh and available, or perhaps they don't know what they want to buy until they see it. In any event, I am trying to do the same — most of the time.

I've also learned how to walk in the channel at low tide — with special shoes and never alone. And I have discovered that I don't have to pay to have all of my favorite products shipped from the States. For most of them, I've found the same product here under a different name or have adapted to their French equivalents. Even Quincie, who eats French cat food but who for a long time refused to eat French cat treats, despite numerous attempts on my part, has finally found one she will eat, so I won't have to have Carla send a supply.

I still have not mastered the art of making a good French salad dressing, but my friends accept my attempts. I have bought a scale for the kitchen to correctly measure ingredients, intending to use it whenever I cook (which is still not often). I've adapted to the hours at the various bakeries and stores. I can make an expresso in my machine that also makes "American" coffee. Thanks to Isabelle, I now have a Carte Vitale along with a French social security number that entitles me to the benefits of the French health insurance system, one available after becoming a resident. I can now answer my brother Marc's question about my status in France. "I don't know if I am an expat, but I do know that I am for sure a resident!"

I am also aware that I am becoming more and more integrated into daily life here. As my friend Joël had said, it is going to be progressively more difficult to leave — should I ever choose to do that — the longer I stay. For the moment, I can't imagine living anywhere else.

Sending emails in French doesn't take quite so much time, partly because I believe I have made some progress with the language but also because I am less concerned about making mistakes. I have added more books to the bookshelves. I am at once scared at how much I am accumulating but at the same time happy to see new titles — the majority in French — sitting beside the treasured few that I brought from the States. As to the other stuff that I said I would stop accumulating but haven't been able to do so far, I will just have to deal with that challenge someday in the future.

I still have not figured out how to program my computer to default to "A4" to print documents. The French words to the Lord's Prayer continue to escape me. And I have not yet figured out what to do about the lack of a bathtub. However, I have come to understand that there is no such thing as a French nose! And that having Quebecois origins is something to be proud of!

Quincie, it seems, has found her home as well. One day, Isabelle and I drove over to Varengeville not very far away to take a long walk. We somehow managed to avoid a windstorm that hit Dieppe. When we returned, I noticed that the dining room French doors were flung wide open. Apparently, I had failed to close them carefully before leaving for our walk, and the wind must have blown them open. I could see no sign of Quincie on the balcony. I nervously rushed upstairs only to find her casually lying on the sofa. She didn't appear to have suffered one bit from what must have been a scary opportunity to venture out onto the balconies.

While she remains ever eager to explore these new spaces, she does seem to be mellowing and losing some of her independence. Lately, I have found her sleeping on my bed when I wake up in the morning. Once, she even reached out a paw for some attention. A friend who had taken care of her when I was in Quebec two years ago noticed recently that she seems calmer and more social. I tend to agree. She is letting me rub her neck more often, and, after she finishes her drink of water from the faucet in the bathroom, she comes to find me to let me know that I can turn off the faucet (of course, in exchange for another cat treat).

Perhaps more significantly, I have given up my goal to master French and have accepted the fact that I will never lose my American accent and will never be able to avoid mistakes. Instead, with Martine's help, I will studiously continue the process of learning the language of my father. It will be enough to be able to communicate clearly, and I don't need to be fluent to do that. Fortunately, I have read that people over the age of sixty do not have to pass a language exam to become a French citizen, in case I ever choose to pursue citizenship. I haven't decided whether I will do that since it is apparently a very long process. My friends, nonetheless, have started planning the party.

After celebrating my fourth Bastille Day in Dieppe, I began preparations for another renewal of my long stay visa, a process that COVID restrictions made much more complicated. And for the first time since I started my "sabbatical," I had no plan to take a trip to the States in January, nor would I have a relative here for the holidays because of the virus and travel restrictions.

In Scott Peck's book about ancient stones, he noted, "Life is a pilgrimage or rather, it can be one if we use it as such."[15]

I reflect on his words and then on the developmental model of Carl Jung that I seem to be following, on some level, even though I am well past what anyone would call midlife. I know I will never lose my reliance on logical, analytical thinking, the skill that took me successfully through high school, through college, and well into both careers — first in banking and then consulting — but it does seem to be fading a bit along with the need to plan for the far future. I do still have to make lists, but they are a lot shorter now and not all items get checked off as completed by the end of the day. And I have not yet created a new five-year plan or a new bucket list, although I know I still need to finish the research on Jeanne's third husband.

At the same time, I have indeed developed a stronger appreciation for living in the moment and enjoying the sensations that surround me, to live in the spaces between knowing and not knowing or half knowing. I feel as if I am giving up some of the need to control what's happening. I can go on a walk with friends and not need to know exactly where we are headed or what time we'll arrive at our destination — at least part of the time.

I still am more serious than playful and more assertive than laid back. I refuse to tolerate bad behavior and will notify the police about a car parked on the street for a longer period of time than legal. And I can apply some of that attitude towards trying to find solutions to

---

15. M. Scott Peck, *In Search of Stones* (London: Pocket Books, 1997), 213.

problems that the French think they have to accept. I am, for example, trying to organize city hall and my neighbors to do something about those noisy motorcycles and scooters.

I haven't stopped being curious or courageous, nor do I want to. Those are some of the fibers that hold together the tapestry of my life. It does feel as if I am adding new threads which can weave themselves into the old ones and in the process create new patterns. I feel those threads being added as I watch the waves come to shore, the clouds form strange shapes above the horizon, the seagulls soar by, and the sun set gloriously in the western sky. Or as I spend time trying to chat with a bird that decides to land on the balcony outside my office window. Or as I experience the warmth of dear friends, kindred souls, and colleagues who could never replace my family and friends in the United States and beyond but who, just as importantly, are adding so much to my life by letting me be who and what I really am.

I wonder, though, how much the basic core of my personality has changed, or whether it could or should. Tatiana once remarked that we can't really change the essential characteristics that make up who we are. However, I do believe I have made some slight but important adjustments around the edges, as I have been forced, and sometimes chosen, to adapt. Can we not evolve?

In one of the scrapbooks that my mother made for me, I discovered a forgotten piece of "art" from a second or third grade class. It's a colorful butterfly. Over forty years later, in one of the last courses I took for my creativity degree, we did a meditation and were asked to

Grade school butterfly

1995 butterfly

Crystal butterfly

draw a picture that the session inspired. Amazingly, I drew another butterfly, this time curiously with a face.

At my going-away party that my colleagues at what was then Shawmut National Bank organized, they gave me a present: a crystal butterfly, perhaps prophetically made in France. It seems that I have been trying to spread my wings for a long, long time, although there have been moments when I wonder if I am going the other way: back into a cocoon, a cozy nest to savor the days, weeks, and years ahead.

I don't believe that I have experienced a transformation or a metamorphosis. However, it is movement forward. I have not totally changed. I am not sure I really want to. But I haven't completed the journey, and I am still learning. It's quite possible that I may never find the "meaning of life," however that's defined. Yet I can accept that it's the search that matters, not the discovery. And perhaps it's in the search that I will find that "second soul" that Charlemagne promised.

I do believe that my movement forward has been helped by my years here in France. On the one hand, it's impossible — or close to impossible — to be bossy or be in control when I can never be sure I totally understand what is going on or what is being said. On the other hand, the culture in France is also playing a supportive role. Life is not only about doing and achieving; I can simply be. So I don't have to be responsible, lead, achieve, produce, and be strong and brave all the time.

Hope Jahren in her book *Lab Girl* makes an interesting and pertinent observation, referring to the growth of plants and trees from tiny seeds: "Something so hard can be so easy if you just have a little help. In the right place, under the right conditions, you can finally stretch out into what you're supposed to be."[16]

That's what France feels like now, a place that is allowing me to spread my branches, with roots much deeper than ever expected.

---

16. Hope Jahren, *Lab Girl* (London: Fleet, 2016), 38.

It turns out I am not on any identity quest, searching to find something I am missing. Instead, I merely needed to weave all the pieces of my life together. In the process, I have found the community I have been seeking for a long time, folks who will definitely come to visit me in the hospital and who will probably miss me when I am gone. But who are, in the meantime, adding a whole lot more to my life in the here and now.

While I had given away too many books, some of the things I did keep are those scrapbooks my mother put together; my letters to my parents from camp in 1956, from college eight years later, and from Russia in 1966; a few other odd letters; and many pictures from my childhood, which my mother had kept over so many years. They all rest now on the shelf next to the letters that my parents wrote back and forth during their courtship, during the war, and later.

Among them, I found a letter that my mother had written to me a year before she died. I am not sure it was ever sent; it might have been discovered by my brothers among her papers after her death. I certainly had forgotten it. In the typewritten three pages, she described in detail our first two years together. I learned more about those years than I ever knew before and more about what she went through having to wait in airports with a three-month-old new baby to make several flight connections from Missouri to California on our way to meet my dad before he left for Okinawa. She sent along some pictures from those days, and she signed the letter, "I love you, Mother." I believe that she did and Dad did as well. They did really love us, in ways that we can only appreciate now. And I have finally come to understand the words of one of the therapists in my past: "Forgive them for showing their love in strange ways."

I certainly did not expect to live out the rest of my life in France, far from my family of origin, and that may not happen. While I am not sure I can ever give up the suitcase that I was carrying around as a four-year-old, I can leave it unpacked for a time and put a temporary, if not permanent, stop to my nomadic life. In that blue travel journal, I had listed a goal of living for six months in France — not for the rest of my life. It has simply evolved this way, and I probably want to let it continue to evolve. Like when I left the bank, without a clear plan forward. My German friend Peter was right: I can jump without a net, and who knows what will happen!

Jeanne's life was full of mysteries that I have not yet been able to solve because of the absence of documents from the seventeenth century. My life is also apparently full of mysteries, twists, and turns because it's clearly not yet finished. As Carl Jung said, this journey is "a lifetime's task which is never completed; a journey upon which one sets out hopefully toward a destination at which one never arrives."[17]

Indeed, not very long ago, one of those twists in life appeared quite suddenly. Although I had managed to complete most of the items in that blue travel journal, there was one — a rather important one — that had still not been fulfilled. In fact, it was item #1 at the very top of the bucket list: "Fall in love with a wonderful man — the other side of me." I had long ago given up hope of ever realizing that goal and had definitely stopped looking. I had even given away my sexy nightgowns, as well as my Carly Simon CD with all those torrid love songs.

Nonetheless, my ancestor Jeanne, whose last name Chevalier translates as "knight" in English, was not going to let that goal remain unfulfilled. She has apparently been by my side, watching over me, all this time. Not long before I finished the first draft of this book, she sent her own knight (without a horse and any shining armor) into my life: a charming, affectionate, good-looking, intelligent, curious, and very funny French man. We'd met, curiously enough, at that historical congress in Dieppe back in November 2019, where I had given a talk on Jeanne's life. He was intrigued, he told me later, by the story and by its author's "adorable" American accent.

Over the next several weeks and months after our first meeting, our relationship developed slowly, partly because of the lockdown and partly, I believe, out of an abundance of caution on both our parts. Since Jacques lives one hundred kilometers south of Dieppe, in the

---

17. Anthony Storr, "Individuation and the Creative Process," *Journal of Analytical Psychology*, 28 no. 4 (1983): 331.

beginning we arranged to meet for lunches in Rouen, a midway point, and kept in contact through phone conversations and text and email exchanges. Our meetings became more frequent as the pandemic-related travel restrictions were relaxed.

In one of the emails my new beau sent, he asked how and for what purpose he could fit into my busy life. At first, I wasn't sure how to respond. It turned out I didn't need to. He found the answer to that question after reading something I had written in a post on my website in late November 2019, not long after we first met. In that post, I wrote that I was finally beginning to accept the fact that my voyage to uncover Jeanne's history was going to take much longer than I first expected and that I might never find answers to all my questions. But then I had added, in line with what my Australian friend Theodora had suggested, "It is also possible that the real reason for this search for Jeanne's story is not so much its discovery, but rather the addition of more joy and fun to my life."

I must thank Jeanne again, this time for sending into my life this wonderful man who brings me such joy and so much laughter and fun. Jacques — along with my family and friends — is helping me find another side of myself that I didn't know existed. The changes this man is rendering in my previously organized celibate life and the lessons he is teaching me about what it truly means to love someone madly and about the many shapes and sizes of love are rather substantial. They are, perhaps, more appropriate for another book.

I started this book with the intention to write about the wonderful people I had met and the marvelous experiences I had had in searching for Jeanne's story. However, the journey of the past four years has turned the story into something more and indeed, something totally unexpected. It's truly been an adventure of discovery of new shores that has changed my life forever.

I came across a French phrase recently, very serendipitously and quite timely: *Je suis à ma place.* It is translated as: "I am where I am supposed to be." It feels as if France is home now. And this is where I am supposed to be.

We always think we are now at the end of our discoveries. We never are. We go on discovering that we are this, that, and other things, and sometimes we have astounding experiences.

Carl Jung[18]

---

18. Carl Jung, *Analytical Psychology: its Theory and Practice (The Tavistock Lectures)* (New York: Vintage Books, 1968), 221.

Appendix I

Les Filles du Roi (The King's Daughters)

Background

In the middle of the seventeenth century, New France (now part of Canada) needed women. The French colony was not growing. Although Quebec City had been founded in 1608 and Montreal in 1642, the French inhabitants in what would become Quebec still numbered less than three thousand in 1663. The men who ventured to New France were not electing to stay. While the climate was certainly a factor, the major reason — at least according to King Louis XIV and his chief minister Jean-Baptiste Colbert — was the lack of women. Louis and his ministers decided that it was time to do something about the situation, to turn the exploration of New France into settlement thereof. Therefore, in 1663, in addition to their other efforts to bolster the colony, they established the Filles du Roi (Daughters of the King) program It was designed to encourage young women — usually orphaned or impoverished — to make the journey to New France, wed the explorers, farmers, merchants, soldiers, and traders living there, start families, and thus expand the population.

Since much has been already written about this program in both French and English and fiction and nonfiction, what follows is only a brief summary of the program.[19]

Precedents

There had been previous French attempts to support the emigration to New France of young unmarried women. In the years before 1663, a woman's passage had been paid for by merchants, family members, or the church. Future brides usually had some sort of family or other

---

19. See the *Sources Referenced* section for additional information.

connection in New France to encourage their decision to leave France. These attempts prior to 1663, however, were not sufficient in number to accelerate growth of the colony.

King Louis XIV's Filles du Roi program was different from previous attempts both in France and elsewhere. These women, who had few, if any, family connections in the colony, were recruited and sent to New France by the king and his administrators. In addition to their passage to New France, the king provided clothes and the promise of a dowry upon marriage. The women also received several other necessary items, including a bonnet, taffeta handkerchief, ribbon, one hundred needles, comb and hairbrush, white thread, a pair of stockings, a pair of gloves, a pair of scissors, two knives, one thousand pins, four string laces for their bodices, and a small gift of money. These possessions, augmented by other personal belongings that had an average value of 300 livres[20], were secured in long wooden boxes called *coffres*.

The Recruits

From 1663 to 1673, 770 young women, the majority of whom were between the ages of sixteen and forty years old, took up the call to serve the king and climbed aboard vessels that left from La Rochelle and Dieppe, France. Most of the ships left from Dieppe, a two-week trip from Paris, made partially by boat on the Seine River and then quite probably over land by foot.

The women came from a variety of backgrounds. Almost two-thirds of these women came from "urban areas." Most women, who — in the early years at least — were usually the orphaned daughters of minor artisans, laborers, servants, and sometimes lower nobility, came from Paris or towns and villages in Normandy or other parts of northern France. Given the lack of mass communication, the widespread illiteracy, and the difficulties of seventeenth-century travel, recruiters — primarily merchants and ship outfitters — focused their efforts

20. The currency at the time.

around Dieppe and La Rochelle. The recruiters received a commission for every woman recruited. The Hôpital Général and La Salpetrière, places in Paris that provided homes for abandoned children, orphaned girls, pregnant women, and even daughters of noble families who had fallen on hard times, were also sources of recruits, with approximately 50 percent of the Filles du Roi coming from these institutions.

It seems that some number of young women simply showed up at points of embarkation, perhaps lured by rumors about monetary gifts from the king. Apparently, despite the challenges of communication in seventeenth century France, the news of the program did eventually spread since one half of all Filles du Roi arrived in the last four years of the program (1669 to 1673).

In the first few years of the program, there were concerns voiced in Quebec that the young women being sent were not accustomed to or physically capable of managing the heavy farm work, harsh winters, and isolation they would have to endure in New France. In response, Louis XIV's chief minister Colbert asked the archbishop of Rouen in 1670 to spread the word throughout the thirty to forty parishes in the Norman countryside to find young women more accustomed to the hard rural life. "They must be healthy, strong," Colbert wrote, "and in no way disgraced by nature and in no way repulsive on the outside!"

Potential recruits went through a careful screening process. Recruiters had to make sure that the young women were not already married; they required each to provide a birth certificate and affidavit from her priest assuring that she was free to marry. (The search continues for these documents, even though they are said to be lost.) A governess on board the ship shepherded each contingent of women from France to Quebec and then watched over them until they found husbands in New France.

The first contingent of thirty-six women arrived on September 22, 1663. These women and the 734 who followed over the next ten years in increasing numbers must have been hardy women. They certainly must have heard some terrible stories of Canadian winters and Amerindian attacks, and they faced a potentially dangerous journey across the Atlantic Ocean. But for probably a variety of reasons, they decided to take a chance on a new life in Quebec.

Reasons for Leaving France

The question is often asked why these women decided to leave France to live in the new colony. Trying to understand the reasons why they chose as they did involves a great deal of speculation because the Filles du Roi left few records or diaries. For most, it must have been a voluntary decision, while it's possible, even probable, that there was some strong encouragement by guardians, parents, officials at the charity hospitals, parish priests, and even recruiters. At a colloquium on the Filles du Roi in Quebec in 2009, famed historian Yves Landry proposed, based on admittedly little evidence, that many of the young women — particularly those in the charity houses in Paris — could have been coerced to join the program.

Even though that may have been true for a large number of them, there are other reasons these women might have left France. Certainly, they must have heard the rumors and stories from Quebec. Life in the New World would have seemed full of dangers and many risks. Yet such an option could have been seen as a way out, an opportunity to improve their lot in life, given their uncertain future in France. Compared to France, marriage in Canada was a virtual certainty for a woman who wanted to marry, so they were apparently willing to take the risk, in historian Leslie Choquette's words, "preferring the prospect of hasty marriage in a distant colony to continuing institutional or familial dependency."[21]

Whatever their reasons, the great majority of these women showed incredible courage. They were probably quite out of the ordinary since, according to Choquette, migration even within France was rare, especially among single women. They were most definitely not fallen

---

21. Leslie Choquette, *Frenchmen into Peasants: Modernity and Tradition in the Peopling of French Canada* (Cambridge, MA: Harvard University Press, 1997), 273.

women, despite myths to that effect arising over the last two centuries. Respected historians seriously doubt that King Louis XIV would have provided so much financial support for the emigration of women with sordid pasts and possible disease, given that his goal was to colonize New France by marrying these women to the men there to create families with descendants for generations to come.

In fact, the Filles du Roi were brave and adventurous women of strong will, determined to take action and make a good life for themselves and their future families in the New World. They were on a mission – for the king and for France.

Results

And fulfill that mission they certainly did. The goals that King Louis XIV and his minister set for the program were achieved. In 1663 at the start of the program, as noted previously, the population of New France was less than three thousand people. Ten years later it had reached 6,700. And the census taken eight years later in 1681 counted over ten thousand men, women, and children in New France, a more than three-fold increase in only eighteen years. Today, the vast majority of inhabitants of Canada and the United States who claim French-Canadian heritage have one, if not considerably more, Fille du Roi in their family tree.

The program ended in 1673 with the recall of the king's administrator for New France, who had been one of the program's champions. It was viewed as sufficiently successful and self-sustaining given the number of births recorded from 1664 on. It's very likely that the war declared on the Dutch by France and England also took the king's attention away from the new colony and further burdened France's already strained finances.

Appendix II

The Eight Creative Talents and Carl Jung

Author Lynne Levesque wrote the book *Breakthrough Creativity* because she believed that everyone is creative and that there are many different ways to be creative. Every individual is capable of consistently producing different and valuable results, the real definition of creativity. It's not necessary to be a genius to be creative, and results don't necessarily have to be original to the world since few results meet that criterion. In fact, most results are built on the work of others. There is also a wide range of creative results from minor adaptations and small solutions to everyday problems to the higher levels of creativity involved in historically significant major breakthroughs. Creative efforts don't have to change the course of history or science, although, certainly for some people who exhibit what could be called "transformational creativity," they do. For most individuals, however, creative results are a bit more ordinary — although still incredibly important and valuable in their own lives and in those of others.

Creative results can be artistic designs or novel inventions or minor fixes that solve customer problems. They can be innovative solutions to tough decisions or problems. Creative results can come from reframing, redefining, or restructuring a problem in a way that generates different solutions. They can be new connections, new arrangements of existing or past data, or novel, new responses, ideas, perspectives and products. They can be big ideas and breakthroughs, or they can be small steps that build on past experience to generate better solutions.

Producing these creative results has a lot to do with the way individuals see the world, take in data and information, define problems and challenges, generate alternative options, and select and implement a solution. To define these different ways, Levesque used the model developed by Swiss psychologist Carl Jung (1888-1961), who spent his entire adult life trying to understand the uniqueness and differences among people, as well as the common patterns that govern behavior. The well-known Myers Briggs Type Indicator® (MBTI®) is also based on Jung's work.

Jung's Theory of Personality Differences

While recognizing the uniqueness of each individual, Jung also found patterns in the way people collect data and make decisions. Jung's model defined these different patterns as preferences. These preferences for looking at challenges, collecting data and information, and generating responses have an impact on one's creativity and one's vision of the future. They can color the type of data that is seen, how the challenge is defined in the first place, and what is done with all this information.

According to Jung, there are four mental functions for taking in and processing data and information. Two functions are used for perceiving or collecting data:

Sensing, which establishes what is actually present

Intuition, which points to possibilities

Two other functions are used for judging or making decisions:

Thinking, which applies logical analysis

Feeling, which uses ideals and values to make decisions

These are functions that everyone uses some of the time. Everyone takes in concrete data about the real world (Sensing), sees patterns and possibilities (Intuiting), uses logic in making decisions (Thinking), and applies personal values as well to the decision-making process (Feeling). People just use them differently, direct them in different directions, get different energy from each, and assign a different degree of importance to each of the four functions.

In addition to the four functions, Jung found that there are two attitudes or orientations to the world:

Introverted (inwardly focused and energized)

Extraverted (externally focused and energized)

At first, Jung believed that people were introverted or extraverted. However, upon more study, he concluded that the functions themselves, not people, were introverted or extraverted. Since each of the four functions of sensing, intuition, thinking, and feeling can operate in the introverted and extraverted worlds, the combination of functions and orientations results in eight preferences — eight different ways for taking in and processing data that produce different creative results and make distinct creative contributions. In *Breakthrough Creativity*, Levesque calls these preferences "talents."

The Eight Creative Talents

When using the four extraverted preferences of sensing, intuiting, judging or feeling, people tend to want to work with others to share their perceptions, ideas, concepts, thoughts, and feelings; generate alternatives; and act on their decisions. With the introverted versions of the four preferences, people tend to operate in a more private space, to reflect and process ideas, thoughts, feelings, and decisions internally; they also prefer to keep their ideas to themselves.

Of these eight preferences, four are used to collect data and information about the world and its challenges:

- The **Extraverted Sensing** preference (the Adventurer talent) helps individuals experiment and play with clever and skillful adaptations based on the five senses and the facts at hand — like photographers and jazz musicians.
- The **Introverted Sensing** preference (the Navigator talent) allows individuals to pull in facts and details to build on what others have already done — like researchers and scientists, who can also add a new twist to what's been done before.
- The **Extraverted Intuiting** preference (the Explorer talent) is used to continually challenge the status quo and generate new ideas and opportunities that might come from brainstorming, teambuilding, and other group activities.

- The **Introverted Intuiting** preference (the Visionary talent) helps individuals ask bold questions, see multiple connections, and provide far-reaching insights into the future, with almost a sixth sense and ideas that come out of the blue.

The other four preferences are used to act on that data or information, to make decisions or judgments:

- The **Extraverted Thinking** preference (the Pilot talent) allows individuals to find designs, strategies and plans to make improvements, get things organized, and make lists to get things done — like disciplined project managers.
- The **Introverted Thinking** preference (the Inventor talent) helps individuals to shift paradigms and build theories and models to analyze and provide unusual insights — like architects and philosophers.
- The **Extraverted Feeling** preference (the Diplomat talent)[22] focuses individuals on people issues and values and helps foster a nurturing environment for the group or team — like humanitarians and civil rights activists.
- The **Introverted Feeling** preference (the Poet talent) encourages reflection, articulation of eternal values, and an appreciation for quiet beauty and elegance — like poets.

It's important to remember that Jung developed his framework of patterns not to label people but to help them be more effective. His model is like a compass that will help individuals understand themselves and their impact on others, to maximize their strengths, and to minimize weaknesses. Like a compass, it's not a detailed map; it isn't meant to be precise. However, it can serve as a guide for exploring strengths and developing greater awareness of self and of others.

Jung believed that individuals are each unique in their strengths, limitations, and talents. He wrote: "Each individual is a new experiment of life in [her] ever-changing moods and an attempt at a new solution or new adaptation." According to Jung, personal development (or what is

22. In *Breakthrough Creativity*, this talent is called the "Harmonizer" talent. Levesque later changed it to "Diplomat" to facilitate translation of her model into other languages.

also known as self-actualization) is a strange adventure, a journey that takes courage and that never ends, but making the journey is worth the risk since the reward is finding one's true self and, Levesque would add, finding one's own particular brand of creativity.

For more information, see *Breakthrough Creativity: Achieving Top Performance Using the Eight Creative Talents.*

SOURCES REFERENCED

On the Filles du Roi

Choquette, Leslie. *Frenchmen into Peasants: Modernity and Tradition in the Peopling of French Canada.* Cambridge MA: Harvard University Press, 1997.

Gagné Peter. *King's Daughters and Founding Mothers*, vol. I and II (no place), 2004.

Lanctôt, Gustave. *Fille de joie ou filles du roi.* Montréal: Les Éditions du Jour, 1964.

Landry, Yves. *Orphelines en France, pionnières au Canada: Les Filles du Roi au xviie siècle.* Montréal: Leméac, 1992

Levesque, Lynne. *Jeanne Chevalier: Fille du Roi*, Boston MA, 2016. (English version)

_____. *Jeanne Chevalier: Une Fille du Roi*, Dieppe FR, 2017. (version française)

Société d'histoire des Filles du Roy. *Mères de la Nation Québécoise.* Colloque sur Les Filles du Roy. 2009 (Two DVDs and One CD)

https://fillesduroi.org/

http://lesfillesduroy-quebec.org/

Other Sources Referenced

Bryson, Bill. *The Mother Tongue: English and How It Got That Way.* New York: Harper Perennial, 2001.

Cusumano, Camille (ed). *France, A Love Story: Women Write about the French Experience.* Emeryville, CA: Seal Press, 2004.

Frame, Rudy R. Jr. "Okinawa: The Final Great Battle of World War II" *Marine Corps Gazette*, (November, 2012). mca-marines.org. Accessed December 14, 2020.

Iyer, Pico. TED Talk, "Where is Home?" July 17, 2013. (French version: "C'est où, 'chez soi?'" September 15, 2014.)

Jahren, Hope. *Lab Girl*. London: Fleet, 2016.

Jung, Carl. *Analytical Psychology: its Theory and Practice (The Tavistock Lectures)*. New York: Vintage Books, 1968.

Kronenfeld, Judy. "Speaking French" in *France, A Love Story: Women Write about the French Experience*, ed. by Camille Cusumano. Emeryville, CA: Seal Press, 2004, pp. 277-286.

Levesque, Lynne. *Breakthrough Creativity: Achieving Top Performance Using the Eight Creative Talents*. Palo Alto, CA: Davies-Black Publishing, 2001.

Moore, Thomas. *The Re-enchantment of Everyday Life*. New York: Harper Perennial. 1997.

Orringer, Julie. *The Invisible Bridge*. New York: Vintage, 2010.

Peck, R. Scott. *In Search of Stones*. London: Pocket Books, 1997.

Poetry House (eds.). *150 Most Famous Poems*. Springville UT (USA): Vervante, 2020.

Storr, Anthony. "Individuation and the Creative Process." *Journal of Analytical Psychology*, 28 no. 4 (1983): 331.

https://www.animalfriends.co.uk/blog/why-does-my-cat-rub-his-face-on-me/, accessed August 16, 2021.

https://www.radcliffe.harvard.edu/event/2013-julie-orringer-lecture

Acknowledgements

The number of people in my life who have been and have never stopped being most supportive of my efforts in the continuing saga of my research on my ancestor Jeanne Chevalier continues to grow. To them all I am most grateful for their patience, understanding, and help and for the lessons they have taught me about friendship. They include:

- My sister Carla Levesque and my brother Dana Cole-Levesque, my nieces and nephews, and the rest of my family;
- The readers of early drafts of this book: Carla, Dana, my cousin Monsignor Peter Dumont, Ann Auburn, Patricia Goletto, Tatiana Lasserre, Brigitte Mason, Paula O'Hara, Pierre Ickowicz, the curator of Dieppe's Château-Musée, and two who shall remain anonymous;
- All my other dear friends in France, the United States, and around the world, whose last names I have omitted to preserve some semblance of anonymity: Arthur, Carol, Helaine, Isabelle, Jacques, Joëlle, Joël, Martine, Nadine, Nelly, Peter, Seta, Susanne, and Theodora;
- Those welcoming members of the Cousins du Nouveau Monde and Les Amys de Vieux Dieppe, and
- My kindred spirits at church, bridge, and the gym.

I owe special thanks to:
- The translators of my book on Jeanne's life: Clyde et Alexandra Dlugy-Belmont, Brigitte Bernaudat, Monique Caplet-Elmosnino, Martine Diamante, Nadine Lefebvre, Florence Levasseur, Yann l'Hostis, and Nelly Mare-Godet;
- Members of the Lévesque Association, Inc. for providing financial support for the plaque in honor of our ancestor Jeanne Chevalier and to Fernand and Marie-Ange Lévesque, researchers at the Lévesque Association, for their help tracing the lineage of Jean-Jacques Lévesque;
- Attendees at the conferences I have given for their feedback; and
- Readers of my first book who sent in so many encouraging comments.

Several historians graciously helped with the initial research for the story of Jeanne's life, which forms the background for this "sequel." They include: Leslie Choquette, Cole Harris, Paul-Henri Hudon, Alain Laberge, Yves Landry, Rénald Lessard, Renaud Lévesque, Ulric Lévesque, Eric Mardoc, Peter Moogk, and Jan Noel.

Staff and volunteers at the following institutions in the United States, Quebec, and France were also very helpful:
- Bibliothèque et Archives Nationales au Québec (BANQ) Quebec at Laval University;
- BANQ in Montréal;
- *La Bibliothèque de Coutances*;
- *La Société d'histoire de Charlesbourg*;
- *La Société de généalogie de Longueuil, Québec*;
- *La Société de Généalogique Québécois*;
- *La Société Généalogique Canadienne-Française*;
- *Les Archives de la Côte-Du-Sud et du Collège de Sainte-Anne in La Pocatière, Québec*;
- Departmental archives in Rouen, Saint-Lô, Caen, and in *le Fonds ancien* in Dieppe's *Mediathéque*;
- The Boston Public Library's Interlibrary Loan Department and the Charlestown branch; and
- The New England Historic Genealogical Society.

Other individuals whom I have fortuitously met along the way and who have encouraged me and provided all sorts of support during my journey:
- Irène Belleau and Gérard Viaud, Société de l'histoire des Filles du Roy;
- Jacques Deschamps de Boishébert and his family;
- Patricia Thomas in Quebec City;
- Veronique Goulle at *Les Archives Municipales de la Ville de Coutances*; and
- Louis-George Simard and Nancy Fortin in Rivière-Ouelle.

I also want to acknowledge with much appreciation:

- The teachers and students in my writing seminars at Grub Street, Boston, Massachusetts, and in my French classes with the Brookline Adult Education Department;
- Mary Carroll Moore for her courses and counsel;
- Dori DeSantis for her incredible encouragement and never-ending creativity;
- Charlie McKee who helped shape the book, even though she was supposed to be doing copyediting!
- Jane Hurford for her help in the final stages of the book; and
- Sylvia Tooker, my faithful webmistress at Bear Data Services.

I hope I have remembered the names of everyone who has helped me along the way, but if I have forgotten anyone, I apologize, and I of course take full responsibility for any errors in this book!

ABOUT THE AUTHOR

*The author at Dieppe's Monument
in Memory of the Fusiliers Mont-Royal*

Lynne's life has been a constant process of embarking on new ventures and enjoying many learning experiences. She then has somehow managed to rearrange these various pieces of her life in a multitude of different ways.

Although half French Canadian by heritage, she was raised in a non-French speaking home. She went off to college with four years of high school French, but decided to start a new language. Her degree in Russian Studies from Mount Holyoke College led her into teaching and then to graduate school at Rutgers University where she earned a Master's degree in Modern European History. Her love for history, particularly women in history, and for the French and Russian languages was, however, put on hold by a seventeen-year business career (MBA from University of California at Berkeley) at two very large financial institutions.

In the middle of that career, a curious chain of events significantly readjusted the course of her life for the next twenty years when she rather serendipitously fell into the study of creativity. After completing her EdD at the University of Massachusetts, Amherst, she let her passion for the topics of creativity and leadership drive her departure from her banking career toward independent consulting and adjunct teaching positions in local colleges and universities. As part of that consulting practice, Lynne published *Breakthrough Creativity: Achieving Top Performance Using the Eight Creative Talents* (2001) and *The Breakthrough Creativity Profile and Facilitator's Guide* (2003, 2012), along with several articles on the topics of creativity and leadership. While still consulting, she spent five and a half years as a senior researcher at Harvard Business School, where she co-authored multiple cases and articles on critical leadership challenges.

Another set of unexpected occurrences led her to leave her consulting practice to start on a different path that eventually resulted in a decades-long search for the history of her eighth-great-grandmother. The journey to uncover her ancestor's story caused Lynne to return almost full circle back to her French-Canadian roots and her love of history, although now more enriched by life's surprising twists and turns. And after teaching, writing and talking about creativity for so many years and urging others to unleash their creative talents, she has now begun to access in depth all of her own talents as a dedicated writer of non-fiction.

She can be reached at lynne@lynnelevesque.com.

About the Cover Artist

Having seen the work of Ilir Stili at a local art exhibition, the author specially commissioned him to create the original watercolor painting that appears on the cover. In the process of working with Stili, she learned more about him.

Stili is a native of Kosovo and had discovered his love for art, along with a fierce curiosity and independent spirit, at an early age. After receiving his diploma in fine arts, he began his career as a portrait artist. Amidst the turbulence that enveloped the country with the dissolution of Yugoslavia, his future as an independent artist was threatened. At his father's urging, he left Kosovo to find sanctuary in France. In his adopted homeland, Stili continues to receive honors and recognition as a professional painter, workshop leader, and teacher of students from five to ninety-five years old.

ilirstili@yahoo.com
◼ ILIR STILI

Made in the USA
Middletown, DE
17 August 2022